Mr Price

27 Years with the RNLI

A lifeboatman's story

Chris Price

First published 2020

This book is available from: info@helstonforensics.com
Tel: 01326 573221, 01326 5611440

Hardback ISBN 978-1-9163535-0-3
Paperback ISBN 978-1-9163535-1-0

Designed and typeset by Simon Culliford
Printed and bound by Booths Print, The Praze, Penryn, TR10 8AA

This book is dedicated to my darling wife
who I stole from RNLI HQ, Poole in 1997

CONTENTS

FOREWORD

I have read Chris's story all through and admire the way he has told it in such an interesting way. Anyone reading it will readily understand that being a lifeboat crew member, at such a busy a station as Falmouth, requires an enormous commitment in time and effort. Also that it demands courage and determination to see a job through often in most challenging circumstances. Despite all the hardships he has experienced as a lifeboat man he has managed, in his writing, to bring out the comradeship, team spirit and humanity that exists at Falmouth and indeed throughout the RNLI lifeboat stations everywhere.

Chris Price (former RNLI Divisional Inspector of Lifeboats)

Authors Note: we share the same name; Chris was one of the dedicated and highly skilled lifeboat inspectors, looking after boats and crews around the coast.

.

Richard Cox Scott in Falmouth Bay, February 2002. Photo: Simon Culliford

Left: Falmouth's Arun class all-weather lifeboat *Elizabeth Ann* in Falmouth Bay in 1987.
Photos: Simon Culliford

ABOUT THE AUTHOR

Chris Price, known as Mr Price by the lifeboat crew past and present, and by many of his friends, has had an interesting life. Fending for himself as a youngster, completing an apprenticeship as a gun maker and building a successful business. Later in his career having gained considerable experience in his trade he became an expert witness assisting courts in understanding the technical issues surrounding the art of gun making, and now lectures in universities and runs a successful Forensic Ballistic Laboratory.

His main passion in addition to gun making is the RNLI, this book gives you an insight on what it took to join a lifeboat crew and work his way up through the ranks, and to, on occasions, take charge of an offshore lifeboat with all the responsibilities that entails.

Having to retire from the active service due to age, he is now the Chairman of the Falmouth Lifeboat Management Group, and therefore is still very much involved in the activities of the Royal National Lifeboat Institution.

Having gone full circle, curling his lip when not chosen from a group of very eager trainees to join the crew on a shout, now he has to stand on the shore when the lifeboat slips her moorings, no longer on the 'A Team' but knowing it is manned by the best lifeboat volunteers in the world!

ACKNOWLEDGEMENTS

I would like to thank all who assisted me in putting this book together, with over 100,000 words I had no idea how long it would take, and as this book describes just a few of the hundreds of shouts I have been on. I have another book brewing.

Very special thanks to Simon who put this book together, Teän who has translated my scrawl into a typed draft. Captain Hugh Fogarty a good friend and recently retired Head of RNLI Operations (Operational Development), and Chris Price (my namesake) retired RNLI Divisional Lifeboat Inspector for all their help with the technical issues. Teän's Nanny, our friend Wendy, Mike Vickers a US Coastguard Rescue helicopter pilot and fellow lifeboat man Graham Hill a volunteer at Chiswick Lifeboat Station for correcting my grammar, and of course Elaine for putting up with me.

Elizabeth Ann on exercise off the Dodman. Photo: Simon Culliford

Mr Price

Photo: Jon Crane

INTRODUCTION

Over nearly 28 years as a lifeboat man I have, like all lifeboat men and women, seen some big seas, the worst of tragedies, grief, illness and death.
This book contains a few of the many hundreds of shouts I have been on; it is intended to give you an insight of what happens on a lifeboat when launched on 'a shout' from the perspective of just one of the crew.

As just one of a crew that is required to operate a lifeboat efficiently, the crew are a team bonded in a common cause, to help people in distress.
A Coxswain once said to his crew *"a lifeboat can go to sea without a Coxswain but it cannot go to sea without a crew"*, just to let them know how important they were!

Some lifeboat crew, probably most, have cast iron stomachs. A few like me are often sick in heavy weather. Luckily I am able to function after being sick (shooting the cat as they say in London), I've tried wrists bands, looking at the horizon, sea sick pills, all a complete waste of time, it's so much easier to just be sick and get on with the job!

Spending many hundreds of hours at sea and getting to know crew well is just the biggest privilege anyone can have. Being a member of a lifeboat crew is one of the most exclusive clubs you could ever join. You have to be accepted by the whole crew and that means trust!

Some of the jobs mentioned have affected me deeply, turned me into a bit of a wimp and I struggle when in the company of someone who is grieving. Even when watching the telly I can get a lump in the throat. When my wife Elaine hears me quietly gasp she says *"need a hankie?"* …. Some jobs are just the funniest and best times you can have, I hope you find the book interesting.

Mr Price caged at an early age.

Mum and Dad with my sisters Phillipa and Pamela and me.

Mr Price mobile at last!

THE EARLY YEARS

I started life as a baby; I can just remember being carted around in a cot to rugby matches and rugby parties, being carried upstairs to bed by Dad, the reassuring smell of tobacco and being tucked up in bed by Mum.

It wouldn't be long before I started running away from home; the first words I had to learn off by heart were *"94 Riverway, Palmers Green, N13"*. If I was lost I had to repeat this to a policeman.

Often on shopping trips I would be found by a policeman and get a ride on his shoulders looking for Mum.

From around the age of 7 during school holidays I was kicked out of the house in the morning with instructions *'be home for tea'*! My favourite past time was to jump on the back carriage of the train at Palmers Green railway station, hide on the floor so the ticket collector couldn't see me and get a free ride down to Kings Cross Station in London, out of the carriage across the tracks and into the bomb sites of which there were plenty.

I would meet up with gangs of similar aged kids and we would go off into the basements of bombed out houses searching for anything, but especially for cartridge cases and shrapnel.

As the years went by, I turned into a horrible child. I wouldn't go to school and had to make sure only Mum saw my school reports as they were so bad.

My best bit of shrapnel from a German bomb, found in amonst the rubble in London.

It became obvious I was not going to achieve anything by going to school; I hated teachers, hated discipline and wouldn't eat my spinach at home.... I cannot imagine what Popeye would have thought!

When I was 14 it was decided my presence at school was a complete waste of everybody's time, so my Dad struck a deal with the school that, if I had a job, I could leave as soon as I reached the age of 15.

As a keen shooter and bomb maker I managed to get a job as an apprentice gunsmith with a weekly wage of £2, taking home £1 6s 8d. Mum and Dad decided to move to Coverack in Cornwall as soon as I started work so my governor, Tibor Takats let me live in the room above the workshop. So that was it, I was abandoned and truly free just after my 15th birthday.

Making bombs is something we all did as youngsters. Weed killer, sugar and Jetex fuse. Trees were our main target and of course the one in our gang who made the biggest explosion was *'the man!'* - Not something you could do nowadays!

Poaching was great fun too. At the age of 15 we all had .410 shotguns, tied to the cross bar of our push bikes. No one had the ten bob (50p) licences from the Post Office and certainly not a ten bob game licence for the pheasants, which were plentiful.

To top up my meagre wages, the sale of pheasant did well in the game season. Another source of income were public phone boxes. In the high street there were plenty of phone boxes, you would put your pennies in the slot before you dialed, press button A if you get through or button B if you didn't, which let the pennies drop back out into a small chrome tray.

For some reason, in my tool box I had some of my Mums crochet hooks, a small device like a knitting needle with a hook on the end.

Straight after work I would do my rounds poking the silver paper from cigarette packets into the button B slot, just far enough up so it couldn't be easily seen. Then last thing at night I would go round retrieving the silver paper with the crochet hook and on average get five shillings in pennies, around a day's pay! I knew then that I was soon going to be self-employed.

Another wheeze if I fancied a pint was to climb over the back wall of the White Swan Public House, grab a few cream soda's, Mackeson and light ale bottles, then pop back round to the front door and cash them in for a pint of the cheapest.

I served my 5 year apprenticeship, occasionally making my way to Cornwall to see Mum and Dad and my two sisters.

Dad wouldn't say much during my visits as he was not very impressed with my academic achievements (or lack of them). He started to speak to me a bit more when I managed to get a job with James Purdey & Sons in London, one of the finest gun makers in the world.

At the age of 22, I moved down to Cornwall to have a go at starting my own business as a gunsmith. A few years of 80 hour weeks and it worked out, the business grew.

Living in the small village of Coverack was great. Everyone knew each other and the village had a lifeboat. This was the hub of the village. Coffee mornings, lifeboat day, lifeboat dinners and, of course, gathering in the pub when the boat was launched, waiting for it to return, often right through the night.

Dad was in the 8th Army. A desert rat, he taught soldiers how to drive tanks in the desert, he hated Montgomery and, like most who came back from the war, didn't talk about his experiences.

Mum started her nursing career as a State Registered Nurse, she was very proud of this; she was a Sister at Middlesex Hospital during the war. The hospital was bombed heavily so Mum was moved to Stoke Mandeville Hospital where she nursed badly injured Polish airmen. She rose in the ranks and retired as a Matron.

Like Dad, Mum saw many horrendous things that she very rarely talked about. She came out of nursing and started a family - the son (me) being a bit of a disappointment I'm sorry

Holiday in Coverack, family car, a Lancia Augusta.

Me looking smart!.

Left: My Mum.

Below left: Mum in full uniform.

Below right: A letter to my Mum from the Polish Red Cross.

CENTRAL COMMITTEE of the POLISH RED CROSS IN LONDON

Patron:
H.E. THE PRESIDENT OF THE POLISH REPUBLIC

Ref. 628/.45/S.Sz. 34, BELGRAVE SQUARE, LONDON, S.W.1.

Telephone: SLOane 9838.
SLOane 9839.
Telegrams: Polredcros, Knights, London.
Cables: Polredcros, London.

Sister Molly Sanderson, 8th January, 1945.
Ward 8x,
Stoke Mandeville Hospital,
Mandeville Road,
Aylesbury, Bucks.

Dear Madam,

The patients in Ward 8 x, have written to us asking us to extend to yourself and the nurses their most grateful thanks for all your great kindness to them, which they appreciate more than they know how to express to you personally.

It is so good of you to make them feel so happy and to attend to their wishes and requirements so well, and we in the Hospital Section of the Polish Red Cross would like to add our gratitude for all you are doing for our wounded. It is so gratifying and encouraging to us to know that such good relationship exists between our wounded and those who look after them and we deeply appreciate your co-operation.

With renewed sincere thanks,

Yours faithfully,
Hospital Section.

(Mrs) Z. Gergovich

to say.

One Saturday afternoon in Coverack a strong south easterly blowing, a yacht had moored in the bay, it was struggling to hold anchor. One of the local fishermen Tony Carey, known by his pals as TC, also a very capable electrician, got into the harbour punt and began to row out of the harbour. The local Coastguard who was on the harbour with the crowd spotted TC rowing round the end of the harbour on his way out into the bay to take the yachtsman off his yacht which looked like it had a good chance of being washed ashore.

"*Get back in the harbour!*" the Coastguard screamed. The crowd on the harbour looked round to see the Coastguard scream out again "*I order you to get back in the harbour*".

TC looked up at him, his expression said '*get stuffed*' he looked away and kept rowing.

The Coastguard, realising he was not God, wound his neck in. The whole village was witnessing a superb rescue. TC drew up alongside the yacht, the yachtsman jumped into the punt. TC rowed like mad and got back into the harbour to a huge round of applause, the Coastguard was seen making his way off the harbour, tail between his legs.

I was just so impressed, one of those moments you never forget… If we ever got a big boat back into Coverack TC would have made a superb Coxswain!

We both joined the crew of the inshore lifeboat at Coverack in 1976. They were great days but could be a bit embarrassing during the

Tony Carey - a true man of the sea.

summer when the maroons were fired in the day times, holiday makers would rush to the harbour to see the lifeboat launch, the big doors would open, and out came the D class 'rubber duck' on a trolley! Launches were pretty unspectacular. Over a few years we had the odd few shouts but the Falmouth Lifeboat or Royal Navy Search and Rescue helicopter from Culdrose would usually beat us to most casualties.

On March 27th 1980 The RNLI decided to close the station. The village was notified of a meeting to be held at the village hall, where a representative sent down from RNLI HQ at Poole would explain why the station was no longer viable.

The day arrived, the village hall was packed to the gunwales. Every person from the village was present, old crew from the 42-foot *William Taylor of Oldham* a Watson class lifeboat with a top speed of 8.3 knots, the shore helpers, the Ladies Guild, fisherman from the harbour, local farmers, in fact the whole village.

The top table situated on the village hall stage contained a selection of elders and the RNLI representative, Les Vipond (known amongst lifeboat crew as V2, V1 being Mike Vlasto). This was Les's first job for the RNLI. I expect headquarters knew the sort of reception they would get from a small fishing village whose life revolved around their lifeboat.

The meeting as you would expect was very emotional, lots of tears, silent periods when Les tried to explain that the station was no longer viable. The majority of shouts were at night and in the winter, and the area was well covered by the flank stations Falmouth and The Lizard, and of course RNAS Culdrose with the Wessex Search & Rescue helicopter.

The meeting broke up at 8 pm that evening and many made their way to the Paris Hotel, the local pub right opposite the Lifeboat House. The pub was packed and the mood sombre.

Coverack Lifeboat *William Taylor of Oldham*.
Photo: RNLI Archive

Les Vipond managed to get out of the village alive, I know he felt our pain, it was one of the worst jobs to get, and it was his first! Before Les joined the RNLI as an Inspector he was a teacher in a sea-school borstal in Blyth, Northumberland, and volunteer Coxswain of the Blyth lifeboat, a 46'9" Watson. So he would have understood the pain better than most.

Les became a District Inspector (DI) and some years later we had him as DI for a few years on the south coast. He was a great inspector, a man of a very few words. He enjoyed smoking his stinking pipe in the wheelhouse, probably to simulate fog! He took the Falmouth crew on its shakedown boat trials when we collected our first Severn class lifeboat *The Will* in 1996; this was his last job with the RNLI before he retired ... Much more pleasant than closing the Coverack station. It was a rough November run from Poole to Alderney then back to Falmouth over 2 days, but more of that trip later.

In August 1981, unknown to any of us Dad found out he had a terminal illness and decided to spare Mum the trauma of nursing him to a horrible death. During the middle of the night he went across the road from their house, into a field and shot himself. He wrote a lovely letter to Mum telling her how much he loved us all, and thanked her for a wonderful life.

The police flagged me down driving to work to say I was required back at Coverack, 'my Dad was missing'. The Coastguards were tasked with searching for Dad by firing a single maroon, (two maroons for a lifeboat). Michael, a Coastguard and local builder in the village found him - ever since that day we had a bond that we never talk about, we both loved my Dad.

I went home that evening and found myself howling like a wolf. I guess it's a kind of crying, I have never done this before or since, it was by far the worst ever day of my life.

There was a big funeral in the village. I can just about remember it, I was devastated, I

ILB days, off Coverack, wearing a proper lifejacket!

Les Vipond on the afterdeck of an Arun, a very different beast to the 46 foot Watson class lifeboat, where he was a volunteer Coxswain before joining the RNLI as a Divisional Inspector of lifeboats.. Photo: West Air Photogrpahy.

Mum and dad at a party after the war.

Dad, a keen angler.

couldn't ever believe my Dad would die. I don't remember much of the next 3 or 4 months, it took a long time to get used to what had happened. Often during the night I would awake having dreamt we were out together in the pub, or fishing together in Dads boat 'The Pelican' a 20 foot fishing boat and his pride and joy. If only I could have been with him that night, I cannot imagine how awful it must have been for Dad, he is the only person I know that would have had the strength to do what he did.

My main job now was to look after Mum; as the man of the house I had big shoes to fill, very very very big shoes!

A few years later I had the great privilege of being asked to become a Liveryman of The Worshipful Company of Gunmakers (Gunmakers Company). This involved being awarded the Freedom of the City of London. To obtain that I had to produce a full birth certificate. I had only ever had a half birth certificate which the Clerk of the Gunmakers Company said wouldn't be sufficient. One evening I asked my Mum if she had my full certificate in the family deed box…. She went as white as a sheet and didn't say anything; I knew something was terribly wrong and had the good sense to say *"doesn't matter, the Clerk of the Gunmakers Company said if it wasn't handy the half certificate would be fine"*…. The colour came back to Mums cheeks but I knew instantly that she didn't want me to see a full certificate.

The following week at work I rang Somerset House and ordered a full certificate, it turned up a week or so later, I opened the envelope marked private and confidential, and saw to my complete surprise that my father was some geezer called Allen Dickson and that I took my Dad's name at the age of 2.

I knew my Dad loved me despite me being baggage that came with Mum and impossible to control as a child. My illegitimacy sort of made sense as Mum had always protected me when Dad was angry.

I never mentioned that I had found out about my past to Mum, and cherished so much the loving looks she gave me every Sunday when I went around to have supper with her after Dad had died.

I got to know Malcolm Rudwick the RNLI District Engineer (DE), I would describe him as old school, and there was nothing Malcom didn't know about engines of all types. He knew how upset we all were in Coverack when we lost our boat and the station was closed.

We kept in touch and I got to accompany him when he arrived down to the west country to look at engines where a launch and sea trials were required. I got a trip out in the Lizard boat, Padstow's boat, and Falmouth, who at the time had a Thames class Lifeboat named *'Rotary Service'* also known as the galloping ghost. The boat was modelled on a Waveney class lifeboat, the RNLI's version of the US Coast Guard 44 foot *'Motor Lifeboat'*. The galloping ghost was too heavy in the bow and used to take to the sea like a pig nuzzling, a very dirty and wet boat, but fast which was more important than anything.

At this time major UK stations were waiting for their Arun Lifeboats capable of 18 knots, more than twice the speed of the older lifeboats they were replacing.

I met Viv (Vivian) Pentecost, the Falmouth Mechanic. He was due to take over as Coxswain from Toby West when 52-11 (the eleventh Arun) *'Elizabeth Ann'* was due to arrive in Falmouth in 1979.

Malcolm got me a trip on the Thames Lifeboat, it was engine trials and a trip up the Helford river to lay alongside the sailing ship where they were filming the Onedin Line. The stars came over onto the lifeboat to look her over and I got to shake hands with '*Captain Bains*' (Howard Lang) and '*Captain Onedin*' (Peter Gilmore), fame at last!

A week or two later I asked Viv if there would be any vacancies on the crew as a trainee reserve, when the Arun arrived and he became Coxswain. "*Well Chris as an engineer we could certainly use you, but living 20 miles away by road you would never make a shout*" Viv said.

"*I'll move to Falmouth*" I replied. Viv grinned, struck his hand out and we shook hands; to me that meant it was a deal. I had to have an interview with the Harbour Master who was the Falmouth Launching Authority and then a medical. Both went well and I found a wreck of a terraced house close to the lifeboat station named by the crew when they saw it as '*The Black Hole*'.

A rough old house, creaking windows and doors, freezing in the winter but only 200 yards from the boat house. It was so small - a real hole – with a curious layout. In through the front door, kitchen sink, cupboard and chair - down stairs (so below road level) one bedroom, storage under the stairs and a small bathroom with toilet, door to the back yard with outside toilet and dustbin space. Upstairs from ground level a small room with a settee, one chair, small table and telly - that was it!

I went onto the trainee list and spent nearly all of my spare time in the boathouse or on the boat helping Roger Lancaster the Mechanic and Donald McLellan (known by all as Big D) the Second Mechanic, changing oil and filters and other routine maintenance of which there was plenty. Within a year I was on the reserve crew list, still lots to learn, never missed an exercise, desperate for my first shout.

In those days, before electronic pagers, we had proper maroons, a sort of mortar bomb with a fuse which was lit and dropped into a mortar box ..... boom, a huge bang that hurled this device (the maroon) about the size of a fat guinea pig high into the air, then a huge green flash followed by a couple of seconds silence then the biggest bang you have ever heard (light traveling faster than sound). Then the second maroon was lit and dropped into the mortar box.

If you were close to the lifeboat house you got four explosions, by the time the fourth went off, if it was in the middle of the night, no one was asleep!

As a reserve I became an 'Emergency Mechanic' and became competent to start and run the engines and keep the boat going. My first shout was to a sinking stone carrying ship called the *Polaris*. The ship was holed below the waterline and drifting in the Manacles area, I couldn't believe my luck, both Mechanics Big D and Graham did not arrive at the boat house, the Second Coxswain John was keen to get going as the report was that the ship was sinking and had crew on board, "*can you run the engines Chris?*", I replied "*yes of course*".... John turned to the crew in the boathouse and said "*right lets go*".

It was approaching midnight on Friday when we launched, fine weather, low swell, a very pleasant evening, but of course not for those on the *Polaris*.

The engines started, the main crew ran the wheelhouse and deck like clockwork, very little talking, everyone knew what to do … I was left to get on with my jobs, monitor the engineer's panel in the wheelhouse and check and record temperatures and oil pressures every 15 minutes, and occasionally check the engine room to ensure everything was in order. Around 30 minutes after launching we approached the *Polaris*, the bow was high in the water, at the rear the accommodation block and bridge were out of the water with centre of the ship under water.

The bulkheads were holding and the ship had stabilised, although somewhat low in the water.

Our job was to tow her slowly into deeper water and await a tug to arrive to tow her to Falmouth.

The job was straight forward, once we had passed the tow we escorted the tug and the *Polaris* back to Falmouth and got back to our moorings at 1130 hours on Saturday. I turned off the engines, checked the oil levels, shut off the sea-cocks and switched off the electrics. My job was done.

John the Second Coxswain said "*thanks Chris*". As he shook my hand, I grinned and nodded. My first job on the boat and I didn't even feel sea sick! A perfect start to my career on the offshore lifeboat.

Abandon ship

Falmouth pilot was on board mayday coaster

OFFICIALS were keeping tight-lipped this week after a coaster struck a rock off the notorious Manacles and suffered massive damage despite having a Falmouth pilot on board.

The 1,600 deadweight tons Polaris was badly holed and sinking when she put out a "mayday" on Friday night. The crew and the pilot had to abandon ship.

It is understood that the eight-year-old Dutch ship struck the Maen Land rock off Dean Quarry pier after loading stone.

A pilot boat, the Falmouth lifeboat, a salvage tug and coastguards were involved in a dramatic rescue operation in the darkness. For several hours the Polaris was in danger of sinking.

But this week, in the wake of what one Falmouth waterfront observer called "a very sensitive episode," no-one was talking publicly about the cause.

Capt. A. K. Boerma, the Dutch skipper, said from his ship in dry-dock in Falmouth: "She has been aground. She hit the bottom and was nearly sinking. We stepped over on to the pilot cutter."

He added: "You just can't say how it occurred. We have to find out. I can't tell you anything about the cause of the accident."

Capt. Frank Sowden is understood to have been the pilot on board at the time. He was unavailable for comment at his office or his home in Dracaena Avenue, Falmouth.

However, a report on the incident is expected to go from him to the chairman of the sub-commissioners of Falmouth pilots, solicitor

By David Rowe

Mr. Michael Richards, who was out of town this week.

Mrs. Susan Exworth, clerk to the sub-commissioners, said: "The report would have to be sent to Trinity House. Trinity House decides if there is an inquiry to be held."

The ship's local agent, Mr. David Haley, of Tamlyns, said that he was not sure about the cause of the accident and could make no comment about it.

The Polaris, he said, had suffered considerable bottom damage and there were several holes. She had been in grave danger of sinking.

He praised the pilot boat and the lifeboat for doing, a "tremendous job" in the darkness.

"The weather was good so there was no problem with the sea. But it is a hairy place to manoeuvre," said Mr. Haley.

He added that the engine room had been completely flooded and the ship's lower accommodation had also been flooded.

Mr. Doug Rowe, managing director of Seawide Services Ltd., of Flushing who led a diving team of three who worked

RESCUED . . . the Polaris in dry dock at Falmouth after being towed away from the Manacles.

for 15 hours on emergency repairs, described the damage as massive.

At crossroads buoy in Falmouth harbour they fitted plywood patches to holes in the ship in a successful fight to keep her afloat.

The Polaris was understood to be on her first visit to Dean Quarry, near Porthoustock, having arrived from Bridgwater and loaded stone for Dover.

According to Falmouth coastguards, who co-ordinated the rescue, the Polaris struck a rock just after 10 p.m. and put out the mayday call. She had lost power because the engine room was filling up.

The pilot boat L. K.

Mitchell was in the area and she took off the five crew and the pilot. The lifeboat was launched and the Falmouth-based German salvage tug Caribic proceeded.

The lifeboat took the vessel in tow to keep her away from the rocks and the Caribic transferred salvage pumps to her. A salvage crew was put on board and the tug towed the vessel, which was well down at the stern, to Falmouth harbour.

As emergency pumping went on through the night, the lifeboat stayed with the Polaris. Two docks tugs towed her in to dry-dock on Monday morning.

Second Coxswain John Mitchell.
Photo: Daviid Barnicoat collection

Newspaper report on the Polaris incident.

The *St Simeon*. Photo: David Brenchley Cornish Photonews

The Arun class all-weather lifeboat *Elizabeth Ann* on service to the *St Simeon*.
Photo: David Brenchley Cornish Photonews

ST SIMEON

OFF TO CULDROSE FOR A BOOZE UP

Thursday 14th February 1985, the wind has been blowing hard from the south east all day, in fact it has been blowing gale force on and off for about two weeks, with temperatures at around zero; sleet and snow, it has been a miserable time for all on the south coast of Cornwall.

In Falmouth there have been very few shipping movements. The fishing fleet is tied up, and most of the pleasure boats crammed in the local boat yards, safe for the winter.

Earlier in the week we had been expecting a shout but as the weather worsened and the forecast for tonight and tomorrow was for storms and severe weather including structural damage to buildings I reckoned no one in their right minds would be afloat.

The lads were looking forward to tonight; we were off to RNAS Culdrose, the helicopter base at Helston for a '999 party'. Extra care was taken to make sure a crew were left in Falmouth, I was to drive; we were looking forward to meeting up with our mates from other lifeboat stations in the area.

At about 2030 hours 6 of us took off for Culdrose. Donald the Mechanic, a big big man, probably 25 stone, big beard, untidy grey hair, glasses and a Londoner (something we are both quite proud of),…. Cliff the boarding boat attendant, he is retired from work and keeps an eye on the boat house. He also runs us out to the lifeboat when there's a call, day or night, Cliff is very reliable,… David, young David, keener than mustard itself, volunteers for everything, even the booze up tonight!... Graham and Tim, two of the younger trainees who were roped in to make the numbers up, it was a cold, wet, black, night, wind blowing south east about a 6 and forecast to go to 10 at around midnight.

We arrived at the main gate in Culdrose Naval Air Station at 2100 hours, showed the pass and entered. We parked close to the doors of the bar we were heading for, it was raining hard, a quick sprint and we were in. We made a bee line for the bar,… it seemed the natural thing to do.

I said to Big D *"boy it's cold in here"* he nodded and grinned, he was always grinning, I looked around, a huge room, half renovated with one complete wall missing but sheeted with heavy polythene to protect it from the weather, the bar was half finished, and to everyone's delight it was open.

A few naval uniforms were huddled in groups chatting and a couple of coach loads of what must have been a local Darby and Joan club, I wondered if we were in the right bar but I guess we were.. *"what do you want bud"* Don grunted, I replied *"Give us a coke mate"*… *"a rum and coke and a coke please luv"* he said to the lady behind the bar; just looking at her you could see she was not happy, in her overcoat and scarf… believe me the coke didn't need any ice! … neither did the lady behind the bar! With the drink in hand I cast an eye around to see if I could spot any lads from the other stations.

In the centre of the room were about a dozen rows of chairs laid out cinema fashion, I guess there must have been about 50 or so from the Darby & Joan Club sat in them, all wearing overcoats, shawls, hats, scarves etc., they looked as if they were waiting for a film to begin, pretty weird; I said to young David *"are we in the right joint?"*, he shrugged his shoulders.

"Price'y… Price'y…" I looked to the back of the room, it was one of the Lizard lads Pedro with a grin from ear to ear. Pedro was one of the crew on the Lizard lifeboat whom I've known for years, a real Cornish fisherman who enjoys his women, booze and fags! We all shuffled over to greet them. They were in what I would call a fortress formation all facing outwards but standing in a circle, as if to hide whatever it was they were protecting, I laughed, it was a gas heater. We sort of broke into the circle as we said our hello's. You couldn't feel any heat at all, the poor old heater was flat out but didn't stand a chance against the blast freeze wind, and 'atmosphere' that was blowing around this huge bar.

Pedro said "*I think its warmer outside, we pinched the heater from the phucking bar but it's phucking useless*" I nodded as we all tightened up to get nearer to the heat. As you can see Pedro is colourful with his vocabulary.

I went up for a round of drinks, caught the eye of a barman in the hope that at least the service would be warmer than that given by the frosty bar maid. I put my arm on the bar, the wind was blowing down through the roof light tubes above the bar. It was freezing, this was unbelievable, I shifted position along the bar I was becoming fed up!

It must have been about 2200 hours, it was blowing a full gale outside and I was shivering. I suggested we go to a local pub in Helston to get warmed up before the drive home, I think the lads seemed keen on the idea, but to 'clinch the deal' I pointed out that I was driving, and I was definitely going. After a final chat with the Lizard lot, who were also freezing…and a few good solid handshakes, we left them to their heater and made our way to the front doors.

We could see the car from the front doors, some bright spark suggested I ran out and unlock the doors in readiness for the rest of them, it seemed reasonable, soon within say 30 seconds we were all sat in the car, the wind was shaking the car violently it was amazing. I started the engine and we were off down to the Angel Hotel for a warm pint and to thaw out. The time was now approaching 2300 hours; we stayed in the deserted Angel for a good half hour.

Damp, miserable, but much warmer, we decided unanimously to have a go at the 10 mile journey back to Falmouth.

Donald the Mechanic had had plenty of rums by now and was much happier. He sat in the front because of his size, he's a big strong lad, (useful ballast), 3 on the back seats and Tim in the luggage compartment at the back of my old Range Rover.

The journey back was slow, the main road was deserted, the wind rocked the car, keeping it on the correct side of the road was difficult, in fact difficult to even see the road, covered in snow with a snow blizzard, the worst we had seen for years, and of course pitch black. It was approaching midnight as I started to drop the boys off, we were due to have an exercise on Sunday, and as each one left the car to make for his front door you could hear the words blowing down the street, "*see you Sunday Price'y*". Falmouth was deserted, just a few dustbins were blowing around the streets. Big D was the last out of the car, I had a job to see his eyes, what with his mop of hair and beard flapping wildly in the gale, as he grinned and nodded and shut the car door.

I got in at about 0015 hours, "*at last*", I thought it was freezing, the rattling noise from the sash windows in the Black Hole, (the nickname for the house) was tremendous, I put on the electric fire, sat on the floor in front of it for 5 to 10 minutes, staring at the glowing bars and listened to the storm outside. The forecast was south easterly non-stop for the next couple of days, I was thinking "it's going to be an interesting exercise on Sunday, this will be the first trip as an enrolled reserve I've been on in a proper gale I hope I make a good account of myself. Will I be sea sick?" If I was very bad it would be the end of my lifeboat career.

I started to nod, it was time to make my way to bed, I curled into a ball and was asleep.

THE DREADED MAROONS

Friday 15th February 1985, 0335 hours, I'm sleep… A blinding green flash bounces off the walls of my bedroom, my head instinctively leapt off the pillow, eyes wide open and then it came… the dreaded bang, I couldn't believe it, maroon, it's a job! I live about 200 yards from the boat house; the maroon must have gone off above the Black Hole.

I was knackered, a long cold night on the booze at Culdrose, the wind was screaming it's guts out of the south east, it must have been blowing violent storm 11 to hurricane force 12!, I've never known a night like it!... I shot out of bed tugging away at handfuls of air in a desperate attempt to find the pull cord to turn the light on. Got it. My heart must have been doing at least 200 beats per minute; I must hurry, I can't miss this one, where's the second maroon,… I ran upstairs, looked at the heap of clothes in the middle of the floor where I normally leave them, what do I put on first?.... pants… trousers, one leg in, stub my toe, start cussing, the faster I go the longer it takes… I must slow down… that's better, I'm waking up. The wind sounded much worse at street level, I had a good idea what the seas would be like; I imagine about 1 ½ minutes must have passed since I was fast asleep, it's now time to sprint down to the boathouse.

I ran out of the house, forgot to lock the door, and was almost blown over before I even began. To get to the steps at the end of my street that lead down to the boathouse I had to run straight into the wind. There was a little sleet in the air that stung as it hit my face. With head down and leaning forward I began to make some headway along the street. To breathe I had to turn my head away from the wind, still no second maroon, that means I must have missed the first one!

I reached the steps that lead to the street below, and in turn to the steep sloping road down to the quay. I could see the light on the quay shining through the window from the changing room of the boathouse, one or two of the lads were by the front door.

I started my way down the steps, 3 or 4 at a time, I was sheltered from the wind by buildings and made good time, I arrived outside the boathouse gasping for air.

In the changing room there were 4 or 5 of the lads some with their gear on. Donald was standing in the engineer's workshop doorway "*get your kit on Chris*" he said, Graham chipped in "*put thermals on, it's bloody cold out there*", I didn't want to, I can't bear to get too hot, but as Graham said, it was very very cold out there. I got changed in the Mechanics room – Well, I say room it is more like a passage - a great privilege to be invited to keep my gear in Don's room. I was quite a way down the crew list, the main crew consisted of 7; I was a reserve member 19 and described on the crew board as Emergency Mechanic.

The boathouse phone was red hot, more crew began to appear at the door, by now I was kitted up, woolly bear, lifeboat gear and lifejacket on. I made my way from the engineer's department into the crew changing room, *"where's the bloody Coxswain"* was said, things were looking bad, the wind was unbelievable, it was high tide, the sea in the harbour was boiling. I said to Don *"where are we going?"*..... *"I don't know bud"* came the rum flavoured reply, although I must say he looked very sober indeed.

One of the lads came off the phone and blurted out *"it's a Frenchman sinking 35 miles off the Lizard"*,... Bloody hell! I don't believe it,... in this weather that's the other side of the world! This is serious I thought.

The boathouse was now crowded. One of the crew said he was too knackered to go; he had been 'working' all day. I looked into Donald's eyes after hearing his comments, I had to grin, Don knew exactly what I was thinking,... we had all been working all day, but some of us had been on the booze all night as well.. still, if he didn't want to go that was fine by me, it meant there was more chance I was going!

Bert one of the main crew, elected to go out and get the Coxswain, we couldn't reach him by phone although we could hear the ringing tones, perhaps he couldn't hear the phone over the screaming of the wind... we found out the next day that most of the phones were out of order in Falmouth.

Bert took off in his car; we didn't see him again that night.

The Lifeboat Deputy Launching Authority (DLA), was in the boathouse and decided he was coming with us, I must take my hat off to him. David Barnicoat is a pilot in the harbour and spends his working time guiding the larger ships into the harbour; he finished dressing, took a call on the phone and spun round, *"come on lads lets go, the Coxswain is coming"*, Viv had managed to phone the boathouse and said he was on his way.

Big D said *"looks like we are off bud, you do the sea cocks Graham will do the heaters, I'll flash up the VHF DF"*, I nodded.

The Arun always has the sea cocks closed when on the moorings. This is where the engines draw sea water to run through the engine heat exchanges to stop the engines overheating, a bit like a radiator. Starting the engines was going to be fun - they would be close to freezing having not run for at least a week due to bad weather.

THOSE OF US THAT WERE GOING..................WERE GOING!

There was a bottle neck at the doorway as we all shuffled to the door at the same time. Donald passed me Zulu (the hand held radio). When we were all on the quay it became obvious who was going and who wasn't, there was no way I was going to miss this job, so I moved around the group towards where the boarding boat was moored, so that I could be first to jump in, (there were quite a gang of us).

The boarding boat is a small 18 foot wooden open boat with an inboard engine. It is moored on an 'outhaul' and stands off the quay by about 20 yards. To bring it to the quay you just haul the rope in... well there were 8 big lifeboat men (the Coxswain was coming to make 9), the little boat was rising and falling in the waves, rolling and pitching, there wasn't a hope in hell that 8 plus the boarding boat attendant could get into that thing and not sink, the floor boards were awash.

I looked around to voice my opinion for what it was worth and saw all these orange suits disappearing towards the inner harbour…. "*What's going on?*" I thought, I ran and caught up to see the lads climbing into the inshore lifeboat; someone had obviously gauged the sea conditions and decided we would never make it to the lifeboat, which was moored in the middle of the harbour, in the boarding boat, and had 'laid on' the ILB.

So much for wanting to be the first into the boarding boat, I was the last into the ILB! I ran and jumped and landed in the middle of the crew. Royston, the senior ILB helmsman was on the controls, he looked at me and said "*well if it ain't ol' Price'y*", I gave him a quick grin as we all tried to get into a position so that Royston could see where he was going.

All eyes looked ahead, we left the shelter of the inner harbour to embark on what was probably the most dangerous part of the journey ahead,… getting to the lifeboat itself.

The harbour was 'alive'; boats of all types were straining on their moorings, yachts masts were pitching wildly, someone pointed out one or two yachts that had sunk on their moorings, with just the tips of the masts showing, one or two smaller open fishing boats had been swamped with only the gunwales just showing.

Royston Prynn at the helm of the A class McLachlan inshore lifeboat used as the boarding boat for this service.
Photo: Simon Culliford

As we approached the lifeboat I could see how violent her movement on the moorings was, she was facing into the sea, as she dipped off each wave the bow sort of plunged in on the next one and the sea broke over her bow. This was most definitely the roughest trip I will have been on, and I mean on the moorings!... What on earth was it going to be like outside in the open sea?

We approached the stern of the lifeboat it was obvious that boarding was going to be 'hairy' as they say; in the trough of the next wave the stern of the lifeboat towered over us. Royston moved his way around to the port side to see if there was a better boarding position. The waves that were breaking over the bow of the lifeboat were washing onto us, accelerated by the wind; it was the equivalent to having dustbins full of iced water thrown over you. We were all soaked to the bone within about 4 waves… this was not the side to board!

Royston put the ILB into neutral and we drifted back fast. As soon as we were a boats length behind the lifeboat he put the ILB half ahead and made his way around to the starboard side. There was a bit of shelter from the green waves that were flying off the bow of the lifeboat. We came alongside about midships, one, two, three, four of the lads leapt sticking like limpets to the side of the boat,… we were blown off, Royston tried to reposition, it wasn't going to work, so he went for bow approach, he drove straight at the side of the lifeboat. As we made contact he held the ILB hard,…. Four more scrambled on, me being a true gentleman let them all go first; to tell the truth I stumbled in an effort to get to the bow and almost got trampled in the rush.

"*Come on Price'y jump*" Royston screamed… '*The cheeky git*' I thought, we were just beginning to drift off as I leapt into the gap between the bow of the ILB and the side of the lifeboat, one thing you can be sure of when in the company of lifeboat men is that when you need a great big hairy arm to pluck you from danger there will be at least half a dozen of them! … well there were… I knew there would be. My knees ended up level with the side deck, my chin level with the top railing… on the outside of the boat! Royton was going hard astern… I was lifted up and over the railings with one movement, "*cheers*" I grunted… then, single file, we made our way along the boat's side to the shelter of the afterdeck.

On a shout it's customary to do these preliminary jobs at double time, the first one down the stairs to the engine room turns on the battery couplings, open's the engine room door, turns on the light, lift the flaps to the seacocks and starts to undo them, you have to spin the wheels quite a few revolutions to open the valves… whilst I was doing this, Graham climbed over me (I was on my knees spinning the valves as fast as I possibly could) and made his way to the engine starter and heat buttons. He pressed both heat buttons, you could hear them 'click in'. The boat was pitching like mad; the engine room was damp and freezing cold.

"*Open*" I shouted, Graham nodded… as he kept the heat buttons pressed, we would need at least 2 minutes heat to pre-heat the engines to help them start.

I stood by the door and waited until time was up, Graham pressed the port engine starter button, the Caterpillar engine turned over slowly, "*come on you old cow*" I shouted… it started to cough and splutter… it seemed like ages and then the roar as Donald up in the wheelhouse cranked the throttle to rev it up. Graham sighed with relief, not that you could hear it, but you could see it in his face, then to the starboard lump, same thing… cranking for ever then a load of coughing and banging… then… both Cats roaring… they drowned out the scream of the wind… a very comforting noise.

Graham and myself both ran up the stairs to the wheelhouse. Deck side crew were clambering over the outside of the boat, preparing to slip the mooring, removing the cover from the flying bridge, securing ropes, fenders etc., the Mechanic side of the crew were busy in the wheelhouse, flicking switches, fans, navigation lights, deck lights, radio's etc. I checked that the cooling water was coming from both exhausts and the after deck, gave thumbs up to Donald in the wheelhouse, he nodded… a bit like clockwork… when you go into '*auto pilot*' very few words are actually spoken, commands, acknowledgements, thanks, watch out, etc. all these gestures are made and understood by eye… very comforting when you trust someone enough to be able to understand what they are saying by just looking at them!

The dashing around slowed down, we were ready to go, Decca navigator was on, radar running, Alan was organising the chart table, Dave came into the wheelhouse and said "*right lads lets go*". He went up to the flying bridge, I took up position in the wheelhouse just behind the radio seat. As a reserve it was my duty to keep out of the way and do what I was told.

THIS WAS THE MOMENT, WE'RE OFF!!

We slipped the mooring… time 0355 hours… the radio crackled… the Coastguard advised… *"the Coxswain is coming out in the boarding boat now"*.. we made our way over to the Docks to get some shelter, as we hit a calmer patch of water I could see the ILB out of the aft wheelhouse door …. well I could see the spray, as the little boat punched into each wave and shot white water into the air as it ploughed its way towards us.

I made my way onto the after deck to greet Viv and give him a hand on board, *"thanks mate, where are we going?"* He was hard to understand because he didn't have his teeth in. I screamed into his ear *"sinking trawler*

Big D - Mechanic Donald McLellan in the wheelhouse of *Elizabeth Ann*. Photo: Falmouth RNLI Collection

30 miles south of the Lizard" Viv's eyes bulged; I cannot imagine what he thought given the sea conditions. He made his way into the wheelhouse, we all piled in behind. Viv slowly looked at each man in the wheelhouse; for a split second, as there were nine of us, I thought he may send someone back… he gave a sort of nod… that meant he approved, of what I do not know,… but it meant to me that he was happy with his crew…. thank Christ!

I found out in years to come it always a good idea to take one or two extra crew on a long or rough shout, just in case of injuries and the sheer physical hard work; just hanging on for hours on end can wear the crew out.

Viv made his way to the flying bridge, this was it, we were really off there was no turning back; we were well and truly committed.

0401 hours, Donald advised the Coastguard on channel zero that we were proceeding, then he passed the crew list, (this was required in case of the unlikely event of disaster), all of the crew list: 1 Viv, 3 Donald, 4 Graham, 8 Alan, 10 John, 12 Mike, 19 Me, 23 Bjorn and Dave Barnicoat. The Coastguard asked if we wanted the weather forecast…. I think we could have told them what it was.. Bloody awful! Anyway Donald said *"we'll take it as read"*, then the Coastguard passed the casualty details, *"the casualty is a French fishing boat Saint Simeon"* it's position 49 degrees 43 minutes north, 04 degrees 54 minutes west. (49°43'n, 004°43'w).

As we cleared the docks and entered the entrance to Falmouth bay, I noticed Governor Buoy slip down our starboard side, range about 25 yards, the seas were very short and steep, the lifeboat was slamming, but not too violently, spray was washing over the boat, shining against the lights of the docks as it rained down on the afterdeck and into the sea behind us. The Governor was dipping almost out of sight in the troughs as we left it behind us, disappearing into the grey/ black of the sea.

Next was Black Rock Beacon and Black Rock Buoy. The beacon is mounted on a group of rocks that is almost in the centre of the entrance to the harbour. Safe passage to the east is marked by a buoy. Once they were sighted astern we were entering the bay and could expect a different kind of ride altogether.

Engines were running at about ¾ revs, say 1500 RPM, they must be getting warm by now. I expect Viv will push the throttles forward soon, and then things start to rock and roll!

I was standing by the wheelhouse door, enjoying the fresh air, Graham was opposite me, I asked "*what was the weather like on the Pirata job?*"… "*This is much worse*" he said as he nodded. Great I thought, I was hopping mad that I had missed the Pirata job, it was a pretty rough job about a couple of months ago. Still, if the weather was worse on this job, this was the one not to miss!!!

We must have been approaching Black Rock by now. Things were beginning to become more exciting, we started to roll heavily as we went across the seas, rolling in from the west,… then the throttles went down! …. Viv mean business, we were going to get to this Frenchman and nothing was going to stop us.

I hung on to a grab rail, and bent my knees, with my legs fairly wide apart, as we slammed, my knees would bend and as we rolled I was able to keep my balance… well after a fashion.

Vivian Pentecost on board the Arun class all-weather Arun lifeboat *Elizabeth Ann*. Photo: Simon Culliford

Things started to fly around the wheelhouse, medical kit left the stretcher, rolled around until it became wedged in various corners, an engine room door came loose and started slamming, Graham popped below and made it fast, I looked around, everyone was hanging on with a vengeance, I hoped I would stand up to the strain (physically). Mentally I was fine,… the elder crew looked fairly confident so if they were happy what did I have to worry about,… anyway, if a French fishing trawler could float in these seas, there was no way an Arun class lifeboat couldn't.

Through the aft cabin door I could see the seas becoming larger. As we left them rolling towards the shore, the mark of the wash of the lifeboat showing, the wind was whipping the tops of the waves off and sending them like streaks of cotton wool into the darkness. If you were to enter the water tonight you would certainly drown. If you could keep your head above water, the air for about a foot above the tops of the waves was full of foam.

We left Black Rock disappearing astern, and then we turned to starboard to make our long run towards The Lizard, making sure we missed the Manacle rocks on the way! We were now in open sea. Diving straight into the waves, the boat took on a completely different motion. Instead of the short slamming hard slaps, we were climbing pretty big waves, rocking as we went over the tops and flying down the back of the wave into the troughs below. Just to make it really interesting, as we had the sea slightly on our starboard bow, we were corkscrewing; this became worse as we drove further out to sea.

0423 hours, more information from the Coastguard *"The casualty is 22 metres long, 150 tons, blue and white, showing 2 red lights, engine stopped in position bearing 141 degrees 12 miles from Lizard lighthouse"* Roger we replied *"our position 2 miles south south east Pendennis Point making heavy weather, 24 miles to casualty"*.

Making heavy weather was a good description, the waves were now very large as they rolled in across the shallow ground of Falmouth bay from their source in the Atlantic ocean. The engines were working hard as they forced the boat up the front of the waves, when we reached the tops and started to dip down they would race, tachos showing 2400 revolutions, when we dipped our bow deep into the trough at the bottom of the wave the boat would seem to almost stop in its tracks, the revs would drop right back as the props dug in, the engines sounded almost as if they would stall! When the boat shook the water off the foredeck and started to climb, the remains of the bow wave would rush over the top of the boat with a hell of a noise and land in the sea behind us, the boat would screw to the side and stern would become awash with the sea, I've never seen this happen before or since. Some water was making its way in through the stern door, it was decided it would be sensible to close the door… the moment I was dreading.

'ENTOMBED' IN THE WHEELHOUSE

No fresh air, the smell of diesel, a wisp of cigarette smoke lingering, and the temperature freezing. The crew were all hanging on, occasionally swearing as we hit a big one, then a moan as we become weightless dropping into the trough, and more swearing as we landed,… the big waves were becoming more and more frequent.

The noise of the two Caterpillar engines screaming, combined with the seas crashing into the wheelhouse was very impressive,… then we came off the top of the one steep one it seemed as if there wasn't any water below us at all, in fact we were truly airborne. When we hit, I ended up on my knees, one or two of the lads were swinging around the roof support poles, others grabbing anything they could to steady themselves with.

0504 hours, the Coastguard advised us that Rescue 80 was airborne from Culdrose, Big D chirped back on the radio *"that makes two of us"*, it brought a muffled chuckle from the boys. We were now 6 miles east of Coverack with about 20 miles to run.

Big D worked his way up to me near the aft door, he smelt like a brewers slops bucket, rum fumes. I had to grin, what a state, hair and beard everywhere, just like he had gone through a hedge backwards as they say. We were all still soaked from the trip out to the lifeboat, and beginning to feel the cold.

We wedged ourselves in on the floor opposite each other, it was very difficult to stand even with knees bent because of the slamming, (sitting wasn't very comfortable either!). I gave Big D a big grin, and got one back. I knew at this moment that at some time I was going to be seasick, but just then I was really enjoying myself!

The pounding got worse; the boys were now beginning to think we needed to ease back. The boat the crew can't take much more before important things like engines become dislodged… "*for Christ sake ease it back*" Dave grunted as we hit a big one, more wheelhouse kit began to fly. The old Psalm 'they staggered around like drunken men, and were at their wits end' (psalm 107, vs27) must have been written by a lifeboat man!

0510 hours things were now very grim indeed, crew were starting to get damaged; I thought if we were going to get knocked down or capsize it would be soon.

I was sort of sitting on the floor opposite Big D who was under the stretcher on the starboard side, as we dropped off the wave, I would leave the floor by about 6 inches and come down on my bum as we 'bottomed out' (excuse the pun).

David had decided on behalf of us all that enough was enough, we would not survive the journey in the wheelhouse at this speed without quite a few broken bones. He asked Barto (John) to go tell Viv to ease back, we were all getting hammered.

Barto had all his kit on, and carefully made his way over the crew that were on the floor to the aft door, as he opened the door and put his first foot out onto the after deck, he looked back, eyes wide open.

It seemed like seconds,… he was back,… thank Christ for that I thought. "*That's better lads*" David said, looking a lot happier, we all nodded, but the ride was still bumpy! I focused on the helm indicator above the wheelhouse driving position. After a while I reckon the old elastic holding my eyes in place was losing strength, they must have started rolling I felt dreadful!

I'd had the 'hot flushes', I was shivering, the tummy was rumbling, the boat was rolling like a pig… right over on one side, then right over on the other; it's only time before I'm going to have to stick my head outside the back door and be sick, how embarrassing, what will everyone think.

I looked around, everyone looked like I felt, they were all swaying together with the boat's motion, it looked very strange.

The jacket I took off when I became hot I soon put back on. I had to do this standing which meant, as I put my second arm into the sleeve hole, I was momentarily unable to support myself,,, needless to say, we hit a confused sea that left me staggering around the back of the wheelhouse, bouncing off the radio, stretcher, Big D and radio seat. This left me with both arms behind me caught in my jacket, laying across the chart table. I raised my head, gave Alan a smile and apologised before wrestling into the jacket, still with my chest on the chart table to give me some support. Dressed, I made my way back to the aft door, the lads were smiling, I felt like a right twit!

If only we could open the back door… let some dam air in!! I was feeling absolutely awful… as it turned out (I'm delighted to say) I was not alone, someone forward in the wheelhouse said "*open the bloody door*", Big D pinned it back,… bliss… I looked at it knowing soon I was going to have stick my head through it!

Graham made me smile, he made his way to the stretcher and took some plastic beakers out of the carrier bag, also some of what looked like airline 'sick bags', and the plastic water container that was wedged in by the bottom stretcher. Graham carefully unscrewed the lid and tried to get some in the beaker, it went everywhere but… at last a little slopped in to the beaker, Graham sipped it very carefully as if on a wine tasting session in the Hilton Hotel, he then sat down on the floor next to Big D. Mike moved aft and took up position between the rear chart table seat and the stretcher. Alan was in the radar seat, Barto was between the chart table and the radio seat, and I was still opposite Big D, with my back resting against the rail that protected the rocket line box.

At last, Graham moved towards the aft wheelhouse door, I could tell by the expression on his face what was happening, he stuck his head out of the door and had a good old cough up. I stood up, held onto the grab rail with one hand and Graham's lifejacket strap with the other, just to give him a bit of a steady back to his position next to Big D, who sort of rolled over towards the door and with both knees on the floor followed Graham's example, there was a lot of groaning and plenty of rum fumes. This was great… I was now feeling extremely sick but very pleased, it looked almost sure I was to be the third to perform.

The boats motion was terrible, it was impossible to guess which way It was going to twist next, which left all those that were not securely wedged in rolling around in an uncontrolled fashion. I looked down at Big D and thought *'you had better hurry up and get out of that doorway or I'm going to be sick all over you'* - my tummy was really bubbling, Big D slid back across to his position by the stretcher, my

The Arun class all-weather lifeboat *Elizabeth Ann* on service to the *St Simeon*.
Photo: David Brenchley Cornish Photonews

tummy started to have 'contractions' a cross between giving birth and an exotic belly dancers performance. I lurched to the door, and coughed and spluttered for about 2 minutes solid, I don't expect the entire contents would have filled an egg cup but believe me I felt brilliant afterwards… I knew now, for the first time that I would survive this job.

A TRIP TO THE FLYING BRIDGE

0526 hours the Coastguard advised us that helicopter *Rescue 80* was now with the casualty, there was some discussion on the chart table and Alan shouted "*I have a course change*", this meant someone had to go to the bridge to advise Viv, there was no chance of using the intercom due to the noise of the wind so a messenger had to go, Big D said "*Chris will you pass the course?*" I nodded, it looked like my turn for a soaking, the time was about 0535 hours, still very dark, we were now approaching The Lizard with about 10 miles to go to the Frenchman, the boat was corkscrewing violently, we were in the tide rips off The Lizard Point, one of the roughest patches of water on the south west coast in a south easterly storm, wind sea and tide all working together to build very big seas.

I checked my lifejacket and received the course, said back slow and loud and got a nod of approval. Now to get to the bridge. I stuck one foot out of the aft door and looked at the afterdeck, it was awash. I decided how I was going to make a dive for the railings that lead up the steps to the flying bridge… go… not the best of timing, I grabbed one rail, missed the other, so put both arms around the one I had and gave it a very firm cuddle, I swung around and ended up sitting on the bottom step, so much for the careful plan. The remains of a wave we had just dived into rained down my neck… I spun around and with one hand on each rail started to climb onto the top of the lifeboat.

As my head came level with the upper deck the wind knocked it back, with wind speeds of approaching 100 mph, and full of salt water, it took me completely by surprise. I froze for a second, unable to breathe, cheeks flapping in the wind, eyes almost closed leaving the tiniest of slits to see what was happening, I hung on for a few seconds, then turned and lowered my head so that it was almost facing backwards so that I could catch my breath.

'*Christ*', I thought, '*I've got a bloody good chance of being blown off this lifeboat; until I get into the shelter of the bridge itself I'm completely open to the weather, with the boat pitching and rolling and slamming I had better hang on very tight!*' I had decided it would be impossible to walk to the bridge, and the only way was to crawl, keeping both hands on the rails each side of the gangway. I edged my way along, turning my head rearward regularly to breathe. I could see Viv and Bjorn's backs as I approached them. They were rolling, and springing up and down as the boat rolled and slammed, they had no idea that I was crawling up behind them. This worried me intensely. If I got blown off they would not see me, if I didn't return to the wheelhouse, the lads may think I decided to stay on the bridge, it was a pretty unsatisfactory situation altogether.

As I reached the shelter from the wind given by the flying bridge, I was able to breathe with my face forward; things were a little less dangerous. I took the opportunity to look around I could see the size of the waves, they appeared to be about three or four times higher than the boat, as we were in the trough of a wave I could see the foam on the top of the wave ahead of us being blown off clean over the top of the boat. As we climbed the wave I looked back, the trough got deeper, and seemed miles away as we went over the top of the next wave, an amazing sight very difficult to describe with words.

I tapped Viv on the arm, he spun round and was surprised to see me, he moved his ear towards my face, I screamed new course twice in his ear, he looked me in the eye and shook his head, I knew he had not received the course. I tapped the top of the compass then held up one finger in front of his face, then four fingers from each hand making 8, then a zero with thumb and fore finger making an 'o'. He nodded then turned his head forward, looked at the compass and brought the boat onto a course of 180, I gave the thumbs up, we both nodded.

It was time to return to the wheelhouse; still in the shelter of the bridge, gingerly I began to edge my way along the walk-way aft. As I lost the protection of the shelter from the wind, I began to accelerate. It felt as if a dirty great big hand was pushing me in the back. I sank quickly to my knees and hung on tight. Carefully I swapped hands and slowly turned around, turning my head rearwards to breathe; I was now facing the flying bridge again, … so slowly I crawled backwards to the steps, then down one step at a time until I got near the bottom, and some protection from the wind. At the bottom of the steps, I looked in through the wheelhouse door, I could see one or two of the lads, Big D noticed me and gave half a nod as an acknowledgement. I made a dive for the door way, perfect timing, straight in, water pouring off me, all over two or three of the lads near the door, one or two moans and groans.

Graham was sipping water from a beaker, he offered me some, I thought he must know what he's doing, I expect it helps reduce the effect of feeling sick. I wasn't feeling too bad, pretty cold but apart from that OK., I had a sip not a good idea, don't expect the sip of water reached the back of my throat before it came flying back out again, instant reject! I coughed and spluttered, wiping my face with my wet sleeve and passed the beaker back to Graham, he half smiled and put it back on the stretcher.

Wheelhouse on St Mary's Arun 52-18 *Robert Edgar* similar to that on Falmouth's *Elizabeth Ann*.
Photo: Gulf Group Marine Brokers Ltd

I decided to try sitting in the chair behind the radio seat mainly to give my knees a rest as they had taken a bit of a pounding by now, especially with the crawling session's upstairs a few minutes ago.

No sooner had I sat in the chair when we flew off the top of a steep one and began to free fall into the trough below … crash. As we fell I left the seat by about 12 inches. I hung onto the arm rests and made the mistake of trying to pull myself back in the seat as we were falling, so when we landed I aided the acceleration effect and sat in the seat very very hard indeed. This in turn impressed the shape of my wallet deep into my right cheek (Bum), deep deep pain. My groans were lost amongst everyone else's as the boat shuddered. I hooked one foot under the rail in front of the chair, and both arms under the arm rails of my chair, determined not to leave the seat again.

I was now securely wedged into my seat, swaying with the motion of the boat. I tried to focus on the helm indicator, and began to daydream. About half an hour must have passed, I was beginning to shiver. I looked across the wheelhouse and could see Mike having a private and very sophisticated cough into one of Graham's sick bags, none of the Big D style cough, splutter, moan and wipe your gob with your sleeve for Mike. The fact that I was feeling a bit sick again was now no problem for me, just about everyone had been ill so, I couldn't have been in better company.

A little while later, almost day dreaming again I started muttering to myself. I can't remember what I was saying, bloody good job no one could hear, what an idiot I thought smiling, Alan looked up at the same time and frowned, he must have thought I was potty, what the hell was there to smile about.

We had around 40 minutes to run to the casualty, a new course change came from the chart table. Most of the crew were on the floor trying to preserve themselves, I got the job... same routine as before, up the ladder, etc. as I hung onto the railings I had a look around; it was getting a little lighter. As we rolled off the top of a big wave you could see the tops of the waves in front for quite a distance, they were much the same as each other, very large and uniform in shape, the wind was still deafening.

Viv was sat on the floor, he looked like a ghost, Barto was driving, Bjorn was with him. Viv must have been absolutely frozen, he had been out in the unbelievable weather for over 2 hours solid, the temperature was zero, add that to a wind speed of 100 mph and you have a good recipe for hypothermia! I gave John the new course and said to Viv *"why don't you come below for a warm up?"* He nodded. Then I made my way below.

I got back into the wheelhouse OK, but I was now shivering uncontrollably. I was freezing, I got down on the floor by the fire hydrant and in such a position so as to be able to see out of the back door,... I didn't want to miss anything.

AT LAST.............DAWN

0641, Dawn had now broken, the sight out of the aft door was bleak, everything was a varying shade of grey, sea, sky, sea, sky, sea, and so on. The radio started to crackle, Alan passed our position. I had to admire him, he had been at it all night. We were in the area of the Frenchman, we asked the Coastguard to ask him for a D/F count. As the Frenchman counted slowly from one to ten we all looked up at that direction finder, the light on the set indicated that he was astern of us port side, someone looked out of the window and screamed *"visual"*, we had

Another shot of *Elizabeth Ann* battling the heavy seas during this service. Photo: David Brenchley Cornish Photonews

him... They must have spotted him from the bridge, as we took up position ahead of him and came round to face east. At last, we were on station and could turn to run with the sea, the slamming stopped, the wind was now right up our backside, the temperature in the wheelhouse dropped instantly to zero, the air became very damp and tasted strongly of salt. I stood up and made my way to the back door, I had to have a look at these mad French men, out in this weather.

As we ran down a wave which took quite a while because we were running 'with it' I looked up at the wave, nothing was there... and then suddenly the bow of *St. Simeon* broke through the top of the wave, it looked like a torpedo, it was right above us... Well it looked as if it was, it was in fact probably about 50 yards away... as we slowly started to climb the next wave we were able to look down on the French trawler as she wallowed in the trough that we had just left. She was old, rusty, absolute junk, certainly not fit to be out in these seas. The height of the waves from crest to trough measured by the helicopters altimeter at 60 feet!

Alan asked me to go up and ask Viv for instructions, so that we could advise the Coastguard of our intentions. I made my way up the bridge with the wind up my backside I had a job to stop myself running straight into the lads on the bridge. Viv was stood up, he was soaked right through…. I screamed *"what do you want us to tell the Coastguard?"* Viv screamed back *"tell them we will stand by"* *"Roger"* I replied… Viv nodded.

I made my way down, and flew into the wheelhouse with the help of the wind. Big D was now on the radio… *"we'll standby"*, I said to him, *"roger"* he said and duly passed the message.

0659, the Coastguard advised us that the helicopter had lowered a pump to *St. Simeon* they were having trouble starting it, could we pass our pump? There was discussion around the chart table,… I was horrified. Can we pass our pump. They must be joking, we couldn't get within 50 feet of that heap of rust without the risk of being smashed to bits! Worse still, if they wanted to pass a pump they may well want to pass a Mechanic with it!! Big D and Graham were fast asleep, this was a short straw I did not fancy drawing!

Great relief… the message that was agreed upon … *"We are not able to pass our pump due to severe weather conditions"* … thank the Lord….

Around 0715 hours the Coastguard and *St. Simeon* were chatting. I say the Coastguard, it was Cyril Hart from Falmouth, a retired teacher who was a fluent French speaker, his sister Mona lives in Coverack and is on the Coverack Lifeboat Committee.

The Coastguard advised us that the casualty had agreed to come with us to Falmouth, we were still running with the sea and making no headway as *St Simeon* was unable to start her engine. She was struggling with the pump in a desperate effort to avoid sinking. We remained on station for the next hour, rolling around. Mike had now gone onto the bridge to relieve Bjorn, who came down and crashed out on the wheelhouse deck, he was, quite naturally, shot out.

Big D was now fast asleep on the floor he had to be buggered, considering the amount of rum he had guzzled the night before! Viv had crashed out on the bridge floor, too knackered to make it down to the wheelhouse, everyone was feeling ill, the boat's motion was unbearable, rolling and heaving, the boat was freezing and damp… and so was everyone on board.

I checked the heater was on, it was totally useless and didn't stand a chance with the wind that was blowing through the boat.

0815 hours from the Coastguard *"The casualty hopes to start her engine in about 30 minutes"*… our reply *"roger"* … another half hour, rolling around, being blown toward the shore. We were all now getting a bit concerned. There was a distinct possibility that we would have to take the chaps off their boat, and that was going to be very dangerous indeed for all concerned.

Almost half an hour passed, we advised Coastguard of our position 159 degrees, 13.6 miles from the Lizard, this was acknowledged. A few minutes later down from the bridge came Viv's message for the Coastguard, 0848 hours… *"conditions deteriorating, the casualty has moved since we arrived and is now closer to The Lizard, what is position re engines?, Coxswain recommends either a tug or the crew to be taken off*" Cyril from the Coastguard had a few words with *St. Simeon*, the reply to us at 0851 hours "*casualty is about to restart engines, will Coxswain wait 15 minutes?*" Our reply "*we will stand by*".

20 minutes passed, we were still being blown onto the Lizard, in every one's mind was the 'Penlee Disaster' just over three years ago, similar horrendous weather, an absolute tragedy that happened due to lack of sea room.

Falmouth's Arun class all-weather lifeboat *Elizabeth Ann* escorting the *St Simeon*.
Photo: David Brenchley Cornish Photonews

0920 hours, the Coastguard has tried to contact *St. Simeon* but with no reply, they asked us *"Can you get casualty to reply to us, are you under way yet?"* Our reply *"No we are still rolling around"*.

ST. SIMEON STARTS HER ENGINE

0924, *"The casualty is now following you"*, the words we had all been waiting for… a muffled cheer echoed around the wheelhouse, at last we were making way, a few more revs, and we began to lead *St. Simeon* in the general direction of Falmouth.

I nipped out onto the after deck to see how *St Simeon* was coping with the seas. Now she was making way, she was certainly struggling. I could see where the shore was still quite a way off, but certainly neither of us would have stood a chance if we got too close, the huge Atlantic swell was smashing into the cliffs, white water all along the coast rising high into the sky.

0946, the Coastguard requested our position, *"our present position 194 degrees, 12.2 miles from the Lizard, steering 040 degrees magnetic, to clear The Lizard, speed reduced to almost heave too"* reply *"roger"*. We continued to slowly steam with the sea, making little headway due to the strong tide and the wind that was now on the starboard bow. *"'In view of the weather we suggest you take the casualty to Penzance and we get the Penlee Lifeboat to relieve you"*. Our reply *"negative, he seems happier steaming into the wind, and a stern wind increases the danger"*, reply… *"roger"*.

1030 hours, it was obvious that we were going to be out here for hours yet, a message came down from above, what's our fuel state?.... Big D looked up at me from the floor, what a wreck.... he said *"would you mind Chris"*… I replied *"do you want an honest answer"*… he said *"thanks bud"*, we exchanged smiles. I made my way forward to the hatch that led below to the fuel tank space, the area stunk of diesel fumes, this made me feel instantly sick, I started to cough as I sank my knees to reach the levers just below the deck level that had to be turned to operate the "sight glasses", I waited and matched the glass tubes so as to make the best guess of the amount of fuel in each tank… each glass rose and fell as we rolled, I decided that we had 100 gallons left in each tank,… we had used 300 gallons in total so far. I shut off the levers and made my way to the steps to get back up into the wheelhouse. I put my foot on the bottom rung just as we fell off a wave, as I went up the boat went down,… I almost fell up the ladder! I reached the wheelhouse deck without climbing any rungs! When the boat hit the bottom of the wave I was laying half way out of the hatch, my chin hit the deck, I clawed my way to my feet and stumbled over to the radio position and muttered to Dave in the radio seat, *"used 300 gallons"*, he said *"OK"*.

I saw Viv out on the aft deck, staggering about, I thought what the heck's he doing out there?... I went to the door and said *"come in mate"*, he nodded and staggered in, he was frozen, he was trying to keep his hands between his legs, they must have been hurting with the cold, I pointed to a spare position on the deck by the chart table and said *"lie down over there for half an hour and warm up"*, he made his way over and got his head down, he was still clamping his hands between his legs, I threw him a towel, he didn't say anything but wrapped his hands up in the towel this kept the cold wet air off them and must have helped, he closed his eyes and was safely tucked up. As a matter of interest, later in the day I found out that the reason he was staggering about with his hands between his knees was because he was bursting for a pee!!!

One of the lads suggested that crew wives were phoned to let them know that things were going OK, this request was passed to the Coastguard who readily agreed, *"what about you Price'y?"* Alan said,… not being married the only person I could think of was my Mum, I was pretty sure she didn't worry about me when we were out at sea, in fact she often didn't know, anyway I thought it would make her laugh if the Coastguard rang and said everything was going well, she may even wonder what on earth was going on, although the weather was what it was and 'Bush Telegraph' as it is in small villages, it doesn't take long for news of all 'types' to get around.

PHONE MY MUM.. PLEASE

Someone passed me the 'mike', *"Falmouth Coastguard this is Falmouth Lifeboat"*… reply… *"go ahead"*… reply… *"I' would be obliged if you could phone my Mum and just tell her everything is OK., just in case she's worrying, her phone number is etc."*… reply *"yes will do"* … reply *"thanks"*.

That message caused my leg to be pulled for many years to come… The Lizard men who I knew well as friends and customers were all huddled in their boathouse in Kilcobben Cove listening to every word, having been unable to launch due to the severe weather conditions, with waves pounding at the lifeboat house doors they all congregated at the boathouse in the hope that the wind direction may turn, or the seas would ease a little so that they could join in the action,… no such luck for them today. Many of the lads we had seen the night before at Culdrose, nothing would have pleased them more than to be out here with us.

1040 hours, from the Coastguard *"are you happy with the Frenchman's course?"* our reply *"In view of our fuel state 200 gallons in wing tanks we would like to be relieved by the Penlee boat so that we can come in to refuel and take on a fresh crew"* reply *"we will come back to you on that"*… reply *"roger"*.

1154 hours the Coastguard called *"Helicopter Rescue 77 is airborne from Culdrose, they will be with you in 5 minutes,."* we acknowledged *"roger"*.

1205 hours we passed to the Coastguard and *Rescue 77 "our present position is 149 degrees Lizard lighthouse 10 miles"*, *Rescue 77* replied *"roger with you in 5 minutes. "* 10 minutes later at 1215 hours, we were anxious for the helicopter, it was battling against the wind to arrive with us, Graham spotted it, far off in the distance astern, Alan looked out of the aft door, he spotted it too, made his way to the radio *"we have visual astern, turn slightly to port"*… *"that's it"*. As the helicopter approached he came over the air to us *"please ask the casualty to steer 30 degrees to starboard"*, the helicopter required this so that when he came into the hover, the pilot would be able to be in position to see the casualty and control the aircraft… our reply *"all communications with St. Simeon are via Falmouth Coastguard as he only understands French"*.

The Coastguard managed to get the casualty to come to starboard and *Rescue 77* was able to lower more fuel for the bilge pump, no sooner was this done, when he said cheerio and disappeared into grey skies astern of us on route back to Culdrose.

By now Penlee had launched, she was an Arun class lifeboat ON-1085, (52-24), 13 boats newer than *Elizabeth Ann* (52-11) moored at Newlyn called 'Mabel Alice'. She was Lizards flank station to the west. At 1246 she called us up for a count for direction finding purposes,

Penlee's Arun class lifeboat *Mabel Alice*. Photo: RNLI Archive

this indicated to us all, that she was closing on our position and it wouldn't be too long before we were relieved, this was good news for all varying degrees of hypothermia and dehydration, everyone was very weak and extremely tired.

1325 hours Penlee asked us for our position,… we gave them our position… "*120 degrees Lizard 12 miles*", 10 minutes later from Penlee "*we have you in visual*", we acknowledged. This was great news… not long before we were officially relieved. We could then push the throttles down and make for home, it would also mean the boat's motion would change from the dreadful rolling that the combination of the sea state and our slow speed was producing.

1345 hours "*we are ¼ mile astern of the casualty and happy to take over the escort*"… Our reply "*roger thank you*". As soon as the Coastguard had completed his message both throttles had gone down, the familiar sound of the two big Cats 'screaming' could be heard in the wheelhouse above the sound of the wind, the bow of the boat lifted, the stern dug in and our speed picked up, at last we were on our way home.

I wondered if Neil Brockman was on board the *Mabel Alice*, Neil turned out for the Penlee shout to the *Union Star* on 19 December 1981, but the Coxswain wouldn't take him as his father, Nigel, the Assistant Mechanic, was on board. All eight of the crew perished that night.

I know Neil and his Mum, Neil's a bloody nice bloke! His Mum just like mine, soft spoken with a kind face. Never knew his Dad but I'm sure he was a bloody nice bloke too. Neil went on to become the Coxswain of the Penlee Lifeboat from 1993 to 2008.

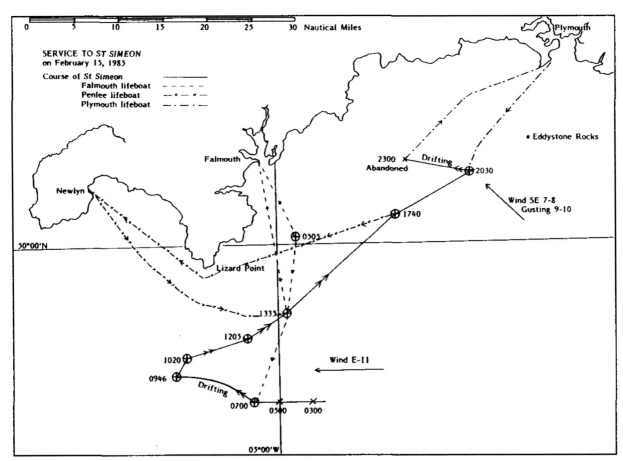

Chart showing the course of the *St Simeon*, Falmouth Lifeboat, Penlee Lifeboat and the Plymouth Lifeboat.
Source: RNLI Lifeboat Magazine

FULL SPEED BACK TO FALMOUTH

As we ran with the sea the lifeboat was broaching as we drove down the waves, this can be dangerous for less powerful boats as they can lose control and turn side on to the wave, the wave will then overtake and swamp you. Our lifeboat has a speed capability of over 18 knots and two engines producing almost one thousand horsepower, our direction can be controlled (sometimes with a little difficulty), so the broaching motion is corrected by steering, the whole process makes for an untidy looking passage through the seas; however as we accelerate down the waves our overall speed is increased considerably.

Things were definitely looking up. The sensation of speed, and the knowledge that we were heading for Falmouth boosted everyone's morale, I sat in the chair behind Dave who was sat in the radio seat. I spent a long time looking out of the port aft window, watching the sea's rolling towards the shore, and looking forward to a hot drink, and the ability to keep it down!

1455 hours the Coastguard advised us that due to the severe weather conditions in the harbour we would be unable to refuel at 'Duchy Warf', and that we could refuel on the '*Ulster Industry*' or at '*Coastlines*', we advised them we would sort it out when we got there. By this time we were steaming across Falmouth Bay, towards the entrance to Falmouth harbour, The Black Rock, and the docks.

I decided it would be good to go up top and join Viv and the other lads who had gone up, the wind had by now eased slightly, the seas were much shorter as we approached the entrance. We could see as we approached the docks that it was still pretty rough in the harbour. At last 1512 hours we heard on the bridge radio repeater that the Coastguard was asking for our position, Dave passed *"approaching Pendennis now"*. Pendennis Point is the short Peninsula of land that forms the west side of the entrance to the harbour, the Coastguard station is situated almost on the point itself, after receiving our last transmission I expect the Coastguard came over to their window to see if they could spot us amongst the waves.

As we steamed in towards the docks we could see in the distance the mess the harbour was in, yachts were rolling heavily on their moorings, many had sunk during the night, a few had broken moorings and were ashore....many of the masts of the yachts that had sunk on their moorings were sticking out of the sea, a strange sight.

Plymouth's Waveney class lifeboat *Thomas Forehead and Mary Rowse II* took all the crew off safely. Photo: RNLI Archive

It was decided we would refuel on the *'Ulster Industry'*, a long fuel barge moored in the harbour. We came alongside heavily fendered to protect the lifeboat. We rose and fell on the waves as they rolled along the fuel barge. As we took on fuel everyone was busy tidying up the boat, re arranging the wheelhouse, putting items back where they belonged and preparing the boat in readiness for service if required.

With the lifeboat topped up with diesel we all waved to the chap that had taken the trouble to struggle out to the fuel barge and make refuelling possible, we then left to go to our moorings.

We closed down with the Coastguard at 1550 hours and mustered on the after deck to wait for the lift ashore. Out came the boarding boat, a wet run ashore but the transfer was completed without incident, the conditions were much less 'hairy' and with daylight at least you could see what you were doing.

As we climbed the ladder onto the quay I was surprised to see the District Inspector of Lifeboats Les Vipond. He stood at the top of the ladder and shook us all by the hand, a very nice gesture I thought... we all shuffled into the boat house for a cup of tea and biscuits, Les Vipond came in and joined us.

Within about 10 minutes the lads started to disperse, I went over to Viv and thanked him for the exciting trip, we shook hands and smiled at each other,... I attach a great deal of importance when gauging a man's character on the strength and firmness of his handshake, Viv's handshake was very much like my fathers was, firm and strong.

St. Simeon went on towards Plymouth, Penlee handed over the escort to a larger French trawler and returned to station; later in the evening *St Simeon* started taking on more water and the Plymouth lifeboat was launched. Eventually she sank, fortunately the Plymouth boat took all the crew off safely.

It took a few days for me to recover, I was covered in bruises of all shapes and sizes, one of them wallet shaped!

Viv was told he was to be awarded a '*Thanks of the Institution on Vellum*' for the '*St. Simeon* job'. The Lifeboat Institution doesn't often recognise services in this way, maybe only 2 or 3 a year. It was certainly agreed by the crew and all the people of Falmouth that Viv's recognition was well deserved. The presentation do that was arranged was very enjoyable… If I remember correctly Big D was off the rum ……..

At the award ceremony Viv received his '*Thanks of the Institution on Vellum*', the rest of us received a '*Vellum Service Certificate*'. After the speeches there was a piss up, a few ended up legless, but of course there was a sober crew available should the maroons go off in the night.

The *St Simeon* service presentation by Lord Falmouth. Left to right: Captain David Banks; Chris Price; George Laity; Michael Wilson; Bjorn Thomassen; Lord Falmouth; Graham Pearce; Vivian Pentecost; Alan Barnes; John Barton; Don McLellan; David Barnicoat and RNLI Divisional Inspector Les Vipond.

This is to certify that

Chris Price

was a member of the crew
of the Falmouth life-boat "Elizabeth Ann"
and took part in the service
which was recognised by the Committee of Management
by the Thanks of the Institution inscribed on vellum
being accorded to Coxswain

Vivian Dudley Pentecost

when on the 15th February, 1985
the life-boat escorted the French trawler "Saint Simeon"
which was sinking thirteen miles south of Lizard Point
and proceeding towards Plymouth
until relieved by the Penlee life-boat
in an easterly violent storm with reduced visibility
because of rain and snow squalls
and a very rough sea.

DIRECTOR & SECRETARY

The 'A Team' on Vivian Pentecost's last day as coxswain on 5 September 1989. Left to right: Don McLellan; Michael Wilson; Chris Price; Vivian Pentecost; John Barton; Graham Pearce; Alan Barnes on board Falmouth's Arun class lifeboat *Elizabeth Ann*. Note the 'proper' lifejackets! Photo: Simon Culliford

Twin Cats in the engine room in St Mary's Arun 52-18 *Robert Edgar*. The V8 engines are similar to the straight 6's that are on Falmouth's *Elizabeth Ann*. Photo: Gulf Group Marine Brokers Ltd

RISING IN THE RANKS

When I joined the crew Viv explained to me that I would join as a reserve, and like everyone I would start at the bottom of the pile. 3 years after the *St Simeon* job Viv gave me a ring at work and said *"I have decided to bring you on to the main crew."* I replied *"thanks Viv that's great"*, Viv replied *"in every private's kit bag is a Field Marshal's baton, see you Sunday"* I had to think for a minute what Viv meant, as I have probably mentioned Viv can be a man of few words, each one chosen carefully, I expect he meant keep your nose to the grindstone and you can rise up in the ranks. Well I was so chuffed I could hardly contain myself!

Elizabeth Ann on exercise on 27 May1989. Taken from Fowey's Waveney class lifeboat *Thomas Forehead and Mary Rowse II* (previously on station at Plymouth). Photo: Simon Culliford

This was a huge privilege, I jumped from number 19 to number 9, I was getting on a bit old for the inshore lifeboat, not too old but have more to offer the offshore boat.

Every crewman has a number, Viv as the Coxswain was as you would expect number 1, I started at the bottom as number 19, eventually over the years rising to number 5 which was in effect the position for the third Coxswain with the title of deputy Second Coxswain, those above being the Coxswain, Second Coxswain, Mechanic, Second Mechanic.

As emergency Mechanic, Big D had already introduced me to the twin Cats, 6 cylinder turbo charged 460 horse power each!,

Our Arun *Elizabeth Ann* weighs 32 tons, 52 foot long with a top speed of 18.5 knots (that's 21.3 miles per hour), we have a range of 250 nautical miles!

Fuel tanks hold a total of 620 gallons of diesel (almost 2 tons!), they are situated just forward of the engine room, two huge stainless steel tanks with an emergency tank below, the pipework in the boat is complicated, Big D showed me how to engage the fire hose, also pump by hand diesel from one tank to another, how to feed both engines from one tank, pump bilges etc. We even carried a special oil Wave-Subduing Oil, to be able to pump into the sea to flatten out the waves, we never used this facility, it was probably left over from days when lifeboats had displacement hulls with a top speed of 8 knots. (Wave-subduing Oil - its effect is to reduce spume blowing off the surface and reduces wind-waves by up to 10%).

The first Sunday exercise following my promotion was great, a few pats on the back, delivered with enough force to dislodge any obstruction should I happen to be choking to death!

In the boat house, Big D stood in front of the engineer's room, well I call it a room, it was more like a corridor, a full length bench leaving just enough room to squeeze down to the end of the room.

"Better bring your gear in here bud" Big D grunted. Although you couldn't see his lips you knew when they were moving, the hairy face totally covered in grey curly hair, big beard, mop of hair, big moustache, when he is talking, if you watched his face, it looked like a large animal making its way through a dense forest. Big D was a real gor blimey Londoner, huge man 25 stone if he weighed an ounce, thick glasses and a blue Breton cap with a RNLI badge with propeller to show he was an RNLI Mechanic.

I knew instinctively when Don was smiling, the ends of the bush moustache twitched and the eyes squinted just a bit, I smiled back, took my kit off the crew rack and put it in the engineers' room… a very proud moment.

As a reserve there was always a scramble for the foul weather gear, one or two of the larger guys like myself looking for the XL jacket and trousers…. I had my own boots because I am size 12, I can squeeze into a size large jacket and trousers but my feet won't fit into size 10 yellow wellies.

To make sure no bar steward took my boots I had felt tipped 'Mr Price' in large letters on each welly, and from the day I did it I was known as Mr Price.

Big D said *"not sure what Viv has planned for us this morning bud, but whatever the exercise is you are mine."*

That meant I was in for a good whipping, starting engines, running the engine log, handing out gear to the deck crew, making the tea and just about every other job you could imagine that involved the mechanical kit on the boat.

The weather was blowing 5 to 6 south easterly, bloody cold as you would expect for November, we could head up to the east and find some lumps off the Dodman or down to the west where the tide around Blackhead threw up some interesting confused waves that would roll the Arun considerably when broached to (rolling heavily when sideways on to the sea).

The steady hand on the tiller

"EVERY time I get home after a job I sit down and work it all out again in my mind to see whether I could have done it better. Every time you go out you learn something fresh. It's never the same thing twice," Vivian Pentecost said.

At 55 he is a steady man in every way, in his movements, his talk, the way he looks you straight in the eye.

Viv is the coxswain of the Falmouth lifeboat. He is secure is his authority, both on the waterfront and among the townsfolk he has known since boyhood.

He joined the RNLI in 1968 as a paid deck-hand after "14 years and 199 days" in the Royal Electrical and Mechanical Engineers, with whom he served in Korea and earned his Sergeant's stripes.

He left knowing a great deal about the vagaries of machinery and little of the sea, so he set about learning all he could as quickly as he could from

Vivian Pentecost

the men of the 70ft. Clovelly cruising lifeboat, which stayed permanently at sea with its crew living on board.

His home was still in Falmouth and two years later he became mechanic of the Falmouth boat. By 1975 he had become so skilful a seaman that the was appointed second-coxswain/mechanic.

Five years later the RNLI changed its policy and told Viv he could not continue in this dual role, so knowing he had still much to give he resigned and waited to see what would happen.

"My notice expired on the day Falmouth's new lifeboat, the Elizabeth Ann, was named," he said. "The crew had asked me to be coxswain by this time and I took the new boat out during the ceremony as second-coxswain/mechanic and brought her back as coxswain."

With the loss of his full-time RNLI job he needed to earn money and Falmouth Technical College snapped him up as a part-time lecturer, first in ropework and then on engines and metalwork.

They were luckier than they had realised at the time because Viv is a craftsman in metal of astonishing ability.

He builds beautiful scale models of military cannon in a tiny but fully-equipped workshop at his home and finds them eagerly sought by collectors.

Viv is a quiet man, less interested in talking about himself than in making sure he is seen as only one man in a lifeboat crew.

"We work as a team. I am very proud of the team spirit we have in the boat," he said.

I have no doubt he will be surprised to learn that his crew are also very proud of him and the certificates marking his outstanding services awarded by the RNLI.

The lifeboat has to be covered for operational calls 24 hours a day and Viv is restricted to travel within the five mile radius of Falmouth that his radio-bleeper can reach.

If he wants to go further afield he has to make sure that deputy-coxswain John Bobin and the second-coxswain John Barton are both available.

"An RNLI coxswain has to be dedicated to the job but that's what it's all about, isn't it, being always ready," he said.

Coxswain Vivian Pentecost - newspaper cutting from the Western Morning News

Vivian Pentecost in his workshop at home.

A class McLachlan inshore lifeboat A-508 with Trevor Wilshaw, Chris Price and Dave Nicoll on board in Falmouth Harbour. Photo: West Air Photogrpahy.

McLachlan inshore lifeboat A-508 in Falmouth Bay during the 1982 Tall Ships Race. Photo: Rose Wilshaw.

There were a good 14 crew in the boat house, both boats were going to exercise, the Atlantic 21 with twin 70 hp outboard engines and *Elizabeth Ann* (Official Number 1058, signifying the 1058th lifeboat built for the RNLI since records began in the late 19th Century). Following the Southport and St Anne's lifeboat disasters of 1886 the RNLI determined that all lifeboats must be built to better standards going forward, and existing boats were tested to new standards. Each of the then 320 or so lifeboats was numbered as and when it was tested.

Viv's car drew up on the harbour, I could see him walking across to the boat house, he came in through the door, had a look around the changing room and across to the Mechanic's door, he looked at Big D and nodded, I could just spot the signs of a grin on his lips ... not a good sign, it meant they had cooked up a long list of tasks for the engineering side, I was expecting fire in the engine room, stretcher evacuation from the survivors cabin (situated under the fore deck), breathing apparatus, and the worst thing of all when there is a sea running, having to wear the dry suit.

The dry suit is great for keeping your clothes dry if you have to go into the water, but for the big guys it is not a pleasant experience, neck and hand seals are covered in talcum powder, sized for skinny 5' 6" whippets, bloody useless for 6 foot 14 stoners with size 12 feet, ... I was aware of the sneaky trick of not doing up the zip properly which means you get soaked, and knew that if you didn't vent the suit by sticking your finger in the neck seal and crouching down to remove excess air you are likely to float upside down!

The boarding boat was full, ten for the exercise plus Viv the Coxswain, Big D grunted to me *"go down below, switch on electrics, open sea cocks and start the engines"* ... I gave a single nod.

The crew massed on the after deck (back of the boat), Big D unlocked the padlock opened the door and let me in, through the aft cabin door is the hatch which is always left open, down the step ladder is the battery bank, we call it the tiller flat where the tea making stuff is situated, from there a small hatch to the steering compartment where the rudder linkage and tool box is situated.

Big D - Mechanic DonMcLellan. Just the best pal you could ever wish for, known by all the lifeboat crews throughout the south of England. There was nothing on an Arun lifeboat Big D couldn't fix!
Photo: Simon Culliford

I made my way into the small dark space and felt my way over to the 2 big levers that switch on the batteries, on came the lights and I could see.

The next job was to undo the engine room door and tie it back to ensure that when I went onto my belly to undo the sea cocks it didn't slam shut chopping my legs off!

Just inside the door were two small checker plate flaps, both with finger holes to allow you to lift them to reveal the port and starboard sea-cocks, two round wheels that had to be spun anti clockwise for what seems like a hundred spins on each until the sea-cocks are fully opened, allowing both engines to draw sea water to keep them cool.

Sea-cocks are always shut when the boat is left unmanned, just in case they leaked, and the boat sank on its mooring.

Both sea-cocks open then forward along the narrow checker plate floor situated between the two huge Caterpillar diesel engines, the starter panel for each engine both face into the gangway about amidships, leaving just enough room to crouch down ready to start the engines.

To start these engines the heater buttons need to be depressed for 2 minutes; this warms up the glow plugs and helps the compressed diesel spray to ignite.

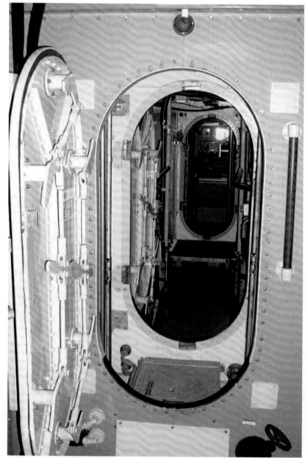

I crouched between the two Cats depress the heat buttons and start counting to 120 ... in the doorway appears Ken the Tea Pot, "*all right mate*" he says with his cockney accent, followed by a big grin, "*yeah*" I replied having forgotten where my count had got to. After what I thought was 2 minutes I moved my finger on the port engine to the starter button, the coughing and spluttering of the engine gave the impression the engine was going to explode at any moment, I kept the button pressed until the engine began to burst into life, the diesel rack arm was moving in and out as Big D cranked the throttle up in the wheelhouse, as the engine settled down Don set the revs at about one third revs, around 700 RPM.

Then the same for the starboard engine. Quite often when the engines were very cold and the batteries also just above freezing it can be very difficult to get the engines started. Always start the port engine first because the alternator can kick in and give the batteries a boost.

Arun engine room from the electrical panal and tea making area, accessed through the aft hatch in the wheelhouse. Note: through the first water tight door are the checkered plate covers that are lifted to reveal the port and starboard sea cocks. Photo: Gulf Group Marine Brokers Ltd

With both engines running it was time to leave the engine room and get upstairs to the wheelhouse, Ken stood back and beckoned for me to go.

Ken had just joined the crew, a big guy, a competent Mechanic with typical Mechanics hands, a solid handshake which is very important in life and a guy you could rely on 100 per cent!

Ken, like me, wasn't blessed with a cast iron stomach, and again like me was known to shoot the cat. He was awarded the name "Ken the Tea Pot" after confessing in the changing room after a lumpy exercise that when he was tasked to go into the tiller flat to put on a brew he felt his breakfast making its way up from his tummy to his throat and said *"reached for the receptacle"* ... there was a unanimous groan from the crew who were all listening intently to Ken's tale, then Pete at the back of the room shouted *"not the teapot"* Ken grinned and nodded his head rapidly ...there was another unanimous groan that could probably be heard in Penryn, two miles away.

"Don't worry boys I gave it a good wash out with sea water", looking around at the expressions on everyone's faces I couldn't help but laugh, John a huge strong man nicknamed *'the winch'* due to his immense strength stepped forward and suggested Ken should present the boat with a new teapot, which he duly did, a really good stainless one that stayed with the *Elizabeth Ann* until she went out of service.

As for the exercise, I was given the lifeboat engineers *'work out'* of a lifetime, the whole crew were obviously briefed to give me a hard time.

A new stainless steel teapot was presented to the crew by Ken after he 'abused' the old one during a lumpy exercise!

Ken 'The Teapot' Avis. One of the best, a Cockney geezer you could rely upon 100% (not often asked to make a brew though!). Photo: Simon Culliford

We had fire in the engine room, emergency steering, launch the *Y-boat*, casualty in the forepeak to be extracted in the Neil Robinson stretcher, anchoring, and to top it off I was volunteered for the dry suit to recover the man overboard.

All of the above was conducted off Black Head, in a strong tide and a south easterly 5 to 6! No time to feel ill, just knackered.

I sat in the engineers chair as we started our run home, Tea Pot came into the wheelhouse *"alright mate?"* I replied *"I will be after a good nights kip"*, Ken grinned, *"Viv wants you upstairs"*.

I went up to the flying bridge, Viv stepped aside from the steering wheel and pointed to it, this meant take the wheel. I looked around, we were on a good course, passing Coverack making our way into the Manacles and on our way back to Falmouth.

"Did the crew give you a hard time?" ..... I looked him in the eye *"of course"* I replied, Viv grinned, *"good"* he said.

On the run home all of the crew in turn came up to the flying bridge .... *"all right Mr Price?"* *"Good exercise Mr Price?"* *"Relaxing morning Mr Price?"* The whole crew enjoyed breaking me in.... to be honest so did I.

Arun 52-11 *Elizabeth Ann* in Falmouth Bay. Photo: Simon Culliford

PARACHUTE JUMP

Mid-summer, a crew fund meeting, 1900 hours at the boat house, the room was crowded almost everyone had turned up. It was a Friday evening, most of the young crew were planning to move off on a pub-crawl after the meeting, on the piss.

Mike being senior was the chairman, "*order please, not much on the agenda, there has been a request for a new waterproof camera for the big boat, Alan can you let us know what you are looking for?*"

Alan stood to address the crew, "*Disney Land* (RNLI Headquarters in Poole) *have turned down our request for a small camera, so I am asking the crew fund to buy one for us, the cost is £85, over to the floor*".

Before anyone had a chance to comment Snowy shouted out "*all those in favour*", everyone raised their hands; that was the end of that.

Mike said "*before we come to any other business I have one more item, RNLI fundraising are looking for two volunteers from each station in the south west to do a parachute jump to raise funds, I am looking for volunteers*".

Normally I would volunteer for everything, my life revolved around the lifeboat, but parachute jump? Bugger that! Every one of the crew knew of my fear of heights, I eased back towards the wall and tried to look as small as possible, the room went very quiet.

Mike said "*as we have two boats at Falmouth we are expected to supply four volunteers, I will put my name down as one, I need three more*".

The room stayed quiet, Big D looked over in my direction. I gave him the big eyes, '*sod off, stop looking at me*' I was desperately trying to convey!

Royston, the Senior Helmsman on the ILB put his hand up "*I'll do it*" he said. Royston is a tough man, he works out of the harbour office, strong, solid, dependable, no fears, obviously with one screw loose if he was going to volunteer to do a parachute jump I thought.

Another long serious pause... "*count me in*" said Trevor, another solid crewman on the ILB, '*come on*' I whispered to myself, just another volunteer and I am safe.

Silence for another minute or so, I lifted my eyes from the floor very slowly hoping no one would notice me, looked across to Big D who was focused on me, again I gave him the daggers meaning '*for god sake keep your gob shut*'.

Snowy stepped forward, I breathed out almost in relief to be mortified by the words "*I volunteer Mr Price*"... '*no way*' I screamed in my mind, but it was too late, the twenty odd in the room simultaneously "*yes, Mr Price*", the next 20 or 30 seconds was a room full of giggling idiots all looking at me!

I looked at Big D and mouthed in big lip movements so any lip reader could understand "*bastard!!!!!*"

Pride wouldn't let me back down, I squeezed my cheeks to make sure I didn't crap myself; I must have been as white as a sheet.

After the giggling subsided, ten or fifteen seconds of silence and Mike said "*I will advise H.Q. we have four volunteers, that will do... Any other business?*"

With no other business the crew fund meeting drew to a close, I received enough pats on the back to make a grown man to sink to his knees in pain... "*well done Mr Price*" "*break a leg*", "*this should help conquer your fear of heights*" and a whole range of other wind-up comments… to be fair I would have done the same if it was someone else. Within minutes there was just Big D and myself, "*all right Bud*", "*no I am bloody not*" I replied and then grinned, I had been stitched up like a kipper.

The jump was planned for 3 weeks' time, a Saturday training and Sunday the jump. These 3 weeks felt like a lifetime, my fear of heights include having to look away if someone on the telly looks down from a skyscraper ledge, it makes my balls tingle and I feel dizzy. Even in a hotel if I'm on the top floor, I can look out of the window but do not like looking down. I have never been in an aeroplane, how on earth am I going to cope jumping out of one!

It's not so bad being winched up in a helicopter. I always feel it would be OK if the winch wire snapped because I would land in the sea, and be all right. Probably not the case but that's how my brain works when it comes to heights.

Saturday took ages to come, 0800 hours muster at St Merryn Airfield in the Parachute Club room, so up early, turn off the lifeboat bleeper and get ready, clean underpants just in case, good breakfast and on the road.

I arrived at 0745 hours, parked up and started to look for Royston, Mike and Trevor. There were dozens of cars and vans in the car park and more arriving by the minute, it was going to be a big turn out!

"*Pricey*" …. I spun round; it was Trevor, "*seen Royston?*" He said, "*no*" I replied... we followed the crowd who were making their way towards two old Nissen huts.

Just outside the hut marked 'Parachute Club' was the fuselage of a small aeroplane with a bit of sawn off wing, it looked like a training aid, and very old.

We both entered through the door and followed the arrow to the club room, it was about half full, lifeboat men from all over the south west, some with lifeboat jumpers, many with casual clothes, even some in boiler suits.

I had my best jeans on, a green woolly jumper and clean underpants; I didn't feel out of place. I saw Royston and Mike making their way over from the corner of the room, Royston was smiling, and we all shook hands, "*why are you smiling?*" I asked; Royston replied "*aren't you looking forward to this?*" "*you must be joking, no sane person would jump out of an aeroplane*" I replied.

I looked around, almost everyone was talking, smiling and enjoying themselves. Am I the only one crapping myself?

I noticed a little guy enter the room, dressed a bit like Biggles, big moustache, leather flying jacket, just missing the silk scarf, he made for the middle of the room, I lost sight as he disappeared behind a few large lifeboat men, they could have been from Fowey!

There was a squeal a bit like an excited pig about to be fed, the high pitched voice,

(Biggles) screamed *"order, order, take up positions around the edge of the room please"*.

After a lot of shuffling we were all lining the walls, Biggles was in the middle of the room, *"all sit down and I will introduce your instructors"* he shrieked.

No chairs, so it meant sit on the floor, everyone sat down on the floor, I cast my eye around, couldn't recognise anyone, I nudged Royston *"recognise anyone?"* *"No, you?"* *"Not a soul"* I replied.

A couple of latecomers came in, full of apologies, quickly filling the gaps... Then in came three instructors, two young blokes and a girl, they lined up alongside Biggles.

"My name is Pete Sampson your chief instructor, with me today are Tony, Bill and Anne, they will be assisting me today and tomorrow with your training" everyone nodded at the instructors who in turn nodded back.

Pete said *"please go around the room and introduce your lifeboat stations so we can all get to know each other, starting with you."*

He pointed at Royston, *"Falmouth"* Royston said pointing at himself, Mike, Trevor and me, the four of us looked to our left, *"St Agnes"* the young guy said pointing to himself and his mate, and so we went around the room, there was one guy from Fowey who I didn't recognise, but he did nod to us after introducing himself *"Fowey"* he said ... No one from the Lizard, not because they are scared of heights, looking at some of the large waves they contend with, probably because the station is fairly remote and they need the

Some of the lifeboat crews at a briefing on how to exit the aircraft. Photo: Rose Wilshaw

entire crew close by in the case of a shout. Pete said *"Anne will tell you what happens today, the training day, and tomorrow we have a final briefing before kitting up and start the jumping."*

Everyone looked very intensely at Anne, not wanting to miss a word, the laughing and joking had stopped. I suspect most in the room, if not all had never done a parachute jump, Anne said *"anyone here done a parachute jump before?"* Out of the 40 odd sat around the walls two put up their hands; blimey I thought, they must be tough, coming back for more!

"Right" Anne said *"this morning we will go through the basics, we will learn how to land, commands from the instructors and chief instructor and some basic do's and don'ts, rules*

of the airfield and safety instructions, is that all clear so far?"

This young lady was confident, talking to a room full of blokes like they were 8 year olds in a junior school class room.

"I have done over 200 jumps at this airfield, we have an unblemished safety record, we are going to keep it that way, understood?" I looked at Mike, gave him the big eye and nodded slowly, he returned the gesture. I drew some comfort that this was at least going to be well organised, even if we were going to be instructed by a complete lunatic female that has jumped out of a plane more than 200 times, and the chief instructor dressed like a first world war pilot.

Anne continued *"this morning we will be outside, I will split you into three teams, Tony, Bill and myself will take you through the jumping and landing drills, after lunch we will go through the kit and how it operates. Tomorrow, weather permitting, we will go through final instructions, do some dummy jumps from the fuselage just outside and then go up in teams of six to complete the jump, right you twelve with Tony, go"*... Anne knew how to give orders, the twelve of us in the first group got up and shuffled towards the door, *"pick up the pace"* she shouted... *"Hitler"* I mumbled in Royston's ear, he looked round and whispered back loudly *"Hitler's wife"* ... but not too loud for Anne to hear (luckily).

'When I say jump you jump!' Photo: Rose Wilshaw

I said to the guy next to me as we formed a circle around Tony, *"which station"*... *"Sennen"* he said, *"how many of you?"* He replied *"just me"*... I didn't bother to ask his name or introduce myself, I got the impression he wasn't up for a chat, and anyway Tony chirped up, *"I'm not as bossy as Anne, but I want you to concentrate, this is important. How you land will decide whether you walk off the airfield or get stretchered off with broken legs"*.

There was complete silence; Tony's few words caught everyone's full attention, *"let's move over to the wooden boxes over there"*.

It was breezy and cool, my best woolly jumper was a good choice, and so far my best pants were still clean!

The boxes were laid out in rows of five, further down the field were more sets of boxes, in the middle group Bill was instructing and at the far end was Anne, bellowing instructions so loud she could have run all three groups.

"*Right*" Tony said "*one box each, stand on top*", the boxes were staggered so everyone could see Tony facing us, standing on his box.

"*When we land we have our knees bent, as we hit the ground we roll backwards like this*" Tony jumped off his box knees bent, crumpled backwards, got to his feet, then said "*have a go*".

I was one of the last, watching everyone else. I jumped off the box, forgot to bend my knees, fell backward and landed heavily on my butt, I gave an involuntary groan, Trevor grinned, "*landed on your wallet Mr Price?*" .... "*sod off*" I replied.

I looked over to Tony, he had spotted my bad landing, he gave a nod to let me know he had witnessed my failure, I felt the tips of my ears burning which meant I had a red face, I thought to myself I must try harder.

This box jumping off ritual went on for around an hour, first the group jumped, them each in turn with Tony watching and commenting on technique.

 My turn "*jump*" Tony said, everyone watching, I leapt off the box, crumpled to a heap, "*bend the knees more!*" Tony bellowed, "*Improving slowly*" he said looking down at me as I lay in agony on the deck, knees buggered, hips buggered, wallet shaped bruise in my left cheek (bum).

"*Comfort break*" I thought it was a Tannoy announcement, it was Hitler's wife Anne at the other end of the training field. Everyone looked down towards where she was gathering her group, we all started walking towards the Nissen hut looking forward to a brew.

Everyone was talking as we lined up alongside the trestle tables with the tea urn at the end, a slow shuffle, pick up a plastic beaker and fill it with hot water, tea bag, sugar for those who needed it.

"*What do you think of it so far Chris?*" Said Mike, "*painful*" I replied; before Trevor could say anything, a screech from the far side of the room "*everyone position yourselves around the room for the next lesson*" it was Biggles (Pete) ... Bill, one of the instructors went to the middle of the room, he said "*we are going to show you how the parachute is made, designed and packed, we pack all parachutes very carefully, never had a failure yet!*"

This was obviously one of his best jokes, a few sniggers, and from me and a few others including Sennen man, just blank stares, not the joke of the century, testing fate a bit. '*I'm trusting my life with a bunch of nutters*', I thought.

Anne 'goose-stepped' into the room and threw the parachute on the floor and stood there with her hands on her hips, a bit like a circus performer waiting for some applause. She certainly wasn't going to get any from me!

Bill began to unclip the bag, speaking at the same time, "*these clips pop open as soon as the rip cord is pulled, allowing the small parachute to tug out the main 'chute.*"

You could have heard a pin drop, Bill was fumbling with the clips and muttering to himself at the same time. The expressions on everyone's face was priceless, the sort of look you would expect if someone had blown off (silently) and no one would own up.

Eventually Bill pulled out the main parachute, he assured us all that although it looked like a birds nest, it would sort itself out with the aid of speed the wearer was traveling at, and then it would fully deploy.

"Who wants to help me repack it?" A chap from the other side of the room stood up and called out *"me"*… I am a compulsive volunteer for anything, but not this time, I could be stuffing my own parachute, into a bag with difficult to open clips. Not on your nelly was I going to step forward on this occasion, anyway I would have had a job to get to my feet after the pounding I took earlier by throwing myself onto a hard dirt floor by jumping off a two foot high wooden box.

The next lesson was for volunteers to have the harness and parachute strapped to themselves. A bit like putting on a lifejacket, but with a few more straps and the parachute bag on your chest.

In front of the bag was where all the clips slotted in, with a big button on the front. This was what you hit to release all clips and remove the parachute…The big warning from Bill *"do not touch this button until you are on the ground and want to remove the harness!"*

What! I thought, *"how the hell am I going to remember this when plummeting towards the earth at 100 miles per hour, crapping myself and ruining my best pants?!!"*

I had a flash back of a shout we had to a flat bottomed coaster from the 'Union' fleet. The ship was called *Union Venus*, a sister ship to the *Union Star*. The Penlee Lifeboat went to the aid of the Union Star, resulting in the loss of both vessels, and all hands, 'The Penlee disaster'.

The *Union Venus* was anchored in the entrance to the Helford River, the captain and first mate both were violently ill with food poisoning but were reluctant to leave the coaster in the hands of the *rookie* crew. Eventually, the Coastguards got them to agree to come off by the lifeboat and get taken to hospital for treatment.

We were launched. My biggest fear as this shout was not that long after the Penlee disaster, was to say by accident on the MF Radio *"Union Star this is Falmouth Lifeboat"*… So I wrote at the top and bottom of every page of my log in huge letters *'Union Venus'*, so every time I picked up the mike to transmit I read ' *Union Venus'*… it took a lot of concentration not to make the fatal mistake of using the wrong call sign, it would have been an unforgiveable mistake.

How was I going to remember not to punch the centre button and leave my main 'chute slowly falling to earth while I accelerated towards a hard landing? I began to whisper in my mind 'not the centre button… not the centre button'!!

We were then introduced to the emergency parachute, a much smaller bag with a small brass handle. My eyes glazed over as Bill began to explain what to do if the main 'chute failed to open … I desperately wanted to put my hand up and declare myself as withdrawing from the whole ridiculous suicide trip! If I did I would have to emigrate, there would be no way I could ever face anyone again. So I just sat there… praying for a forecast of a gale for tomorrow.

"Right lads, we will break for lunch, back here by 1400 hours when Pete will brief you on the drill in the aircraft".

Everyone nodded at Bill as if to say 'understood' and we began to file out of the hut, with very little talking. All the crews were beginning to understand how dangerous this was going to be, I think we were all focused on how hard it had been for Bill to unclip the main 'chute bag!

I had a sandwich in the car. We all agreed to meet by Royston's car for a relax and chew over the morning briefing.

I felt the need to be honest and said to Royston, Mike and Trevor, "*I hope it blows a gale tomorrow*"; the three of them looked at me and grinned, enjoying my fear!

It seemed like minutes and it was 1400 hours, everyone back to their positions around the room. I sat leaning to the left to take the weight off my right cheek (bum) to ease the wallet shaped bruise obtained in the morning with the box jumping off practice.

Pete stood in the middle of the room, legs wide apart, hands on his hips looking around the room at his students, smiling to himself…

"*Quiet please… it's now time to discuss what happens in the plane. I will be accompanying each team on the flight, I will be giving instructions to each one of you, my instructions will be clear! Anne will you show us how we jettison our main chute and deploy the emergency parachute*".

Pete stood aside and into the centre came Anne; the audience was totally silent, concentrating on every syllable uttered by the instructors.

I spotted Sennen man about five away to my left, he looked very concerned, I expect he was like me, crapping himself.

Anne was wearing the main 'chute on her front, just below it was the emergency 'chute, contained in a smaller bag, with a D handle on the front.

In a high pitch voice which reminded me of the song 'Tragedy' and in a similar pitch to the Bee Gee's she screamed "*to jettison the main chute you just punch the main button in the centre of the harness like this*" …thwack… with a thump that would have floored a big man, she wacked the front button, the harness flew to bits and the bag dropped to the floor… "*then, to deploy the emergency parachute you pull hard on this D handle*", she slowly turned around so everyone could see she was pointing violently towards where I expect her belly button was situated. Then she pulled out the handle, clutching it aloft in her hand like an actor holding an Oscar. I felt like giving her a round of applause, but luckily contained my excitement, which was controlled by the feeling of possibly having to conduct this emergency operation myself to stay alive!

Pete stepped back, legs apart like you might have to on the afterdeck of a lifeboat if the weather was lively and you wanted to remain in one position instead of staggering around the deck and bouncing off the railings and wheelhouse like a ball in a ping pong machine.

Well I say he stood there with his legs apart, they were so wide apart it looked like he was attempting the splits!

"*well, thank you Anne… you have seen what we need to do if we have to deploy the emergency 'chute*"… a long pause…"*when you are on the wheel plate, holding the wing spar, you will look at me and I will give you the command "jump". This will happen when the pilot dips the wing to give you a clear airspace so you will not impact the tail plane".*

I looked across to Sennen man, he had beads of sweat on his forehead, his eyes were bulging. He could have given Marty Feldman a run for his money! All lifeboat men were looking very anxious, the thought of wrapping yourself around the tail of the aircraft did not sound like an attractive option.

Pete continued … "*now in the very unlikely event the wire attached to your main 'chute rip cord gets snagged and you remain attached to the plane, you will find yourself trapped against the fuselage of the plane, you will look at me, put your hands on your head, I will cut the wire, as soon as you are free and clear of the aircraft you jettison your main chute, then you deploy your emergency 'chute…"*

"*What!*" I screamed, (one of those Tourette's moments) obviously flagging up that I was the most frightened in the room! …. 40 pairs of eyes were looking at me, waiting for the next outburst … I mutter "*bugger*" a bit too loud …. I looked to my right, Royston looking straight at me, the loudness of my outburst had made him jump… "*he must be phucking joking*" I whispered at the top of my whispering voice which I expect everyone heard.

There was plenty of shuffling going on, I could see many having similar thoughts to me…. what am I letting myself in for?

I expect at this point on other classes, Pete will have seen many walk out, declaring "*this is not for me*".

He looked around the room, a deadly silence, he said "*don't worry, this never happens but, just in case it does we have to be clear on how to deal with it*". …. Long pause "*tomorrow we will practise moving around in the plane and preparing to jump, using the training fuselage outside; time for a cup of tea I think*".

The room went from complete silence to everyone talking at the same time. One or two came over to me and shook hands, without exception smiling having enjoyed my outburst, no doubt saying exactly the same but under their breaths.

We milled around for about 10 minutes before Anne screamed "*right, let's get seated for the last session of the day*".

We all shuffled back to our same spots around the room, I moved forward a little quicker and grabbed Sennen's arm. "*Come and sit with Falmouth*" I said. He looked relieved, he knew no one, and, like me, was very afraid of what was to come.

"*Ever done this before*" I said, "*you must be joking*" he replied with a strong Cornish accent.

"What's your first name?" I asked, Trevor, Mike and Royston were with me, welcoming Sennen into the Falmouth fold, "*Ben*" he replied… "*what do you do on the Sennen boat?*" I asked Ben, "*I'm deck crew*"… "*did you know Eric Pengally?*" I asked "*of course*" he replied, "*a brilliant Coxswain*" he said. "*What's your day job*?" Trevor asked "*I am the publican at the First and Last, I really am not enjoying this*" he said… "*Don't worry it will be fine, these guys know what they are doing*" I replied.

Everyone sat down, some still talking, we were in a little group trying to give each other comfort, I thought it's time for a poem to cheer everyone up, (not for the whole room, just our little gang), *"we did poetry at school"* I began, *"this nearly got me expelled"*.

"I was dared by my best mate Jim, to say it in class", the teacher asked *"has anyone got a new poem for us*?" I put my hand up and stood up, knees knocking … the class waiting in anticipation ...

"There was a young woman from Leeds,

Who swallowed a packet of seeds,

Out of her arse grew blades of grass

And out of her fanny grew weeds"

Most of the boys nearly pissed themselves, the girls were all looking at each other with mouths wide open, I looked at Jim, knowing that was not a clever move, the teacher screamed *"headmasters office now*!"…. My Mum saved me from Dad's wrath by apologising to the headmaster, and regretfully I was not expelled.

I recited my poem to Ben to cheer him up, everyone within earshot laughed, Ben smiled, most certainly for the first time since he had arrived at St Merryn Airfield!

"Order" Anne screamed, looking straight at me as if I was a trouble maker… everyone settled down.

Pete took up his 'doing the splits' stance, *"right, now you have successfully left the aircraft, the static line will automatically deploy your 'chute, you will feel the 'chute open, you will stop falling quickly and begin to slowly float to earth, as soon as the chute opens you will say "one thousand, two thousand, three thousand, check canopy"* … right all say it"*.

'One thousand, two thousand, three thousand, check canopy!' Photo: Rose Wilshaw

We all chanted *"one thousand, two thousand, three thousand, check canopy"*, it was like being at school, a distant and unpleasant memory!

Pete inched his feet together a few inches to stop himself falling flat on his back *"if our canopy is not open properly, we ditch the 'chute and deploy the emergency 'chute,"* he looked towards Anne, who punched herself between her bosoms then clutched an imaginary D handle from her waist area, holding her hand aloft in almost a Nazi salute, my lips moved into grin position, soon to move back to blank expression as Anne cast her evil eye around the humourless students.

I expect most in the room were now considering rushing home and writing a will!

Pete gave a cough to bring the nervous group to order, *"we will finish up with a quick tour through the parachute packing shed so you can see how carefully your parachute will be packed"*… this was no doubt going to be in an effort to reduce the tension and make sure everyone comes back tomorrow for the jump.

The parachute shed was well used, one of the packers gave us all a demo on the procedure, I watched intensely, very very impressed! The detail for packing was meticulous, there was a lot of chatter, the mood picked up considerably, a good ending to a frightening day.

We all mustered in the car park and shook hands. Mike looked me deep in the eyes, *"see you tomorrow?"*, *"of course"* I replied.

I drove home slowly trying hard not to think of what was in store for Sunday, there was no way I could back out of this, so what's the point in worrying.

I had difficulty getting to sleep, all I could think of was being battered against the side of the aircraft with Biggles screaming at me to release my 'chute, then plummeting to earth at 100 miles per hour clutching a 'D Handle' plucked from the emergency parachute.

Sunday morning, best underpants, best woolly jumper, jeans, cup of tea, out of the Black Hole. The run to Perranporth was uneventful, empty roads, blue skies, slight breeze, so little chance the big jump was going to be called off.

I met up with Royston, Mike and Trevor; we strolled into the Nissen hut for the morning's briefing. Everyone took up their places, identical to yesterday as if the places were the property of each lifeboat crew.

Sennen man (Ben) stuck to us like glue, the RNLI is a great big family, as far as we were all concerned Sennen was one of us…. *"Alright mate?"* I said *"yes"* he replied, lying through his teeth, I expect like me he had his best underpants on, and like me, he wanted to keep them clean!

In marched the kamikazes … Biggles (Pete), Anne, Tony and Bill. The three stood almost to attention, while Pete stood legs apart, then wiggled his feet until he was half way to the splits, hands on hips. *"Right"* he said… pause… *"we are going to break into teams of six, first six outside and take up position near the training fuselage, the rest back to the boxes to practice landings, we will rotate until all teams have had jumping instructions."*

Luckily Royston, Trevor, Mike, Sennen and I all kept together, we were joined by one Salcombe lifeboat parachute volunteer, good guy. We made our way over to the *'landing boxes'* shaking hands and exchanging pleasantries. We could hear Pete giving instructions to the first six by the fuselage, the rest of us got onto the boxes, ready to jump off and practice our landings.

Arms in the air, *"jump!"* Tony bellowed, everyone stepped off their boxes and crumpled into heaps on the well-worn dirt patches in front of them, plenty of groans: *"again!"* Tony cried out… the drill seemed to last for ages.

From the Nissen hut came the cry *"next team of six"*… that was us…. This is going to be interesting I thought.

Pete stood by the sawn off plane, legs as always apart *"right lads, each team of six will board the plane, into the fuselage, the heaviest closest to the door, the heaviest is first to jump."*

I stepped forward with my hand up *"I'm the heaviest"* I declared, I probably was but I didn't want to get into a weight bidding auction, I just wanted to be first to go, probably to reduce the chances of me backing out…. or worst of all blacking out!

"OK" Pete said looking at me, *"you will be first, I will be at the front of the plane, next to the pilot, I will call you forward. When I pat you on the shoulder you will put your right foot out of the fuselage, onto the chequer plate on top of the landing wheel, your right hand on the spar… then your left hand on the spar, swing out of the doorway, put your left foot next to your right, you will hold position, look at me and wait for the instruction 'jump', that is when you let go"*.

Pete looked at us quickly in turn, *"is that clear?"*… everyone said *"yes"* at the same time. *"let's try it"* Pete said… we all piled into the fuselage on our hands and knees, me last, all facing forwards, Pete got in right up the front facing us all.

I was next to where the door used to be, just an open hatch. Pete was on the other side of the door looking straight at me *"you OK?"* … I *said "of course"* I must have been as white as a sheet…. *"Right exit plane"* Pete screamed, I guess to simulate the need to overcome the noise of the imaginary engine and wind noise.

I stuck my leg out of the doorway, my foot making its way to this plate fixed over the landing wheel, the plate about the size of a dinner plate, I thought how on earth am I going to get two size 12's on that!?

Trevor kitted up and ready to go. Photo: Rose Wilshaw

Right arm out, grabbed the spar then with my left arm lunging forward to grab the spar I was almost out, with two hands on the spar I swung my left leg out and over to meet my right leg, all I could think was this is bloody dangerous, what is it going to be like 10,000 feet above ground?

I looked back into the doorway… *"jump"* Pete screamed at me, I jumped backwards, distance from the ground about 18 inches… I stepped back and watched each of the team do the same thing.

Out stepped Pete *"everyone happy?"* … I looked at Trevor my eyes spelling out *'no I'm bloody not'*.

Off to the tea room for a brew, slowly the teams came in, up to the tea urn and back to their position around the room.

With everyone present, in came the instructors, Pete addressed us *"the wind is forecast to increase later this afternoon, so to make sure we get you all in we will start jumping in 1 hour, first team into the parachute shed to get kitted up"* … Off they went.

"The next team (us) will wait by the runway, do not come forward to the plane until it is stopped and I call you." Then Pete left. About 10 minutes past, in the direction of the runway, I could hear the coughing and sputtering of what sounded like an old motorbike engine revving into life, then the scream of the engine as the plane made its way down to the runway.

Royston Prynn , Trevor Wilshaw and Chris Price kitted up and ready to go. Note: I'm not smiling!
Photo: Rose Wilshaw

Anne screamed *"next team!"*, I want to scream back *'we're not bloody deaf'*, but thought better of it.

We made our way over to the parachute packing shed. Parachute club members were there and took us in pairs to our 'chutes, I put my hand on Sennen's shoulder and we went to our parachutes to get kitted up. I was now crapping myself, Sennen was too, just looking at his face you could see he was very unhappy.

The six of us shuffled out of the shed, laden down with bulky parachutes, over towards the edge of the runway. In the distance I could hear a big guy in a field shouting instructions to parachutes floating down having jumped from the aeroplane.

I looked up, the plane was making its way down and lining up to land, it's the first time I have seen it. After a heavy touch down it ran past us, went to the end of the runway, turned round and made its way back to our position.

It was a real old banger, not that I'm an expert on planes, having never been in one. A single propeller, a wing over the top of a flimsy fuselage, two spars and the dreaded chequer plate. No door, no seats except for the pilot's seat and an empty seat next to his.

The engine was on tick over, the prop spinning slowly. Smoke from the exhaust did not give confidence; it really was an old banger. I drew strength from the fact Biggles felt it was safe, he wasn't wearing a parachute so he obviously had faith in its ability to land in a controlled manner.

He stuck his head out of the hole where the door should have been, "*ready!*" he shouted, giving a hand signal for us to approach and board the plane …. I hung back determined to be the last on and first out! The boys on our team began to board, the floor on the plane was waist height, with minimal head room. They crawled in and crawled into position in the fuselage. There was just enough room for me behind the pilots seat, he looked at me and smiled and nodded. I tried a smile and nodded back; he must know by looking which jumpers were excited, and which like me were dreading the experience.

I was right next to the doorway looking out to the spar and over to the wheel covered by the dinner plate size checker plate, then across to Biggles, he looked at me with concern. He probably thought I was close to fainting. I gave him a grin, he instantly relaxed, looked across to the pilot and gave him a nod. They, like lifeboat men, obviously know each other well and convey instructions just by facial expressions and head nodding.

The pilot leaned forward and pulled on a knob, it was obviously the throttle; the plane began to shake and move its way down the runway.

This was it. Will I survive the next 10 or 15 minutes? Will my best pants survive? The runway tarmac became a blur and before I knew it we were airborne.

The whole plane was vibrating, I looked behind me, 5 lifeboat men all looking forward, no one smiling. I looked back at Pete, he was really enjoying himself, in his element.

I looked out of the hole, I was only inches away from the edge. Fields became a patchwork of colour, green and brown, small blobs were cows, the odd building roof. I quickly looked back into the cockpit. The pilot looked like a complete lunatic tugging away at the joystick contraption, swaying. He could have been singing but the noise of the screaming engine drowned out any chance of hearing a song.

On the lifeboat in heavy weather at night, I looked at something to the front of the wheelhouse to concentrate on to try and delay the onset of the inevitable creation of a pizza.

I focused on a pop rivet in the pilots Meccano' type seat, it was revolving in its hole, the complete seat was close to collapse, all the rivets moving like live woodworm in a rotten piece of wood.

We circled and circled and circled and climbed for what seemed like ages, but probably just 7 or 8 minutes.

Pete tapped me on the shoulder, *"look!"* he screamed in my ear, pointing out the door towards earth, *"see that field? That's what you will be aiming for"* ... what an idiot, *'see the field'* ... there were hundreds of them, pinhead size dots that must have been cows, I closed my eyes and nodded as I looked back into the back of the pilots chair ... I thought *"how does he think I'm going to be able to steer towards a particular field?"*, I would be happy with any field, my big concern was being skewered on a telegraph pole or gate post!

Pete tapped me on the shoulder *"get ready!"* he screamed... I could feel my heart pounding, my knees were quivering, hands shaking, a complete nervous wreck, my main focus was not to pass out, Pete clipped my pull cord to the fuselage.

He pointed to the chequer plate *"foot out!"*... here goes, foot out, the wind nearly took it off, we were doing at least 100 miles per hour probably a lot more, foot on plate, leg quivering like a bow string, hand out, grab the spar, second leg out, bum off ledge... I was now in position you would be in if you were standing having a poo.

Eyes streaming, difficult to breathe, complete face rippling in the wind, I looked back into the hole, Pete looked at me and grinned... the prop noise changed the wing dipped to starboard, *"Nowwwww!"* Pete screamed... I just let go of the spar and I was gone. Upside down, tumbling, the scream of the wind, I'm going to die, no control. I had no idea which way I was facing, then suddenly a spine jerking tug, within a split second I stopped accelerating towards earth, almost silence, the faint sound of the plane engine in the distance... I'm going to live; I'm the right way up ... I opened my eyes, I was facing Lands' End, I could see the end of Cornwall, the curvature of the earth, it was unbelievable, and I had never been so high up.

I had certainly forgotten about the one thousand, two thousand, three thousand, check canopy... my hands were clamped firmly by my side, I looked down, the fields were still a small patchwork but getting bigger.

The bellowing Scotsman was on the ground shouting *"can you hear me?"* I looked down *"yes you"*, I couldn't see him but I guess he was shouting at me, *"if you hear me open your legs"*, I opened and closed my legs a couple of times... it wasn't going to be long before impact, hopefully in a field, and not down someone's chimney pot or into a green house.

"Steer your bloody canopy!" he screamed, I really didn't want to raise my hands in case I slipped out of the harness (of course this wouldn't happen). Slowly I plucked the courage to grab the steering toggles, turned the 'chute left then right, I was almost beginning to enjoy the experience, but another look below and impact was imminent.

The ground got closer and closer, it felt as if I was accelerating; a couple of seconds later I hit, both legs rigid, no knees bent, (forgot all the training). I must have looked like the pole when they toss the caber in the Highland Games! I stuck in then I keeled over, splat, flat out in a muddy field, then a tug as the chute wanted to drag me along. I rolled over to my belly, got to my knees and quickly began to gather the chords, got on my feet and walked towards the 'chute, which collapsed, allowing me to gather it all up.

One of the parachute club came running towards me *"you OK?"* *"yes"* I replied with a big grin, the first for a few weeks, the ordeal was over, I survived, the whole episode did nothing for my dislike of heights!

The rest of the team were now on the ground, we all got together on the slow walk back to the parachute shed. The plane was touching down at the end of the runway in preparation for collecting the third team.

I looked at Sennen, a different man, smiling, happy, face full of colour *"fancy another go?"* I said to him *"no chance me ansum"* he replied *"you?"* I said with conviction *"only a complete idiot would want to jump out of an aeroplane, although to be fair I could understand wanting to jump out of that"* nodding towards the single prop Meccano kit as it was loading the next batch of jumpers.

That evening everyone met in the local pub in Perranporth to celebrate the day, a charity jump for the RNLI. The minimum that had to be raised by each jumper was £100… I dislike asking people for money and decided at the beginning to ask myself for a donation of £200, which of course I agreed to… from the few who mentioned their money collecting achievements some struggled to make £100, others managed a small fortune.

Falmouth crew having survived the jump! Photo: Rose Wilshaw

The four of us from Falmouth grouped together with Sennen, my chest stuck out so far with pride for not bottling out, I could have been mistaken for a women. My ugly mug spoiled the possible illusion.

There was a call for order, Biggles (Pete) in the middle of the room, legs apart, I could just see the top of his head, called out *"a toast to the RNLI and its fantastic parachute team"*… a huge roar of approval as everyone took a swig of their beer...me with a pint of orange juice looking like a doctors urine sample, had a swig too!

Sennen shuffled like a small peacock, pint of lager in hand, he looked totally at home, chirping like a canary,… a new man, we shuffled around the room as a team of five…. All very happy to be alive!!!

Copter crash probe

Experts sift wreckage after loss of three lives

DID the huge twin-engined Sea King helicopter from 706 Squadron Culdrose drop out of the sky, dive straight into the sea or crash land and sink?

These are the questions which crash investigation experts will be asking when they piece together the wreckage of the aircraft which went down on Tuesday evening three miles off Dodman Point with the loss of three lives.

The pilot and captain of the aircraft, which was on a routine night training exercise, was Lieut. Mike Johnston, aged 32, of Mullion. He was found soon after the crash in a critical condition, but died on his way to hospital. He was married with a son of four years.

The observer, Lieut. Paul Smith, aged 25 of Helston was found strapped in his seat by the Falmouth life-

By Stephen Ivall

boat. Lieut. Smith was also married and his wife Frances is expecting a child in six weeks.

The third member of the crew, 26-year-old Lieut. Neil MacBean, second pilot, was missing. He was married and had a three-year-old daughter.

● An intensive search throughout the night failed to find any trace of Lieut. MacBean and the Portscatho Cliff Rescue Company as well as two Wessex helicopters from Culdrose resumed the search at daylight.

The whole of Culdrose

Lieut. Neil MacBean.

Lieut. Mike Johnston.

Lieut. Paul Smith.

was in mourning on Wednesday as flags flew at half-mast. Commanding officer Capt. Jimmy James sent a message to all personnel. On Wednesday the recovery ship Seaforth Clansman was heading for the area

from Scotland in an attempt to lift the wreckage, which had been marked by buoys.

Officials at Culdrose were saying little, but it was understood that the pilot of the doomed aircraft had

notified Air Traffic Control that he was experiencing engine difficulties. He later sent out a May Day.

It was just after 8 p.m. on Tuesday night and weather conditions were reasonably good with a force seven wind and a slight sea. All three crew were wearing dry suits, which would have given **Turn to page 3.**

THE grim scene at Falmouth.

Copter crash probe

From page 1

them a few hours' survival in the cold water had they not been injured.

District controller of Coastguards at Falmouth, Tom Coppin said the suits would enable crew members to survive for about five hours. He would not hold out much hope after that in the conditions experienced.

Both the Falmouth and Fowey lifeboats searched the area with other helicopters, but nothing had been found of the third crew member by Wednesday afternoon.

Wreckage, however, was being washed up along the coast and police and Ministry of Defence officials asked members of the public to leave well alone and contact coastguards if they found anything.

"We want to find out what went wrong and we must have every piece of wreckage we can find," said a spokesman.

The Sea King helicopter can fly on one engine if necessary. It carries sufficient fuel for about four hours of flying and its fuselage is designed to float after what the Royal Navy term "controlled ditchings."

The aircraft has a reasonably good record and although it is due to be replaced remains one of the world's most modern and advanced helicopters, particularly in its role of submarine detection.

The 706 version of the Sea King is used for training and while it is not so sophisticated as frontline helicopters, can carry out all the same manoeuvres.

PORTUGAL

Tuesday's crash was the first fatality at Culdrose for some time, although Sea Kings from the air station have been lost elsewhere.

In February, 1983, an aircraft from 820 Squadron was lost off Portugal and the pilot killed. In the early 1980s there were a number of controlled landings on the water in Falmouth Bay and on one occasion the crew of a helicopter "drove" themselves ashore safely.

A Sea King from another squadron was lost in the Falklands and the civilian version, the Sikorsky, has had more than its fair share of problems.

The Isles of Scilly helicopter crash led to a number of improvements being made, but aircraft

used on regular North Sea oil routes have also been known to crash.

Captain James said this week that it was a tragic incident that had shocked everyone. "Our thoughts and prayers are with the families," he said.

"We will give them all the support we can. If anyone wants to make a tribute the best way is to get back to the task in hand and serve the Fleet Air Arm in the professional manner which has become our tradition," said Capt. James in his broadcast to the air station.

Newspaper cutting from the Falmouth Packet week ending 28 February 1987

SEA KING DITCHED

A Sea king HAS 5 helicopter similar to the one lost in this incident. Photo: Simon Culliford

Like many rough weather services at night, the launch to the ditched Sea King helicopter on the 24 February 1987 was, on the face of it, routine,… for me personally it continues to remind me to this day how cruel the sea can be, and how it can bring such tragedy to those connected with it… and their families.

On Tuesday the 24th the first radar course was due to start at 1830 hours in the RNLI's mobile training caravan. It was parked outside the Lifeboat House, down on Custom House Quay. The caravan is towed around the UK coast by the instructor, it is used to train lifeboat crews in the finer points of the use of radar at sea, and in particular how it is applied to the fleet of offshore lifeboats when on service.

The caravan is modern, fitted out with 8 students 'booths', each fitted with a radar simulator. Up at the front the instructor's booth has a monitor. He can, by computer and other modern complicated gadgets, plot the progress of his students, and if he is so disposed, throw the 'odd spanner in the works'.

I arrived early, around 1800 hours; our instructor for the course (which ran for 2 nights a week for 3 weeks) was a jolly little chap. I introduce myself, shook hands with him *"my name is Mr Price"*, *"I'm Jock Stewart"* we grinned at each other. I went into the caravan to find I was the fourth to arrive, I exchanged the usual unpleasantries you tend to do with likeminded mates, *"good evening Mr Price you old bugger"*,…one of the younger monkeys in the corner chirped, *"cheeky git,"*… I replied, I'm sure you can imagine how it all goes… all good fun.

The wind earlier in the afternoon had started to whip up from the east, a south easterly gale was forecast, and it was cold and blowing quite a bit, just what you expect in February. The caravan was creaking and rocking a little as the odd gust clipped it.

More of the lads arrived, the caravan began to get a little crowded, the heater was trying hard to keep the unit warm. At around 1930 Jock called for order, we all took our seats, and the lecture began.

The radar is an amazing bit of kit, in good sea conditions at night or in fog I find it easy to use, in rough weather things are a little different,… when the boat is pitching and rolling you hang on to the radar with both hands, and look through a rubber lipped funnel into the screen. The picture consists of yellow shapes that glow bright and then fade as the sweep arm passes around, like a second hand on a watch (but going much faster)... as it passes around it re-energises the picture, the rest of the picture is speckled due to the pitching of the boat, and rough seas, making it difficult to identify anything but the largest of ships. They appear on the screen as a good echo, or very faint, it really depends on the angle of the radar as it sweeps over the area that the ship is in. In the largest waves the boat can be pointing up towards the sky, or down towards the sea bed.

After 15 to 20 minutes with my head in the radar in lumpy weather, I am totally disorientated, you completely lose touch with the boat's motion, in fact if I have to shift to another position in the wheelhouse after coming straight off the radar I feel quite giddy!

The lecture was getting off to quite a good start, Jock was used to all the wise cracks, no doubt he had heard them all before, from other lifeboat crews around the coast.

The wind was picking up by the minute, it was due to reach gale force by the end of the evening, Jock had to speak up to make himself heard, the caravan was rocking gently. As the odd gust hit, it would creak and rock a little more vigorously. One or two of the younger lads looked at each other as the caravan rolled and shook,… it was a little like being at sea!

BLEEP BLEEP BLEEP

At 2025 hours the big boat bleepers started to bleep… Jock stopped talking and stepped back away from the door, he could see that the door was not a safe place to stand by. The inshore boat crew got out first, we were all keen to be the first out the caravan and all arrived at the door at the same time; as we wriggled to get out we became jammed, it was just so funny, I saw Jock out the corner of my eye he was creased up with laugher. *"I'm first"* Dave shrieked. Three of us all laughing pushed him, he popped out the caravan door like a champagne cork, we all followed, we made our way the few steps from the caravan door to the lifeboat house in a matter of seconds.

If you are lucky enough to get into the boat house before the rush begins, you stand a good chance of getting your waterproof kit on in comparative safety, when eight or nine are trying to get 'kitted up' at once it's a bit like a 'ruck' on the rugby field, pushing, shoving, elbows, arms, shoes, wellingtons.

I take size 12 wellies. The main crew have their own kit due to the huge range in sizes, small to extra-large, then to Big D. Any crew who arrive from lower down the list will steal anyone's kit, if you are not geared up when the Coxswain arrives you stand little chance of getting picked as an extra to join the main crew!

To make sure no one takes my wellies I have written Mr Price in huge letters on each one, not that I'm particularly precious about my wellies but they are the only pair in the boat house (with the exception of Donald's) that I can get my feet into.

As the newly appointed wireless operator, I made straight for the phone, called the Coastguard to get a brief sit rep, so that I would be able to brief the Coxswain as he got his kit on. *"This is the boat house"* I said, the reply *"we've got a Sea King ditched three miles south of the Dodman, launch immediate"*, I replied *"Roger I'll call you on 16 shortly"*… *"Roger"* was the reply… I put the phone down.

Second Coxswain John Bobin.
Photo: Simon Culliford

By this time the Coxswain Vivian Pentecost had arrived, John Bobin the Second Coxswain was in, so to was Donald the Mechanic… I said to Viv the Coastguards exact words he nodded to me to indicate he had received the information; he didn't utter a word, but looked very concerned. It was by now blowing a full gale; it looked like this wasn't going to be a jolly… which turned out to be the case.

About 5 minutes has passed since the bleeper sounded, the crew room had about twenty four bods milling around, main crew, ILB crew, trainees even Jock the radar instructor was ready to go if required, it was chaos. Cliff, the boarding boat attendant, appeared at the door to let Viv know he was ready to run us out to the lifeboat.

Viv looked around, nodded to his main crew, which consisted of John Bobin, (Second cox) Don (Mechanic), Graham (2nd Mechanic), Barto, Alan and Mike, and myself as radio operator. As we started to move towards the door Viv called out "*Bjorn and Tim*", those two lucky reserves that were to go with us this evening… disappointment for those that couldn't go, but their turn would come, as they move up in seniority, as the years go by.

Tim Julian later in his RNLI career when he was the station mechanic. Photo: Simon Culliford

We ran down to the boarding boat. As this was a 'hurry up job', there's no time to chat. The main crew know their jobs off by heart. When we 'hit the lifeboat' things run like clockwork, very few commands are uttered, they are just not necessary.

On the run out to the lifeboat in the boarding boat, as we cleared the quay the spray from each wave as it hit the bow sprayed over the crew, we all kept our heads down in an attempt to keep as dry as possible. Viv told the younger crewmen to take the cover off the flying bridge, this was their job, as soon as they boarded the lifeboat, he didn't bother to tell anyone else what to do. Viv normally stands on the afterdeck out of the way and keeps an eye on things, nodding with approval, as the boat is prepared for sea at double time.

It normally takes about 5 minutes to get the lifeboat rolling from a 'cold start'. As Cliff brought the boarding boat alongside the starboard side of the lifeboat there was a mass scramble to get aboard, I normally undo the padlock on the aft wheelhouse door and open it. Don and Graham the first and Second Mechanics go in first, they make their way below to flash up the engines, the first one below flips in the battery coupling switches, the lights come on in the wheelhouse, Alan makes his way forward to the throttles, he checks them for neutral and stands by as those below open the sea cocks (for the cooling water for the engines), and prepare the engines for starting.

Until both engines are running the navigation equipment cannot be switched on, while Alan waits for 2 minutes or so, I make a start on the radio.

"*Falmouth Coastguard, Falmouth Coastguard this is Falmouth Lifeboat, over*",… reply: "*Falmouth Lifeboat this is Falmouth Coastguard, over*" … "*Falmouth Coastguard this is Falmouth Lifeboat, we are launched and proceeding, request casualty position, sit rep and time check please*",…

Bjorn Thomassen.
Photo: Simon Culliford

By this time both engines were revving, fans are switched on, electrics, navigation lights, even a blue flashing light, Alan starts up the radar and Decca Navigator. Meanwhile Viv is in position on the flying bridge, he has indicated to two of the crew on the foredeck to let go the moorings,… we start to move off.

I continue with the Coastguard…"*Yes Falmouth Lifeboat, a Sea King helicopter is down,*

Coxswain Vivian Pentecost and crew coming aboard Falmouth's Arun class lifeboat
Elizabeth Ann. Photo: Simon Culliford

position 180 degrees from Dodman Point, range 3.8 miles, one crewman picked up, critically injured, 2 crew missing, over". I had the main facts scribbled down on my note pad, and replied "*Roger, I will pass the crew list shortly*". I made a note of the position on a separate piece of paper and passed it to Alan at the chart table.

By now we were leaving the Docks and making our way from the shelter of the harbour, and out to the open sea.

LEAVING FALMOUTH

The revs were picking up as Viv opened the throttles, we had got away from our moorings in under 5 minutes,… before we were abeam of the Governor Buoy (just beyond the Docks)… Don passed through the intercom to the bridge, "*both engines warm*",… Viv pushed the throttles right forward, the boat picked up to full emergency speed of around 18 knots, we were running flat out.

As we hit the open sea the boat begins to pitch, I am checking my notes, and the crew list before calling the Coastguards back to pass it. They beat me to the draw… 2050 hours on channel 16… "*Falmouth Lifeboat this is Falmouth Coastguard, go to channel zero*",… "*roger, channel zero*"… "*Falmouth Lifeboat this is Falmouth Coastguard, pass your crew list and ETA the casualty*". Alan shouted "*35 minutes*". – my reply "*crew list, 1, 2, 3, 4, 5, 6, 7, 13, 17, 18, total P.O.B .ten, ETA. on scene minutes 35, standing by zero*"… the

Coastguard's reply.. *"Roger"*.

My next job was to inform Lands' End Radio on the big MF long range wireless on the distress / calling frequency 2182 that we had launched on service. *"Lands End Radio this is Falmouth Lifeboat, over"*,… *"Falmouth Lifeboat this is Land's End Radio. Good evening sir, you are loud and clear"*,… *"Lands' End Radio this is Falmouth Lifeboat, good evening sir, you are loud and clear also we are launched on service, listening 2182, over"*,… *"Thank you Falmouth Lifeboat"*.

By now we were well into the bay. It was a dark, cold, windy, rough night, we were heading up to the east towards the Dodman, my log was made up. I had a little time for reflection before we reached the search area... the pilot lifted from the sea was in critical condition, two others missing, things were not looking good, the seas were short and steep, I had this terrible feeling that their chances of survival were very poor indeed,… as long as they were not injured there was a chance, I crossed my fingers.

The VHF crackled, Fowey Lifeboat had launched, they were opening up with the Brixham Coastguard. I advised Viv on the intercom that Fowey had launched, and advised him that I would open up with them shortly… he was happy with that. Fowey had a Brede class lifeboat, it's a small boat, built on a Lochin 33 foot hull,… strictly speaking she wouldn't be out in this weather as she is restricted to force 6 … still the lads on the Fowey boat are a pretty tough lot, and I can't imagine any weather they wouldn't launch in.

A couple of minutes later I copied Fowey advising Brixham Coastguard she was returning to station with an engine problem… I bet the lads were jumping….

2110 hours, the Coastguard called up with an update *"we have an update on the datum point… 193, 3.5 nautical miles Dodman Point,"* we replied *"Roger, we are searching in the Gull Rock area, we have a helicopter searching in our area, our position is Nare Head 200 true, range 3 miles, we will proceed to Dodman, continuing to search to the datum point, over"*… *"roger Falmouth Lifeboat, all copied"*.

As we left the Gull Rock area to cross the bay towards the Dodman we hit one or two fairly big waves, then without warning what can only be described as a black hole,… a very deep trough, it took us all by surprise, we continued in free fall for a second or two, and as the bow dug in, the kit in the wheelhouse went flying, including my good self! I caught one of the upright poles in the wheelhouse to stop myself crashing into the radar seat, I pivoted round and caught my bum on the corner of the chart table,… deep pain!

We continued to motor on, I retrieved as much gear from the floor as I could find… there was an extremely strong smell of diesel in the air, I thought that perhaps there was a problem below,… Alan stepped into the wheelhouse to check our position and check that I was all right… *"OK?"* he said … I replied *"yes, OK, can you smell the diesel?"*… *"yes, it's the helo's fuel oil, it stinks outside"*. That explained the smell, it was almost overpowering, a constant reminder that this was a true disaster!

Things were beginning to hot up, activity on the radio was increasing, Fowey Lifeboat advised Brixham Coastguard it had repaired its engine and was proceeding from Fowey for the search area… helicopter traffic was short and precise, there were three on the scene, criss-crossing the datum, I could see search lights in the sky ahead of us.

2112 hours, from Falmouth Coastguard to us, *"The datum point is 50 degrees 08.30 north, 004 degrees 49.10 west, will you please carry out a sector search with tracks of three quarters of a mile"*. Our reply *"yes, all understood"*.

Alan was still in the wheelhouse, I made a note of the new datum on a scrap of paper and passed it to him…He began to prepare the chart, the rest of the crew were up top, eyes peeled, the two searchlights scanning, one port and one starboard, it was now blowing hard, with a little sleet in the air.

THE LIFERAFT

Viv came down to have a look at the chart, no sooner had he entered, when John who took over the wheel on the bridge altered course, and passed down on the intercom that he had spotted a strobe light and was proceeding to investigate … Viv said *"pass that to the Coastguard"*. As he left the wheelhouse on his way back up to the bridge, I replied *"Aye, Aye"*, … I don't suppose he heard,… he was disappearing through the aft wheelhouse door as I spoke.

The time 2125 hours… to the Coastguard, *"We are going to investigate a strobe light, our position to follow, stand by"*… (Alan took our position from the radar and advised me)… *"Our position is Dodman bears 060 degrees range 4.39 miles"*, Reply *"Roger"* I completed my entry in the log, then moved forward in the wheelhouse to have a quick peep through the window… I could see the strobe; I crossed both fingers and prayed (mentally and with my eyes open) that both aircrew were safe in the liferaft that we suspected the strobe was coming from.

2130, Viv called me on the intercom, *"we are alongside the liferaft, no one in it"*. *"OK Viv"*… my heart sank. I frantically noted Viv's message ready for accurate transmission… 2132 to Coastguard *"we are alongside liferaft, no one in the liferaft, what shall we do with it?"* … the reply *"Is it attached to anything?"*… Viv was monitoring the transmissions on his bridge radio, came over the intercom *"no"*, my reply to the Coastguard *"No, negative"* they replied *"what is the wind speed and direction"*,… I said *"stand by"*… *"what's your best estimate Al"*… Alan replied, *"south east, five to six"* I passed it,,… they replied *"Roger"*.

I stood by waiting for the Coastguard to answer my original question, I imagined they were all in their ops room, saying to each other *"what shall we do"*… it seemed as if hours were ticking by, we were wallowing in short seas, waiting by the liferaft…waiting …. waiting, I imagined by now Viv was getting very impatient.. I was right.. *"what do they want us to do"* Viv snapped on the intercom, *"Falmouth Coastguard this is Falmouth Lifeboat do you wish us to proceed with the search?"*… the reply *"Yes proceed"*. My reply *"Roger"*, my tone of voice and choice of words suitably relayed Viv's impatience, and I am sure reminded the Coastguard that we required fast reply's and top quality decisions!!

Viv grunted *"proceeding"* on the intercom as he increased speed and turned the boat back towards the three helicopters searching in the distance.

2140 hours, from the Coastguard *"There is a helicopter in the area who will flash his landing light at you, proceed to him, that is the datum point"*,… *"Roger"* I replied… Viv came over on the intercom, *"ask them has the helicopter sunk, and that we are proceeding to the datum point now"*.. *"OK Viv"*.

To the Coastguard *"from the Coxswain, has the ditched helicopter sunk?, we are proceeding to the datum point now*", the reply "*stand by*"... 3 minutes later... "*proceed with caution, if you sight wreckage use as the datum point*", I didn't get a proper answer, I really didn't want to labour the point with the Coastguard as it would bog us down in trivia... luckily Viv who has a lot of experience was thinking the same... he said over on the intercom "*we will do our own thing*",... a great feeling of relief, he had obviously heard the message and like me felt there was no need to continue asking for instructions, as we

Fowey's Brede class lifeboat *Leonore Chilcott* Photo: John Mitchell collection

were best placed to make the decisions regarding operational matters.

We were now in the search area. It was cold and very dark, we started to track across the search area... As we turned north on a new course, we had the wind up our stern, the strong smell of fuel oil blew straight into the wheelhouse, the smell was awful... Alan decided to go up onto the flying bridge with the rest of the lads, leaving me in the wheelhouse... With the combination of the boats motion and with the strong diesel smell I could have used some fresh air too!!

Things settled down for about 10 minutes, Fowey Lifeboat called up Brixton Coastguard to advise them she was approaching the search area and was now in Falmouth Coastguard's 'patch', they then had a radio check with Falmouth Coastguard.

2156 hours, the boat slowed, over the intercom, "*we are alongside a yellow marker buoy*",... "*Roger*". I made a note of the lat and long from the Decca navigator.... "*Falmouth Coastguard this is Falmouth Lifeboat... our position is 20 degrees 09 02 north, 004 degrees 51 78 west, we are alongside a yellow marker buoy ... stand by*". As I was advising the Coastguard Barto pushed in through' the aft wheelhouse door "*it's a grey bouy*" he said, I passed this.. The Coastguard replied "*Roger... the helicopter flashing his landing lights is over the datum point*",... "*Roger*" I replied. I passed the Coastguards message up to

Viv... we picked up revs and we made our way towards the helicopter.

2159 hours... "*Both lifeboats this is Falmouth Coastguard please act independently, Falmouth Lifeboat to act as on Scene Commander*". We both in turn acknowledged the Coastguards transmission. As we were both acting independently nothing much changed. Viv called down "*Chris can you make a note of Decca reading every 10 minutes*" I replied "*no problem Viv, I have been for the last half hour*", reply "*thanks mate*".

Tim one of the younger lads slipped in to the wheelhouse to get a pair of gloves, "*it's bloody cold out there*", he said, he looked cold too, he put on a pair of gloves, and disappeared back outside.

The boat was pitching and rolling as we criss-crossed the search area, on every turn and new heading we took on a different motion. The wheelhouse was cold and dark, except for the glow of instrument panels, the flashing of the radar as the arm swept over the land and 'relit' the picture on the radar screen, and the glow of the panels on the various radios.

Not knowing which way the boat was going to roll next made it awkward to stand, hanging on to something solid was essential. 5 minutes had passed, not a word on the radio, just the noise of the engines, and the occasional wave splashing against the wheelhouse windows, the Coastguard called up ... it made me jump (I was day dreaming)... "*what is your position?*" I checked the Decca and passed "50 degrees 09 06n, 004 degrees 52 35w"... Like all of us in the search area the Coastguard must have been getting anxious for results...the chances of a good result were very slim indeed but there was a chance!...

The combination of cold and the boats motion made me feel quite ill... well I say ill the last thing on my mind was a big greasy breakfast! The radios were completely silent, the helicopters were still busy ahead of us, they were working a different frequency to us, so all our contacts with them were through the Coastguard, they must have been feeling terrible... as every minute passed it reduced the chances of survival of the two lads we were all looking for.

2213 hours, from the Coastguard "*have you located any wreckage yet?*" What a stupid question I thought to myself as I replied "*negative*"... I felt like saying "*we will let you know as soon as we find anything*"... but I appreciated what it must have been like for them. When I was a trainee on the lifeboat, I used to rush down every time the maroons went off, hoping that there be a place for me... many times there wasn't... there is nothing worse than listening to the action on the radio, from the crew room... very frustrating!!!

At 2220 hours the Coastguard called up, "*we have a new search area, boundary 50 degrees 08 50n, 50 degrees 10 00n, 004 degrees 52 50w, 004 degrees 48 50w*", I replied "*Roger all copied*", I made a separate note for Alan in case he wanted to put it on the chart, although I couldn't see the point, we were following the helicopters as the datum point drifted along the coast.

JOHN BOON'S HELMET

10 minutes later things began to happen, we went half astern and began manoeuvring, Viv had obviously spotted something, Alan rushed in and said, "*We've spotted a helmet in the water, there could be a body underneath it*"... I went sort of numb with fear, please

don't let it be a body I thought... there was a lot of activity on the after deck,... I read the Decca reading and prepared a message to send to the Coastguard... I hoped and prayed it wouldn't have to be a body.

I popped out on deck to have a quick look, the search light shone down on the helmet; I dashed back into the wheelhouse to man the radio... Then someone shouted in, *"it's just a helmet"*... thank God I thought... I picked up the mike, *"Falmouth Coastguard this is Falmouth Lifeboat"*... *"go ahead"*,... *"Coastguard, Lifeboat, our position is 50 degrees 09 29 n, 004 degrees 51 27w, we have found some wreckage, we have sighted a helmet wait one"*... one of the lads called out *"we've got a helmet, it's got some writing on it"* ... Mike brought it into the wheelhouse and gave it to me.. *"Coastguard, Lifeboat, the helmet is old and well used it bears the name John Boon"*... *"Roger, from your present position carry out a sector search"*, I replied *"roger"*, I then called Viv on the intercom and advised him of the Coastguards request... *"OK"* he said...

The Coastguard must have informed the searching helicopters, because within 2 minutes the area around us was well lit from the sky by their powerful searchlights.

Fowey Lifeboat was abeam our starboard side. Viv asked me to advise them to carry out a sector search, them to go east, and us west, I did this and we were off... We were now amongst the wreckage... the chances of finding the two lads were much better, it had been around 15 minutes when activity became intense, the helicopters were gathering ahead of us.

THE WORST TYPE OF NEWS

2245 hours, a helicopter was flashing us, he had obviously found something and wanted us to go over to him, Viv altered course... As we moved towards him, the Coastguard called up *"Kilo 91 has found a body in a seat please recover"*... I replied *"Roger, we are making our way over now"*.

My heart sank down to my boots, it felt as if we had failed this young man... I didn't have much time to dwell on the news, we were fast approaching the pick-up point... as the engines slowed, we were under the helicopter searchlights... I noted our position... Graham came into the wheelhouse, *"We need some rope Chris"*, I passed him the heaving line, he didn't say anything, he looked as if he was in a state of shock... it must have been a dreadful sight,... a young man strapped in a seat, in the sea.

2253 hours, *"Falmouth Coastguard, this is Falmouth Lifeboat, our position is 50 degrees 09 32n, 004 degrees 51 54w, we are recovering the body now"*, the Coastguard replied *"please identify the body as soon as possible"*.. I replied *"stand by please"*... I stepped out onto the after deck... the lifeboat was beam on to the sea, we were rolling like a pig, four or five lads were recovering the seat and its occupant on the port side, using the 'A' frame and ropes, it was a difficult operation... Viv was looking down from the bridge, I nipped up to him, he looked at me... I could see he was choked... I said the *"Coastguard wants me to pass the chap's name, are you happy for me to do this on the VHF?"*... He looked at me for a second or two as he thought, and nodded,... *"OK"* I said.

Viv's not keen on names being passed on VHF,... with so many people listening in, including the press, all confidentiality is lost... This was different... As I came back down to the after deck I said to Barto *"I need the chap's name"*... I could see some writing on the helmet the young man was wearing … Barto said "*Smith*"… I nodded I went back in to the wheelhouse and called up the Coastguard.

"*We have recovered the body… the name on the helmet is Smith*"… the Coastguard replied "*Roger*".

There was quite a struggle to get the helicopter seat and body onto the lifeboat, the lifeboat was rolling heavily, attaching lines was very difficult. Eventually this was achieved and the seat was winched on board, using the 'A' frame with a rope and pulley, As soon as the seat was inboard Viv turned the boat head to sea, this stopped the violent rolling motion and left the boat rising and falling by the bow, pitching, this helped the lads who were securing the seat in position on the side deck.

Donald, Graham, Bjorn, Tim and John Bobbin came into the wheelhouse, they were all soaked through… freezing and looked like they were in a state of shock… I expect looking down from the flying bridge of the lifeboat and seeing a young man strapped to his seat, breaking the surface in large waves, illuminated by the helicopter searchlights must have been a terrible sight… I threw Donald a dry towel, "*Thanks bud*", he muttered as he began to dry his face.

Viv called down from the flying bridge, "*we are returning to Falmouth to land the body*"… "*OK... I'll let the Coastguard know*"….to the Coastguard "*We are returning to Falmouth to land the body, do you wish us to leave the body in the seat*"… reply "*yes*"... our reply "*roger, our ETA 35 minutes*".

Bjorn went back on deck to give Barto and Alan a hand… Barto came in and said "*have you got a blanket*"... He looked like the other lads, shocked... I said "*yes, no problem*". As Barto went back onto the after deck I collected the blanket from the forward cabin. I also picked up the wheelhouse carpet as I thought this would be useful to put on top of the blanket, Barto was obviously very anxious to protect this young man on the return trip to Falmouth and ensure that he was not knocked around in anyway.

We were steaming for Falmouth at about half speed. Viv could see that there was still activity on the port side deck, with the securing of the seat. I started to put my lifejacket on in the wheelhouse, it's not easy trying to stand still especially when both hands are busy securing the lifejacket, as the boat rolled I staggered and started to accelerate… tottering towards Graham and Donald who were by the aft wheelhouse door They spotted me heading for them, out of control… they grabbed me and held me still whilst I finished securing my lifejacket,… I didn't bother to say anything… but they saw me grinning as I cursed the boats untimely roll!

I picked up the blanket and carpet and made my way out onto the after deck, it was windy, there was light spray in the air, put up by the bow dipping into the waves, it was pitch black ahead of the boat. You couldn't see the waves, only the spray as it flew back over the boat, illuminated by the deck lights that were left on to help the lads on deck who were still tidying up and fixing down all the loose ends. I couldn't get to the seat from the aft deck. There were two lads in the way, so I nipped around the starboard side, across the foredeck and down the port side to the 'scene'…

The young pilot was sat in his seat, a big black aluminium contraption, covered in straps and bits of angled metal that looked like dexion shelving legs. There were jagged edges sticking out where the seat had been torn from its fixings… The seat was leaning back slightly, as if it was a rocking chair on the backward tilt, the body was intact, the young man was wearing his green flying suit, covered in pockets and zips, helmet and dark visor, all appeared in good condition. I looked up at Barto, he nodded, I took hold of the pilots arm and folded it across his lap, and then the other… I held his hand it was cold, I looked at it, it was very small and very white, almost like a young child's hand, it made me shiver… I carefully put the blanket over him, Barto took the other end and we arranged it to cover as much as we could, Bijorn came up to help,… he took the carpet and placed it on the pilots lap to help hold the blanket in place,… all this would at least keep the heavy spray off.

THE SILENT RUN HOME

Barto said "*I'll stay out here with him*", I nodded and made my way back around the foredeck to the wheelhouse, leaving Bjorn and Barto to stay with Lt Smith.

Viv increased the revs to ¾ throttle, we picked up speed, it was now 2314 hours,… Alan came down from the bridge, said "*ask the Coastguard to receive the body at Custom House Quay*", I nodded as I wrote the instruction down on my log,… to the Coastguard "*please arrange to receive the body at Custom House Quay*", … reply "*Roger*".

It all seemed very cold and efficient, we were all referring to this chap as '*the body*', I suppose there was no other way to describe him, especially over 'the air', I couldn't help thinking someone was getting ready to confirm the worst to his loved ones, who by now would have heard the helicopter was missing… the thousands of men and women connected the RNAS Culdrose were not enjoying this evening,… this sort of news spreads like wildfire, on the evening news, in the pubs and clubs, by phone… '*have you heard*'… etc.

Mike who was on the radar said "*We're approaching St Anthony*", no one said anything, we were grateful for the information, it meant we would soon be turning north into the entrance to Falmouth and calmer waters, everyone could start to get busy, it would help them to stop thinking of the evenings events.

2323 hours the Coastguard called us up, "*We have arrangements to pick up the body at Custom House Quay with a Navy ambulance, you are requested to return to the search area afterwards*" my reply "*roger*".. I passed the message to Viv who said "*OK.*"

As we rounded the lighthouse and turned to the north, we had the sea up our stern and began to surf a bit, the spray from the bow stopped. Graham started to tidy up the wheelhouse, Don went below to check the engines, we were approaching the docks.

2344 hours we rounded the docks, Custom House Quay was about 200 yards to run. Viv reduced speed to quarter throttle, fenders were made ready, starboard side, I called the Coastguard "*we are approaching Custom House Quay now, over*"… reply "*roger*".

The lads were tense, we had on board one of the Culdrose lads we desperately wanted to find… but not in this sad state…It showed on the faces of everyone. I cannot remember a word spoken from the crew from the time we passed the Black Rock at the entrance to the harbour. All preparations for landing were carried out in slow motion, everyone was cold and wet, faces without expression, engines went to neutral, I could see the flashing lights of police cars, a few uniforms, naval and police, some of the lifeboat crew who didn't make the shout, but stayed on in the boathouse and …. the press.

We coasted into the steps, a few slight corrections with the throttles and Viv had us laid alongside, we passed ropes shore side, Donald came into the wheelhouse and cut the engines.

Viv came down to the afterdeck and had a chat with one or two of the lads, then Viv went around to the starboard side to advise our Hon Sec Captain Banks that he requested that no filming was to take place of the transfer of the pilot to the ambulance. Captain Banks heard Viv's words and, rather than conduct the discussion in public, came down the stone steps to the railings of the lifeboat and had words with Viv.

I didn't hear what was said… the discussion was not heated... but I can guarantee you that it went something like this: '*Captain, I am not moving the pilot off this boat until the cameras are removed*' reply '*The press have a job to do*'.. Viv '*My word is final*' then Viv would have looked into the Captain's face … Captain Banks would then have known that to argue would have been a complete waste of time, and that unless he got on with job of explaining the situation to the press, Viv would have slipped ropes, taken the boat away from the Custom House Quay and stood off in the harbour until the quay was cleared.

Captain Banks climbed the steps and went to the press, a group of men with a large television camera, some with microphones and electric recorders and similar devices hanging from their shoulders, and began to explain the problem… the 'Press' were not happy, there was some heated discussions. One or two of the crew from the boathouse were amongst the crowd … the situation could well have got out of hand. One or two of the crew on board were beginning to get angry … Barto instructed one of the younger lads to go up to the flying bridge, switch on both search lights and train them on the man with the television camera … this was done,… it brought a protest from the camera crew... I'm pleased to say it was totally ignored from all on the boat.

By now Viv was on the foredeck. As one of the larger, more agile of the crew on board (I was in those days) I was called around to give a hand to carry the body and seat ashore, to the naval ambulance. I came along the starboard side, up around the foredeck… gave Viv a nod, and down the port side to the seat, we removed the carpet and re-arranged the blanket to cover as much as possible. It was extremely awkward to lift the seat in the narrow passageway of the starboard side, the gap between the wheelhouse and the railing barely gave room for two at the front and two at the rear. … We struggled and managed to get the seat to the foredeck, there four or five more crew rallied around and the job became easier … up over the railing, up the steps and straight in to the ambulance.

Dave caught his hand on some of the jagged seat base, a little blood but he didn't make a fuss, the situation was totally over whelming.

As we loaded the ambulance there was a hell of a commotion going on behind us, I turned to have a look, it was at least 10 lifeboat crew struggling to keep a human wall together, denying the press access to the '*loading area*', the frustration the boys of the press must have been feeling at the time brought great joy to my heart… I thought to myself those bastards would have been delighted to have broadcast pictures on television of the undignified return of a young naval pilot to land, to have been seen by the families and friends of all naval personnel throughout the country.

I stood and watched as the doors of the small naval ambulance were closed. The driver and his mate were in uniform, they were obviously deeply distressed, the driver thanked us… then went straight around to the front, his mate stood and looked at us, as if he wanted to say thanks, but didn't speak… I stuck my hand out… we shook hands… he seemed relieved that he didn't need to say anything, he just nodded a couple of time and turned and made for the front of the ambulance.

They slowly drove up Custom House Quay to the road above and were gone.

A QUICK CUP OF TEA

Back on board we gathered in the wheelhouse to see what was going to happen next… Viv came in; it was just after midnight … still blowing and raining hard. Viv said, *"we will leave the boat here and go round to the boat house for a quick cup of tea before returning to the search area… is there anyone who would like to be relieved?"* Bjorn said *"I've got to be at work early this morning"*… Viv said *"OK …. anyone else?"*, there was no reply.. I think we all felt the same... this was personal… it wasn't a matter of want or not want, everyone was going… and as Viv would sometimes say *"my word is final"*.

"Notify the Coastguard" Viv said as the lads began to pile out of the aft door… *"Falmouth Coastguard this is Falmouth Lifeboat over"*… reply *"Go ahead Falmouth Lifeboat"*… *"Coastguard, Lifeboat, for the next few minutes we will be available in the boat house"* the reply.. *"Roger"*… the time was now 0006 hours.

Crew member Dave Nicoll.
Photo: Simon Culliford

I caught the boys up within yards of the boathouse door, the crew room was full, ILB crew, reserves, one or two wives, and as always when the lifeboat returns from a job at night (no matter what the time is) Mrs Nicholls. She is the mother of one of the lads on the inshore lifeboat crew (Dave)… Mrs Nicholls keeps in touch with the Coastguard by phone when the lifeboat is launched… she listens on the scanner, (her marine radio) and from years of experience can tell when the lifeboat will return, tea and biscuits will be needed in the boathouse. As we pile into the crew room a big smile… *"tea, coffee, or chocolate?.. Tea, coffee or chocolate?... What would you like Chris?"* As always I reply… *"tea please"*.. the thought of drinking chocolate or even smelling that horrible drink is enough to make me feel ill… talking of feeling ill I was OK in the boathouse, but I knew full well that if I had a couple of biscuits and a cup of tea that as we rounded the lighthouse on the way back out in a few minutes time, that the tea would pass my lips for a second time… (on the way out!).

The crew were all sitting around the crew room, sort of forming a square circle if that makes sense… all looking into an area of carpet in the centre of the room… sipping tea, coffee.. I'm not sure if anyone was drinking Mrs Nicholl's hot chocolate… there was very little talking... Bjorn stood up and said to Viv… *"I must be off now"*… Viv nodded… no one said anything... Bjorn left. It was approaching half past midnight, Viv stood up, then Donald,... then within about three tenths of a second so did the rest of the crew,... I could hear David (son of Mrs Nicholls) say to Viv *"I can take Bjorn's place"*.. David was as keen as mustard ... *"No, we've got enough"* Viv said,... David's bottom lip curled with disappointment.

There was a jam at the boathouse door as we all tried to get through at the same time; it brought a few silent smiles... the first I'd seen for a few hours.

As we got to the boat the quay was almost deserted, the press had gone, one or two of the younger crew came across to cast off the ropes. Graham started the engines, *"Already below?"* Viv called on the intercom, *"all yours Viv"* Donald replied... Viv came astern; we left Custom House Quay to return to the search area.

RETURN TO THE SEARCH AREA

0042 hours *"Falmouth Coastguard this is Falmouth Lifeboat, over"*,... *"go ahead lifeboat"*... *"We are now proceeding back to the search area, our crew list is 1,2,3,4,5,6,7,13,18 total POB nine, over"*... *"roger all copied"*.

By now we were leaving the docks behind us, making our way back out to the harbour entrance,... both throttles forward, flat out. Just as I looked out of the starboard window towards the Coastguard station up on Pendennis Point, they called us up... *"The search has been extended from 0200 to 0300, if you locate any wreckage note it's position"*... *"Roger"* I replied,... I passed this up to Viv who muttered *"OK mate"*.

We had learnt about 20 minutes earlier in the boathouse that fleet tender vessels *Headcorn* and *Heava* were preparing for a first light search of the area, I thought to myself as we passed the lighthouse and entered Falmouth bay... in a few hours from now as we make our way back in past the lighthouse... we will see the lads on *Headcorn* and *Heava* on their way out.

The seas were just as large as when we left them on our way in, the boat was running well, slamming quite a bit but we were making good speed, the tea in my tummy was beginning to react,... that sort of frothy feeling... I knew I wasn't going to hang on to it for long.

As we left the lighthouse disappearing astern of us the smell of fuel oil returned to the wheelhouse, the seas were steeper, most of the crew were inside the wheelhouse, John Bobbin the Second Cox was in the forward driving seat, the boat was being helmed by Viv up on the flying bridge, so John didn't have anything to do, ... Mike was in the radar seat, the radar was on... but the boats motion didn't make for a good indication of our position. Graham was at the chart table, he like me was feeling the effects of the boats motion... it was great comfort to us both to know we weren't suffering alone. I was sat in the radio seat, feet up on the back of the seat in front, well wedged in...my head cocked over to one side and resting on the rim of my lifejacket which was acting like a pillow.

We continued to punch our way out to the east... towards the Dodman, and the search area... then... out of the blue, we found the same 'Back Hole' that we hit on the first run out... off the top of a biggish wave, then down and down for what seemed like a lifetime... the boat was pointing down the wave at quite an angle... there was a sensation of weightlessness.. it gave us time to find something to hang on to... (this reaction came naturally)… then we dug in, the boat buried herself into the next wave…

What a picture it would have made, I reckon we must have almost disappeared under the wave as it broke over us… the engines juddered almost to the point of stalling… then the boat bobbed up and shook the wave off, we started to continue our journey.

Things began to settle back into normal routine, confidence began to grow, I felt reasonably confident that there were no more trough's like the one we had just been through ahead of us,… and therefore I decided… well I say decided… I don't think I had a lot of say in the matter… to make my way to the aft wheelhouse door, and deposit my cup of tea on the after deck… what appeared to be a complete cup full shot out in one violent 'whoosh'… that was much better… I sensed the odd snigger as I made my way back to my seat… by the time I sat down, most of the boys were smiling, I made a point of looking around with an '*I don't know what you are smiling at*' expression on my face… that made it even funnier. The Second Cox swung round in his seat and looked at me… I shrugged

my shoulders as if to say '*what did I do?*'… He smiled… everyone had a good laugh… the incident helped to '*break the ice*'.

It was now about quarter past one in the morning we had approximately 20 minutes to run to the search area, Viv called down on the intercom, "*man the search lights, we will start searching from here*"… the wheelhouse soon emptied, the Second Coxswain John stayed in his seat and kept an eye on the radar,… We were now abeam of Gull Rock, with about five miles to go... It was cold, dark, still windy and the smell of fuel oil was very strong indeed.

Viv reduced speed as we approached the search area, searching shore side of the datum we slowly zig zagged up towards the area where there was still a Sea King helicopter carrying out his search pattern… his search light shining down onto the sea.

0134 hours, the Coastguard called up, "*what is your position?*", John looked out of the window towards the helicopter for a second or two and said "*one mile north of the datum, searching, we will advise you as soon as we arrive*", I passed this… the Coastguard replied "*Roger*".

10 minutes later, Viv called down, "*we will start our sector search from here, first leg to the west,*"… I replied "*OK Viv*"... I looked across to the Decca Navigator for our latitude and longitude position and made a note in my log… ready for passing to the Coastguard.

0144 hours, "*Falmouth Coastguard this is Falmouth Lifeboat our position is 50 degrees 0878 north, 004 degrees 5048 west, we are starting our sector search from here, first leg to the west, over*", the Coastguard replied "*roger*".

For the first leg to the west we ran with the sea, the ride was quite comfortable… we were in the right area… Alan came down below to check that all was OK in the wheelhouse... I gave him the thumbs up… "*haven't seen a thing yet,… Fowey are about half a mile on our starboard beam*" he said, … I imagined what it must have been like in their boat, very uncomfortable, it's much smaller than ours,… their wheelhouse is very cramped... they are also fairly low in the water,… they must have spent most of the night awash with spray from the short steep seas… not a very good platform from which to conduct a search!

The Coastguard called up at 0153 hours and said "*we expect you to find flotsam in position*

50 degrees 10 north 004 degrees 51 west" I replied *"roger"* … I called up to Viv *"did you copy the Coastguards last"*… *"yes.. we will continue our sector search"* Viv replied.. I 'keyed' the mike twice to acknowledge receipt of his comments… they expected we would leave our search pattern and rush off to the position someone had in his wisdom decided there was wreckage… if only they could be out here with us for a few minutes... just to see what it was like…

We continued to steam in the various directions the sector search took us through... the search pattern can best be described as a cartwheel pattern… we would run up one spoke,… then around the rim for a short distance to the next spoke and back to the centre, through the centre and up the opposite spoke… and so on, until we complete the search by covering every spoke the search pattern is ideal for lifeboat because we run to a stop watch, as the tide takes us along on the surface of the sea it influences our position... we therefore move with the datum... to explain... the datum is the point where floating wreckage is expected... this drifts with the tide.. and is therefore usually on the move,, our search pattern does the same... so If we start with the hub of our search in the right area and run on spokes of say one mile long, we will have covered a circle surrounding the moving datum of two miles in diameter upon completion of our search.

About 15 minutes had passed since our last communication with the Coastguard.. it seemed like hours,… I felt a little rough… I coughed.. I didn't expect anything to come out, as I had already jettisoned my cup of tea, John turned to look at me just at the moment I coughed again, to my complete surprise approximately a quarter of a cup of tea flew out and landed right on top of my radio log.. I couldn't believe it... of all places to land, my log was soaked… I quickly wiped it off... looked round at John... I gave him a grin as I wiped my chops with the sleeve of my jacket… he chuckled and sitting around to face forward again he was still laughing, I knew because I could see his shoulders bobbing up and down.

The writing on the radio log was smudged but still readable,… I picked up the biro to see if it would still write on paper soaked in 'second hand tea'... no luck… I got a fresh pad out of the drawer, and thought to myself… if I feel like coughing again, I'll do it by the wheelhouse door… no sooner had I got myself organised when the Coastguard called again for our position… I replied *"50 degrees 08 60 north 004 degrees 50 47 west"* the reply... *"roger"*.

We continued searching, nothing at all was found, the minutes passed very slowly ... the search was due to terminate 0300 hours… then at 0258 hours the Coastguard called up *"Falmouth and Fowey Lifeboats this is Falmouth Coastguard, we are terminating the search please return to your stations, over"*… I felt a sense of relief… everyone was mentally and physically exhausted. Fowey Lifeboat called back to the Coastguard almost immediately *"all received Coastguard, we are returning to station"*… the Coastguard replied *"roger"*, I checked with Viv that it was OK to confirm we were returning too, he said yes, I called up the Coastguard *"this is Falmouth Lifeboat, returning to station"*... their reply *"roger"*.

LEAVING THE SEARCH AREA

By the time I had passed my message we had turned to the west and increased power to full speed… one or two of the lads came down from up top… very cold and wet.

I called up Fowey Lifeboat....*"Fowey Lifeboat this is Falmouth Lifeboat over"*... reply *"go ahead Falmouth"*... *"Fowey Lifeboat this is Falmouth Lifeboat, the Coxswain thanks you for your help and excellent services this morning, we wish we could have had a better result, have a safe journey home, over"*... reply *"thank you Falmouth Lifeboat safe journey to you too"*... I keyed my mike twice to acknowledge... Viv called down on the intercom *"thanks mate"*... Viv likes that sort of message... it promotes friendship with flank stations it's also good for our station, because transmissions are heard and talked about by many who listen in, after they hear the two bangs when the maroons go up... they tend to gauge the quality of the job by the way the radio is used... I suppose it's all they have to go by.

We had a good three quarters of an hour steaming ahead of us before we reached Falmouth, time to settle down and reflect on the events of the few hours that had passed... both Caterpillar diesels were purring away at two thousand revolutions a minute, the lifeboat was swaying from side to side... the odd thump as the bow cut through a wave... the motion became almost monotonous... I looked out of the corner of my eye to see half a dozen of the crew 'strewn' around the wheelhouse, heads swaying and nodding to the rhythm of the boat... as we rode down a wave the lads all leaned forward as we hit the next wave and began to climb, all heads rocked backwards... I was wedged in my seat, elbow on the radio table and supporting my head in my hand... thinking of the lads on the Sea King Squadron back at Culdrose, and their families... none of them getting any sleep this night.

I passed our ETA to the Coastguard at 0330 hours *"our ETA Falmouth 0355, over"*... *"Roger"* was the reply... hardly a word was spoken in the wheelhouse on the run home... everyone was mentally and physically drained... this was the worst job the station had been out on for years... it seemed as if the boys that had died that night were like our brothers... or member of our own crew, you could see by the expressions that the crew were deeply affected... over the years we have enjoyed many exercises with the helicopters from Culdrose, the team spirit.... Brilliant...

At ten to four in the morning... we were approaching the docks... I gave our boarding boat attendant Cliff a call on channel 16... *"Lifeboat Zulu, Lifeboat Zulu this is Falmouth Lifeboat over"*... Cliff who had been up all night waiting for us to return replied *"Falmouth Lifeboat this is Lifeboat Zulu go to channel 6, over"* I replied *"roger channel 6"*... then on channel 6 *"Lifeboat Zulu this is Falmouth Lifeboat, we would like to refuel, over"* reply *"yes Chris the hoses are all ready"* ... *"OK Cliff thanks"*... then an exchange of twice keyed mike's to acknowledge each other... Cliff has this habit of leaving formality and calling me Chris or Mr Price on the wireless... it makes me smile... and I tend to lapse and reply in the same way... it's a relief from being all starchy and 'professional' ... and lets in the human element.

Viv brought the boat alongside with his usual skill... no fuss... low revs... no bumps,... we passed ropes up to the crew shoreside... four or five of the younger crew who had sat in the lifeboat house for the last several odd hours, waiting to lend a hand when the boat returned... needing to be involved... we re-fuelled and made our way back to the moorings.

0421 hours *"Falmouth Coastguard this is Falmouth Lifeboat, we are back on our moorings, ready for service, switching off the wireless and going ashore, over"*... reply *"Falmouth Lifeboat this is Falmouth Coastguard RNAS Culdrose has asked us to extend their thanks for your assistance"*... I replied *"Thank you very much, from the Coxswain and crew, we all feel their loss… good night"*… reply… *"good night lifeboat"*.. Viv likes that, he was in the wheelhouse beside me when I closed down; he gave me a pat on the back. At that moment I almost burst into tears… Viv looked at me and said *"alright mate"*… I didn't have any words left... I managed to regain my control and nodded.

The following events need to be mentioned as they were in a way part of the job.

BACK ASHORE

By the time we got back to the boathouse, got changed and had a cup of tea… it was gone 5 o'clock… I walked up the hill thinking shall I go to bed… when I got in, I went to the bedroom, kicked off my shoes and lay on top of the bed,… and nodded off… at 0700 hours the alarm radio came on... the local station was playing,, News time, it was a bleak story for the newscaster to tell… *"Yesterday evening while on exercise a Sea King helicopter from the Royal Navy Air Station at Culdrose with three crew on board crashed into the sea, three miles off Dodman Point,… one crew was picked up from the sea by another helicopter and taken to Treliske but sadly died on route, Falmouth and Fowey lifeboats were launched, Falmouth lifeboat recovered one body from the sea, the search continues for the third crew member"*.

It was time for a cup of tea, (one I could keep down!)…then off to work.

My job the day after was to prepare the radio log… I took it to work and got it typed up during the day to hand to Viv that evening… for checking before it was handed into the Hon Sec for forwarding to RNLI Head Office in Poole as the official record of our activities during the service.

About a week later, just after the private funeral of Lt Smith, his wife, through Lt Sealey, a pilot on the same flight, asked if she could come over to the lifeboat house to give her thanks to the crew who were aboard the lifeboat and had recovered her husband. This was duly arranged for the following Saturday morning, Mrs Smith, Lt Sealey and his wife would arrive at 1030 hours.

On the Saturday I arrived at around 0930… Viv and Donald were in the boathouse crew room chatting, I knew the next hour or more would be an upsetting experience, Viv said *"I had quite a chat with Doug Sealey, Lt Smith was one of his best friends, Lt Smith's wife's about seven months pregnant, she's taking her husband's death very hard... we'll play the visit by ear, but I don't want her to be upset too much"*,, Donald and myself nodded.

The rest of the crew drifted in one by one… all arriving early; we were all dressed the same, lifeboat jumpers, black trousers, black shoes... Viv ran through his requirements again to us all,… the mood was sombre.. I was not looking forward to the visit at all… it was going to be very difficult to remain composed in the presence of a young lady who was going to have an emotional meeting with the crew who *'brought her husband home'*. Graham, who is a bit of a *'softie'* like myself, muttered to me *"I'm not looking forward to this"*… I nodded and muttered *"me neither"*…

A car pulled up outside the boathouse, it was obviously them. Lt Sealey got out of the driver's seat and went around to the back door; he helped Mrs Smith get out of the car.

I could see all this going on through the window… Mrs Smith was obviously in an emotional state... she wiped her eye… Lt Sealey's wife went around comforting her, she was crying with her head buried in Lt Sealey's chest, they were all crying; it was going to take a few minutes before they could get ready to enter the lifeboat house.

Viv had us all lined up in the crew room… eventually Mrs Smith, Lt Sealey and Mrs Sealey entered… Mrs Smith was in a near state of collapse, her eyes were red,… she raised a smile as she looked at us all,… then Viv introduced us all one by one,,, after shaking hands with us Mrs Smith said *"thank you all so much for taking care of my husband"*… she wanted to say more but obviously couldn't.. Mrs Sealey helped her out of the crew room into the changing room… we could hear her crying.. a moment I will remember forever... you could have heard a pin drop in the crew room… fortunately Doug Sealey started to talk to Viv, we all shuffled around and started to chat... it helped to relieve the tension.

I looked out of the window, and could see Mrs Sealey helping Mrs Smith into the car, she was still crying… I 'made eyes' at Viv, he looked up… Doug Sealey turned and looked… I nodded to him to look out of the window… he could see it was time to go… he thanked us all, and left.

A few days later, the funeral took place of the third crewman from the helicopter; he was recovered with the wreckage from the sea bed.

That afternoon an observer on the same flight as the helicopter that crashed came into the shop... he's been a customer for years … I asked him if he knew why the helicopter crashed… *"we don't know yet, it could have been anything,… everyone on the base is keen to know"*.. I said *"we had met Mrs Smith the other day, she looked like she's taking it pretty hard"*… he replied *"Yes, the wives on the flight are looking after her, there all quite concerned, what with the baby and all"*…

That evening I rang Doug Sealey *"Do you think Mrs Smith would like a bunch of flowers from the lifeboat crew?"* He replied.. *"yes Chris, that would be a good idea"*... I took his address and arranged to drop them in the next day… I rang Viv and told him what I was doing and he agreed, it was a good idea... we agreed the card should read '*From the Coxswain and Crew of the Falmouth Lifeboat*'.

I decided in due course to collect a pound each from the crew to go towards the cost of the flowers… not for the money, but to make sure that the flowers were truly from us all.

On the way home from work on the following Saturday I called in on Viv for a cup of tea, we sat in his workshop and chewed over matters in general, Viv mentioned that there was a memorial service to be held in Helston, and that he was asked to provide two representatives from the crew, *"I would like you and Donald to go, I've spoken to Donald, he's OK to go."*..

"Yes I can go, no problem"…*"good"*, Viv replied… Just before I left, I remembered the pound I wanted from Viv... *"oh, by the way Viv… quid for the flowers please"*… (holding out my hand), he put his hand into his pocket,… grinning as he put the pound into my hand… *"Here's your quid son"*… rubbing his nose at the same time…(inferring I was of 'Jewish' extraction)… It's a sort of joke we have whenever discussing money.

Some weeks later Donald and myself attended the memorial service… it was a formal occasion, the three things I remembered most about that service was… the 1 minute of silence before the '*Last Post*'... the Last Post itself… and an electronic watch playing one of those silly tunes during a quiet moment during prayers.

Our observer customer came into the shop some weeks later, we chatted about this and that... then inevitably the conversation came round to how Mrs Smith was getting on, "*she's had a little boy… she named him John after his father… he's the spitting image of his father*" I replied…"*that's good news... I'll tell the lads, how is she in herself?*"... "*Not so good… she's still grieving… and to make things worse… her father in law John's dad died two days after the memorial service*"… that was terrible news.

I'm pleased to say that things turned out well in the end, Mrs Smith came to terms with her tragedy… a few years later she re-married… she's had another baby... and still keeps in touch with her friends at Culdrose.

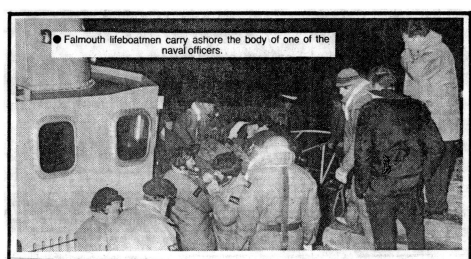

● Falmouth lifeboatmen carry ashore the body of one of the naval officers.

HELICOPTER BASE MOURNS LOST FLIERS

THE town of Helston and the huge helicopter base at nearby RNAS Culdrose were in mourning yesterday for two members of 706 Squadron who died when their Sea King crashed into the sea off Falmouth on Tuesday night.

A third member of the crew was still missing yesterday morning and a search for him was continuing.

The dead were named yesterday as Lt. Michael Johnston (32), the pilot, of Mullion, and 26-year-old Lt. Paul Smith, the observer.

Lt. Johnston and his wife, Julie, have a four-year-old son. Lt. Smith also lived locally, with his wife, Frances. Both men were veterans of the Falklands campaign.

Wreckage found

Lt. Neil MacBean (27), the third member of the crew, also lived in the Helston area. He and his wife, Rachel, have a daughter, aged three. He was a pilot trainee and won the Queen's Telescope award at Dartmouth after coming top of his course.

Some wreckage from the helicopter was found in the Portscatho area yesterday and a Culdrose spokesman said the Navy were now looking for the main bulk of it.

Lt. Johnston was picked up from the sea by another helicopter, but died on the way to hospi-

● A liferaft recovered at Portscatho yesterday.

tal at Truro. The body of Lt. Smith, still strapped to a seat, was recovered by Falmouth lifeboat.

The tragedy occurred while several helicopters were taking part in a night exercise three miles off Dodman Point.

Falmouth and Fowey lifeboats searched for Lt. MacBean. It was

resumed yesterday morning when more helicopters from Culdrose and Naval vessels scoured the area for wreckage. The public were asked to tell the police or Culdrose if they found any washed up along the coast.

The ill-fated helicopter managed to send an emergency signal before crashing. The nine-man Falmouth lifeboat, under coxswain Viv Pentecost, was launched soon after Falmouth coastguards received a request for assistance from Culdrose.

Pilots at the base have a good safety record. The last fatality at Culdrose was ten years ago when three members of the Sharks helicopter display team were killed.

There were no casualties among Culdrose personnel during the Falklands campaign; four men died off the islands in 1985 when their Sea King was in collision with a plane.

Another newspaper cutting, this one from The West Briton and Royal Cornwall Gazette, Thursday 26 February 1987.

A Sea King helicopter from 771 Naval Air Squadron during a winching exercise with Falmouth's Arun class lifeboat *Elizabeth Ann*. Viv the coxswain is concentrating on holding course and speed, keeping an eye on the compass and safe water ahead, on this occasion with me updating him on the exact position of the helicopter and diver who is being winched up or down. In effect I am the eyes in the back of his head. The pilot has a perfect view of the lifeboat and keeps a watchful eye on the flag man who is stood on the bow. Note the plaque Viv made for *Elizabeth Ann* which now sits inpride of place in the crew room.
Photo: Simon Culliford

PR TO COVERACK

Public Relations (PR)

During the summer much spare time for the crew is taken up by 'PR', the lifeboat is cleaned and prepared for visits to neighbouring ports, demonstrations, and bringing alongside the harbour wall for people, and groups, to look over. There is something going on at least once a week in the summer. The majority of the visits are annual... Porthscatho, St Mawes, Portloe, Helford, Flushing, Coverack etc. some are Sunday evenings where a helicopter demonstration precedes a religious service, followed by the boat being made available for inspection by the public. This gives the holiday makers a chance to have a look at the boat and equipment, and to talk to the crew... very important considering it's their money that make it all possible.

Every year around mid-August we have a midweek PR visit to Coverack,... a beautiful village, that once had its own famous lifeboat station, and was at one time Falmouth's 'flank station'. The visit to Coverack is one of the best runs of the year... Falmouth Lifeboat is always made very welcome and many traditions live on from year to year. For instance Mike Eustice who was Mechanic of the Coverack Lifeboat *The William Taylor of Oldham,* comes down to the lifeboat every year when we come alongside and presents a 'bottle' to the Coxswain... (booze), he also always gave a pot of cream to Viv when he was Coxswain... now he gives us a pot to take back to Viv when we return to Falmouth... Another interesting tradition is that when the boat is tied up alongside I accompany the Coxswain to visit Mona Hart who lives in a cottage overlooking the harbour,... Mona is the Coverack Lifeboat Branch Secretary and has for many years supported the lifeboat. What a character she is... Out comes the scotch and a few tales from the war ... After Viv retired, John was keen to carry on the tradition, as was Alan who succeeded John as Coxswain .... Mona's brother Cyril was a school teacher at Falmouth and he also has a great affinity with the Lifeboat Institution... He was the interpreter up at the Coastguard station on the '*St Simeon'* Job.

Many of the old crew of the Coverack Lifeboat still live and work in the village, the branch is made up of dedicated committee members (of which my mother is one) who all remain very active, collecting a considerable amount of money each year, to go towards central funds.

Another charming tradition, which continues to bring a lump to my throat, is that whenever the Sennen Cove lifeboat comes past Coverack Bay, on passage from Sennen to the boatyard at Falmouth, it comes into the bay and circles once, blowing it's hooter in respect to its Coxswain of a few years ago, Eric Pengelly, who is buried in the Coverack churchyard overlooking the bay...

Eric who was known by his crew as Mr Pengelly was a real gentleman. He and his family are originally from Coverack... Sennen have a new lifeboat now, I'll bet Eric is very proud when he sees the crew salute him every time they pass by Coverack.

THE CREW FOR THE DAY

As the Coverack run drew closer John Barton the Coxswain rang round the crew to find out who was available... as a midweek PR it isn't easy to get all the main crew. Employers are happy for crew men to leave work for an emergency, but a jolly is a different

The day John Barton took over as coxswain from Vivian Pentecost in September 1989. Left to right: Don McLellan, Michael Wilson, Chris Price, John Barton, Graham Pearce, Alan Barnes and Steve Datson. Photo: Simon Culliford

matter. The crew for this Coverack run was John the Coxswain, Big D, myself as Second Mechanic, Roger, Ken the Tea Pot, Trevor and Snowy. Roger works on the pilot boats in Falmouth and works shifts, guiding large vessels in and out of port. He was delighted to hear that the Coverack PR was on one of his leave periods… Ken is known as Ken the Tea Pot, because he donated a new tea pot to the boat when he was enrolled as a reserve crew member, partly because he makes a good cup of tea, but mainly of course was because he was sick in the old teapot! Trevor who is an inshore lifeboat Helmsman, and Snowy who is the Deputy Senior Helmsman of the ILB.

We had a good crew for the day, all the steady reliable types… John also likes to take a guest on the run… in years gone by we have taken on occasions the DLA (Deputy Launching Authority) but as John and the launching authorities haven't seen eye to eye for a

Crew member Roger McClarity. Photo: David Barnicoat Collection

Crew members Ken 'The Teapot' Avis (left) and Snowy Angove Photos: Jon Crane

while, and there is a reasonable amount of friction at present, the DLA will not be going… or asked to go this year. Peter Richards was asked instead, he is a Falmouth Lifeboat Branch member and was delighted to accompany us. Peter is a keen supporter of the lifeboat, he is responsible for many functions, and runs many events each year to raise funds. He also runs the annual dinner and dance and the 'fun run', his wife and daughter are Coastguards… a very nice family. Peter is a good choice. The plan was to muster at the boat house at noon on Wednesday the 21st August.

1200 hours, the crew mustered, we needed to arrive in Coverack Bay by 1430 hours to rendezvous with the helicopter from RNAS Culdrose, a Sea King from 77 Search and Rescue Squadron, so plenty of time.

We took a slow trip out to our Arun, the *Elizabeth Ann* (52-11). The previous year she had been in the boatyard having a re-fit, the latest navigation equipment and some modifications to other electrics.

During this time we had the relief boat *Ralph & Bonella Farrant* (52-22) Official Number 1081, so the 22nd Arun and number 1081 RNLI Lifeboat since recording began.

My favourite relief boats were *Sir Max Aitken* (52-17) ON-1071 and *Duke of Athol* (52-46) ON-1160.

The *Ralph & Bonella Farrant*, like *Sir Max Aitken* and the *Duke of Athol*, have V8 Caterpiller engines, much easier to start and more responsive than our station boat *Elizabeth Ann* with her straight 6 Cat engines.

Clifford dropped us off on the Arun, as I cast off the boarding boat I said '*thank you Clifford*', he replied with his cheeky grin, "*my pleasure Mr Price*".

This was one of Big D's last PR visits as Mechanic as he was due to retire early next year, we started the engines together, Big D flashed up the radar and other electrics, checked the intercom with John who was up on the flying bridge and I prepared the crew list ready to pass to the Coastguards.

Weather was westerly 5, we slipped the mooring and chugged out of the harbour towards Black Rock and the lighthouse and into the open sea, I passed the crew list to Falmouth Coastguard and advised them we were out to Coverack for a PR and would be keeping a listening watch on 16, zero and 2182.

As we rounded the Manacle Buoy, I chanted *"the old home town looks the same"*, something I sang in the wheelhouse every time we passed Coverack, going to or returning from a job, or if we were on passage.

"Put a dry suit on Chris". John said through the intercom from the flying bridge to the wheelhouse. Ken grinned, I drew the short straw, the dry suit meant I was to go in the water just before the helicopter was due to arrive, the lifeboat stands off, I fire off a red smoke, then the helicopter comes in to pick me up and return me to the afterdeck of the lifeboat.

The dry suit is like a bloody great boiler suit, made of a rubber material with wellington boots built in. I needed an extra-large, not because I had a big fat belly but because my shoe size is 12, the large suits have size 10 boots which are agony to wear.

The cuff seal and neck seal are rubber powdered with Johnson's baby powder; I pushed my head through the neck seal and was greeted with a large cloud of baby powder, leaving the wheelhouse smelling like a poof's hand bag!

With everything on, hands out of the cuff seals and feet firmly in place in the size 12's, the next job is to get someone reliable to do the large zip up at the back. That ruled out Ken the Tea Pot and Snowy straight away! They would be sure not to do the zip up properly which meant I would fill with water!

Ken said *"do your zip up bud"*, I replied *"sod off, where's Roger or Trevor"*, Trevor appeared at the aft wheelhouse door, I pointed to the zip, turned round and Trevor zipped me up.

The final job before putting on my life jacket is to get the surplus air trapped in the suit out.

Looking like the Michelin man I carefully put two fingers into the neck seal, pulled the rubber seal away from my neck and crouched down, the air pushed through the gap spraying me in more baby powder, when the air stopped hissing I let go of the neck seal and stood up, looking a bit like I had been shrink-wrapped. Life jacket and bump cap on, I was ready to jump off the stern on the Coxswains command.

We were now entering Coverack bay at about half speed, helicopter due in around 10 minutes. The deck crew were busy securing the loose ropes and any other equipment that could hinder the helicopter transfer.

John took the lifeboat around the bay at full speed to show the gathering crowd on the harbour what an Arun lifeboat looks like traveling at 18 knots, it's really impressive, huge wash, roaring twin turbo charged diesels.

The helicopter called up for a radio check and advised they had 4 minutes to run.

I took up position on the after deck and looked up to flying bridge for instructions, expecting the boat to slow down. John gave me the hand signal to jump, he was grinning, I scowled back and jumped off into the huge wake of the lifeboat moving along at full speed clutching my smoke flare.

As I floated to the surface and lay on my back I looked to the north and saw the spec of the helicopter, struck the flare and the red smoke poured out of the small cardboard tube.

The helicopter went into a hover and prepared to move in to drop the diver...the flare went out so I let it go, the helicopter came lower and crabbed its way towards me sideways, the cabin door was open, the diver sat in the doorway and gave me the thumbs up, I returned the signal and he gave a big single nod.

The diver pushed himself off the edge of the doorway and plummeted into the sea with a big splash, the water around us was beaten flat with the rotor wash; I had a job to breathe what with the spray and the pressure of the downdraft of the helicopter.

The diver swam up to me and screamed into my ear "*alright mate?*"

I replied "*yeah*", he passed the strop under one arm and around my back, got hold of it under my other arm clipped the loose end onto the carabiner at the end of the winch wire that had been lowered from the helo, then clipped himself on, looked me in the eyes and nodded

Falmouth Lifeboat crew member being winched from the water by a Sea King helicopter from 771 Naval Air Squadron. Photo: Simon Culliford

with eyes that looked like they were saying '*ready*' ...I nodded, he tapped the top of his crash helmet and with a violent jerk we were out of the water and moving towards the helicopter.

I have to say I wasn't enjoying the experience as I do not like heights, the helicopter was climbing as the winch wire was bringing us closer to the cabin, the sea suddenly looked a long way down.

With my back to the doorway as we were level with the edge I was whisked into the cab, the diver climbed in alongside me. The three guys in the cab were all smiling which I found a little unnerving, the pilot glanced around caught my eye and nodded, I nodded back and off we went, at high speed doing a circuit of the bay, my feet dangling out the cab, and a very reassuring hand gripping the straps on the rear of my life jacket to make sure I did not slip out. I also noticed I was still attached to the carabiner on the winch wire

Elizabeth Ann on a training exercise with a Sea King from 771 Naval Air Squadron in Falmouth Bay. A lifeboat crew member can be seen on the bow of the lifeboat holding a red and a green flag.
Photo: Simon Culliford

and still had the lifting strop under my arms.

I could see the Arun taking up position for a slow run into the bay. This would allow the helo to move in and position itself over the stern of the lifeboat so they could lower me down.

As we begun to formate over the afterdeck the three guys, still grinning, all patted me on the shoulder, the swimmer gave me the thumbs up and nodded, still grinning. I thought perhaps they were all high on drugs, it was really weird, why would they all grin, did I have '*dick head*' tattooed on my forehead?

I thought I better grin back, I nodded, then felt a push to my lower back, and within a split second knew why they were grinning, they had left me with about 2 feet of slack on the wire, free fall for 2 feet doesn't sound like a lot but when the wire goes tight and you stop dead … a big shock.

I spun my head round on the wire and found myself looking in under the helo, I looked up to see three grinning faces, I grinned back and mouthed '*bastards*', like the three wise monkeys they instantly burst out laughing.

I was now slowly being lowered towards the deck of the lifeboat, Trevor was right on the bow holding a green flag high and holding a red flag in the other hand which was pointing to the deck and alongside his leg.

Flags are used to give a visual indication to the pilot that the Coxswain is happy with his course and speed, and if for some reason he wants to abort the transfer the Coxswain will indicate to the flag man on the bow *'red flag'*. The helo pilot would see this and would terminate the transfer.

Flags are used for two reasons, one being that all wireless transmissions cease when winching up or down is in progress, to ensure it does not interfere with any voice exchanges within the helo, also a red flag being held up is an instant signal to the pilot that the lifeboat wants to cease the transfer immediately.

As I approached the deck I could see Roger moving around the deck with the earthing pole, getting ready to touch the winch wire, to earth the wire and static being produced by the helo. The pole is a good 6 foot long with a metal wire hook on the end, attached to the hook is a thin chain with the end resting on the deck.

If the wire is not earthed it is effected as soon as one of the deck crew grabs my legs to stop me swinging and guide me onto the deck.

Grabbing an unearthed diver or anyone coming down on the winch wire without being earthed would make superb entry for *'You've Been Framed!'* The electric shock can be severe and usually brings extreme joy to those who are spectators.

Lifeboat crew member on *Elizabeth Ann* holding the earthing pole used to earth the winch wire. Photo: Simon Culliford

Roger was standing around on the deck looking like he was trying to get into a position where he could stick the pole right up my jacksy... luckily he *'earthed'* me before I hit the deck by touching the wire just above my head.

Safe on deck the strop was unlocked, whisked away from under my arms and let go, the helo was astern of us and winching in the wire. Thumbs up and big grins all-round the helo rose high in the air.

To complete the display we went out into the bay and waited for the helo to drop the RNLI flag on a rope under the cab, we both sped back into the bay, the helicopter did a circuit, with the guys in the cab and pilot waving to the crowds and as quickly as that it was gone, a spec disappearing to the north and back to the Royal Naval Air Station at Culdrose, some 10 miles from Coverack.

The time was approaching 3pm, Ken the Tea Pot gave me a hand to get out of the dry suit and Barto said through the intercom *"get ready to drop anchor"*.

Roger, Snowy and Tea Pot went forward to the foredeck and prepared the anchor ready for dropping, we took up position just off the old Coverack lifeboat slip close to the harbour and dropped anchor, the tide was coming in, soon we would have enough water in the small harbour to get the lifeboat alongside, so we could open the boat to the general public, show them the wheelhouse and some of the kit, (the engine room was out of bounds). We are always keen to show everyone what the latest and best gear looked like, after all they paid for it!

I made everyone a quick cup of tea or coffee, made a note of the engine dials and advised the Coastguard on channel zero that we would soon be going alongside Coverack harbour and will be keeping a listening watch on channels 16, zero, and 2182 (the long range radio).

Mr Price chatting to two Coverack fishermen during a PR visit while we wait for enough tide to get in to the harbour to allow the publice to look over the lifeboat.

We all mustered on the after deck drinking our tea and enjoying the warm stiff breeze, the boat was rolling in the swell, not violently but enough to remind us the weather was freshening. 1530 hours and shoreside advised they thought there was enough water in the harbour for us.

The deck crew raised the anchor, as always very little was said as all the crew were so well versed with the manoeuvre.

With anchor stowed, the big white fenders were retrieved from the lockers where they were stowed to keep them out of the way for the helo.

The crew strung them along the port side of the lifeboat, and set out the ropes we would use to moor alongside the harbour. Two 'breast ropes' one for the bow and one for the stern, and two 'springs' tied diagonally from for'ard to aft, and aft to for'ard to stop the boat surging alongside the quay, and to hold her steady. The crew took up position ready to pass ropes as Barto eased the boat into the harbour and alongside the quay, no shouting and bawling, no screaming orders, just the odd nod of the head, and clasping hand

2 Thursday, August 17, 1995   HELSTON & THE LIZARD NEWS EXTRA

Lifeboat Day brings crowds to Coverack

COVERACK's annual lifeboat day was, once again, a real community effort, said Colin Lynn, chairman of the local branch of the RNLI who expected about £2,000 to have been raised from the various activities around the harbour.

Mr. Lynn said that all the women of the village provided food and refreshments, served in the Coverack Fishermen's Rest, and local people chipped in as well, donating competition prizes.

This year's lifeboat day at the picturesque fishing village also benefit-

ed from a good turn-out of visitors, their numbers probably swelled by the fine weather.

Said Mr. Lynn: "It was a lovely day, and there was a tremendous turnout. We certainly think it was better than last year . . . we usually raise more than £2,000."

Two lifeboats were on hand for the afternoon, the David Robinson (The Lizard) and the Elizabeth Ann (Falmouth) which people queued on the harbour to board. There was also a search and rescue display involving a helicopter from RNAS Culdrose.

●The scene at Coverack with the Falmouth lifeboat Elizabeth Ann alongside and The Lizard boat David Robinson under way beyond.

Newspaper cutting from August 1995 - a typical Lifeboat Day at Coverack

drawing into the body to indicate tighten on the rope.

With the engines in neutral and on tick over Barto appeared at the aft wheelhouse door and said "*finished with engines*", this was my cue to switch off the engines, wind down the radar and prepare the wheelhouse for the influx of holiday makers who were keen to look over the boat.

Barto continued Viv's tradition of visiting Mona in her cottage in the village, so the two of us made our way up the quay and left the boys in charge of the boat and looking after the visitors.

I had *'Lifeboat Zulu'* the portable VHF over my shoulder, I checked it was on zero and adjusted the squelch knob till it was just off squelch, squelch being sandpaper noise it makes when it is tuned just a little too fine to receive the faintest transmission. Fine tuning so the squelch noise just stops means it is perfectly set.

"*Falmouth Lifeboat this is Lifeboat Zulu radio check on zero, over*" I said, a few seconds later Big D came back "*loud and clear, over*" I replied "*loud and clear also, out*".

On our way through the village that was crowded with holiday makers for lifeboat day we bumped into Mike Eustace, he was the Mechanic on the Coverack Lifeboat *The William Taylor of Oldham*, a short stocky man with arms like tree trunks, always happy, always very smart and much loved in the village, a true gent if ever there was one. "*on your way to Mona*?" he said as we all shook hands, "*yes*" I replied as we walked off.

As we approached the cottage Mona stood in the door way, "*the kettle is on*" she said.... "*unless you would like something a little stronger*". I said "*tea would be great*" Barto nodded.

On the stern of Elizabeth Ann with my best mate from school, Jim, leaving Coverack after a PR visit.

We all sat on the small floral pattern three piece suite crammed into the small sitting room, *"how's Viv?"* Mona asked, *"he's fine and sends his love"* I replied, we chatted away for around 5 minutes kisses on the cheeks all round and we left, Mona passed me a carry bag and said *" a few scones and cream for Viv"*. I replied *"I'll see he gets them"*. We made our way through the village towards the harbour, and lifeboat.

The lifeboat at 52 feet long tied up alongside the harbour, surrounded by small fishing and pleasure boats of around 18 to 20 foot the lifeboat looked huge.

The general public were crawling all over it like ant's. I said to Barto *"I'll go back to the boat to relieve a couple of the lads"*, *"right I will be in the pub"* he replied.

At the top of the harbour is the Paris Hotel the local pub. The lifeboat crew love their 'pint' …. I gave up drinking when I joined the crew, not being able to hold my beer very well, there was no chance I was going to miss a shout because I was half cut!, and as a wireless operator being half pissed was out of the question, what with at least a thousand ears tuned to channel zero every time the maroons went off and the lifeboat was launched on service.

I managed to ease my way through the line of holiday makers all patiently waiting to get aboard and have a look around, into the wheelhouse (very crowded) caught Big D and Rogers eye, *"nip up the pub if you like"*, I passed the hand held radio (lifeboat Zulu) to Snowy as he rushed past me in the wheelhouse.

The wheelhouse normally holds a crew of 7 to 8, there must have been 40 crammed in, all asking questions at once.

The weather was certainly freshening outside in the bay, later that evening a gale was forecast, but it was still OK inside the harbour, the boat moving gently against the harbour wall, one or two ladies looking anxious feeling the gentle movement and declaring *"it's getting rough"*, I had to smile, thinking to myself when it gets rough on board the boat whilst I quite enjoy it, my tummy doesn't.

What does this do? What does that do? What are those knobs for? The questions seemed sometimes to be rather silly but to be fair some of the holiday makers had actually never stepped aboard a boat of any type …. ever!

The wheelhouse was very full, I was pinned up against the VHF and MF radios answering questions when a call came through on channel 16 *"Falmouth Lifeboat this is Falmouth Coastguard over"*, I picked up the hand mike and replied *"loud and clear over"*, the wheelhouse fell quiet everyone listening ….. *"Lifeboat this is Falmouth Coastguard, we have a dis-masted sailing yacht 4 miles south east of The Lizard Point, are you able to attend, over"* I replied, *"yes, we will leave Coverack now, I will call you as soon as we are under way"*.

I looked towards the doorway and said to Tea Pot who was looking after the after deck, *"we need to get everyone off the boat"* Ken nodded and announced to everyone *"We need to launch, every one off the boat please"* … the public began to move to the foredeck which was level with the quayside, and step off the lifeboat.

As the wheelhouse began to clear I gave around 10 short blasts on our fog horn to get the attention of Barto and the crew who were in the bar at the Paris Hotel at the top of the harbour, they were out like a shot.

Snowy called on Zero from 'Lifeboat Zulu' the handheld radio, *"what's up Chris?"* I replied *"we've got a shout, yacht 4 miles south east of Lizard Point"*.

The crew made haste through the crowded quay, in the meantime I checked the throttles were in the neutral 'detent' and flashed up both engines using the two start buttons on the engineer's panel in the wheelhouse.

As the crew jumped aboard and took up positions to let go the ropes, Barto popped his head through the aft wheelhouse door, *"are we launched?"* I nodded and said *"the Coastguard have asked if we can attend the yacht"* and I replied *"yes we are on our way"*. Barto replied, *"tell them approximately 30 minutes"*. *"Roger"* I replied.

We have approximately 8 miles to run to get a position roughly 4 miles SE of Lizard Point, which was going to take around half an hour at our full speed of 18 knots, and because there was a strong wind blowing from the south east the yacht would be drifting in our direction.

I suspect the Coastguard called us because they knew we were in Coverack on a PR visit. A gale was forecast for later in the evening and there would be no point in launching the Lizard Lifeboat as they would take some time to muster and launch, also if they were to attend the casualty they would need to tow it back to Falmouth, which would leave their patch without cover. Another consideration was that they would be unable to recover their boat back on their slip way in the south-easterly gale forecasted and would therefore need to seek shelter in Falmouth until conditions eased.

The Lizard boat and crew are very able to work in heavy weather in the Lizard area,

Mr Price speaking on the wireless, wearing his best "Ted Tuckerman" jumper......"tight lines"

where the seas can be huge without doubt some of the largest in the UK, but, as with all boats that live in a lifeboat house and not on a mooring, they rely on reasonable weather to be able to recover their boat onto their slipway. This is a difficult manoeuvre requiring the Coxswain to line-up the keel of the boat with the keelway, a 12-inch groove down the middle of the slipway, reverse into the keelway and hold her there whilst his crew haul on board the winch wire and connect it. In the case of The Lizard there is no way they can recover the lifeboat and get her back in the boathouse in a south easterly gale.

The launch was great for us, to get a job on a flank stations patch means we hoist the '*skull and crossbones*' flag, A Falmouth tradition, not that anyone notices it, but it signifies we are stealing another stations job!

As we made our way out of Coverack harbour both engines went to full speed, the deck crew were busy stowing ropes and fenders.

I was busy writing up the radio log and preparing to advise the Coastguard we were under way, together with our ETA.

Big D was at the radar position tuning in the radar and adjusting the squelch on the VHF direction finder. This is a strange looking instrument, a bit like a clock but with a compass for a dial with North, South, East and West, the outside dial surrounded with small LED lights, the VHF DF is tuned into the channel we would listen in on, in this case channel 16. As we receive a transmission the light would go around the disc and illuminate the position the transmission was coming from. Normally, to get a good signal, we would ask the casualty to transmit a description of the crew on board, male, female, their physical condition, and confirm they are wearing lifejackets or, if we had already established that, we would ask for a slow count to 10.

I called the yacht on channel 16, advised them *"this is Falmouth Lifeboat we are launched on service, we will be with you in 25 minutes, please advise number of persons on board and is anyone injured, over"*.

The casualty replied *"this is yacht Mangareva 3, we have four persons on board, no one is injured, we have lost our mast and unable to start our engine, we are thirty six feet long, white hull, and we are rolling heavily in the steep seas, over"*.

Big D said to Barto on the flying bridge *"got them on the DF they are right on the nose, looking for them on the radar"* …. Barto replied by keying the mike button twice …. This saves removing it from the mike holder.

The lifeboat was rolling from side to side as we ploughed through the short seas that were growing steadily.

Then on channel Zero we received a very sharp and angry transmission from the Deputy Launching Authority (who wasn't invited to this year's PR to Coverack) *"Falmouth Lifeboat this is the Lifeboat Launching Authority, I have not given permission for the lifeboat to be launched, you are not launched on service, over"*.

I spun round to Big D, Snowy and Tea Pot who were in the wheelhouse, Snowy and Tea Pot were getting ready to go up to the flying bridge to keep a look out for the casualty.

My mouth was open, eyes bulging, *"what"* I exclaimed raising my hands into the air, Big D shook his head in despair, Ken grinned from ear to ear and Snowy looked to the floor shaking his head.

What the hell was I going to say in reply to that transmission I thought …. and before Barto could bark out the reply he wanted me to say came:

"Tell him to phuck off Chris, he can't phucking talk to you like that, tell him to phuck off, who the phuck does he think he is!!"

It was Pedro the Mechanic on the Lizard Lifeboat, I knew him well, he was obviously listening on zero in the Lizard Lifeboat house.

Pedro unlike our old Coxswain Viv (a man of few words), was a man of many words, each one interjected with a swear word!

Oh dear I thought, this is not going well, I imagined the whole of the south coast listening into every word being said, I decided how to respond.

"All copied Pedro, thanks, out"… the '**out**' being a firm indication I did not require a response, (whereas the word '*over*' prompts a response or answer to a question).

The airwaves went silent. I took some comfort from the fact that this '*phuck*' conversation was being conducted on zero which is a channel reserved for VHF emergency services and is not available on normal yacht VHF radios.

I gave it half a minute to compose myself before replying to the DLA,

"Falmouth Launching Authority, this is Falmouth Lifeboat. We have been tasked to assist the yacht Mangareva 3 who is dismasted 4 miles south east of the Lizard Point our ETA

20 minutes, two zero minutes, over".

Almost instantly came the angry reply:

"*You are not launched by the RNLI I have not given permission for you to launch, over*".

What the hell can I say to that, should I say we will leave the yacht to drift ashore and let crew get dashed on the rocks …. of course not, anyway, if the stupid conversation was to continue I know Barto would advise me to switch off zero and ignore any further transmissions.

Probably twenty seconds went by, "*tell him to phuck off Chris*" Pedro said in a loud and clear voice … I knew the Coastguard and the DLA would have heard that, plus probably 1,000 keen marine radio enthusiasts tuned to Zero!

"*All copied, out*" I responded so as not to invite a '*phucking*' conversation.

Thankfully channel zero went quiet, Big D started giggling, I couldn't hear it, but you could tell, his shoulders were moving about as if he was being electrocuted and his whiskers were twitching violently as if there were a bunch of sparrows having a punch up in effort to get the best roosting place.

I have to confess that, although serious, it was very funny, an anonymous voice telling the DLA to '*phuck off*'.

From the flying bridge Barto called down on the intercom "*casualty in sight*", I gave two keys on the mike and made to the casualty on channel 16 "*the Coxswain has you visual, we will be with you shortly, I will advise of the Coxswain's intentions as soon as I have them*"

Mangareva 3 replied "*thank you lifeboat*".

We came up on the casualty. She was wallowing in the swell heavily, Big D and myself were looking out of the forward wheelhouse windows, "*bit of a mess*" Big D grumbled, the yacht had the mast hanging in the water, sails strewn over the deck, some of the railings were wiped out and two of the yacht's crew were in the small cockpit at the rear.

Barto slowly approached the yacht. Being mindful of any trailing ropes, we stood off, the lifeboat rolling heavily in the swell too. "*Mr P, advise the casualty we are going to put a man aboard to help clear the deck, and bring the mast inboard, then we will rig for tow and take them to Falmouth please*" … "*roger*" I replied.

I advised *Mangareva 3* of our intentions and advised them we would be putting a crewman on board.

It was early evening, all quiet from the Lizard Lifeboat house.

Big D passed me our position which I duly passed to the Coastguard on channel zero.

On the afterdeck the deck crew were rigging fenders on the lifeboat's port side ready for the crew transfer. Tea Pot came into the wheelhouse and said "*Barto wants the big wire cutters, he's going to put Snowy on the Yacht, he needs to clear the deck of all the crap and rigging*"… Big D said "*they are in the big tool box in the tiller flat*"… Tea Pot nodded, looked at me and grinned, he was enjoying himself. We stood off for what seemed ages before a lull in the big seas presented itself. Without hesitation both engines engaged full ahead and we shot forward, within five seconds we were alongside and Snowy stepped aboard, clutching the big wire cutters, engines full astern and within five seconds we were at least two boat lengths astern of the yacht, just in time as a couple of large swells came through.

Barto took us off a reasonable distance and we watched Snowy and the two yachtsmen starting to clear the deck of the birds nest of wire, rope and jagged ends of the mast.

We were only fifty yards or so away from the yacht, it was now disappearing in the trough of each wave, we were certainly going to have a long and uncomfortable ride home.

Eventually Snowy came over on channel zero, using the hand held radio "*Lifeboat this is Lifeboat Zulu, over*" I replied "*loud and clear Snowy*", he replied "*the mast is lashed on the deck, we are ready to accept a tow, one of the female crew has a sprained wrist and both ladies are comfortable in the cabin, although both suffering from sea sickness, the two male crew want to remain on the deck, and although feeling sea sick are OK*".

Barto gave two clicks on the mike to indicate he had copied the transmissions.

Tea Pot and Trevor had rigged for tow, attached to the heavy tow rope we have an orange heaving line. Trevor stood on the aft starboard side of the lifeboat ready to throw the heaving line, Barto slowly passed the yacht upwind kicking the stern in as we passed her bow. Trevor threw the line high in the air, the near gale force wind took it straight over the foredeck of the yacht, Snowy grabbed hold and looked up to the flying bridge and gave a huge nod indicating to Barto he had the line and was ready to take on board the tow rope. Our tow rope is housed in a locker just outside the aft wheelhouse door on the afterdeck.

At the stern on the lifeboat is a large opening in the rails (a 'gob-eye') to allow the tow rope to swing from side to side when attached to the '*Sampson post*' positioned in the centre of the afterdeck.

Trevor passed the heaving line through the after rails and tied it off firmly to the heavy tow rope, he put two turns on the Sampson post and we were ready to pass out the tow rope.

Ken the Tea Pot looked up to the flying bridge and gave two thumbs up indicating we were ready to pass the tow rope to Snowy, who was rising and falling on the bow of the yacht, it must have been like sitting on a bucking bronco machine.

As we moved slowly ahead of the yacht Trevor paid out the tow, Snowy retrieved enough of the big tow rope on board the yacht to make it fast (tied firmly around the yacht's towing post), he gave the signal that the rope was made fast by crossing his arms, this meant we could put a little weight on the rope as it was paid out, to bring the yacht's bow head to sea.

With the two turns on the lifeboat's Sampson post Trevor paid out the tow, Ken busily bringing the tow rope out of the locker.

After paying out the tow we were beginning to lose sight of the yacht in the troughs, Barto needed to make sure the tow was paid out so the lifeboat and the yacht climb their respective waves at the same time so as not to snatch the tow rope, this is extremely

Clock on Falmouth's current Severn class all-weather lifeboat *Richard Cox Scott*, simililar to the one on *Elizabeth Ann*, showing the green silent periods for 2182 transmissions. Photo: Simon Culliford

important in heavy seas if the towed vessel is heavy, as a big snatch on the tow rope could result in it parting. That is very upsetting for the deck crew as it means recovering the heavy tow rope, getting out a new heaving line and beginning a dangerous operation of passing a new tow, dangerous for both boats, and for Snowy who would have to go back up to the bow of the yacht.

Parting the towline is also dangerous as the tow rope has some elasticity in it. If it parts under heavy tension it springs back at a fast rate. If a crewman gets caught by a tow rope it could cause a very serious injury or at worst a fatal injury.

We were now under way and engines slowly being brought up to the towing speed, normally around 6 or 7 knots. Big D looked into the radar and estimated we had 18 miles to run, it was now 1830 hours.

"Falmouth Coastguard this is Falmouth Lifeboat on zero, over" *"Lifeboat this is Falmouth Coastguard, loud and clear, over"* *"we have the casualty under tow, our current position 4 miles south of Lizard Point, ETA Falmouth 2200 hours, over"* the reply *"all copied, out"*.

Trevor went up to the flying bridge to keep Barto company, Tea Pot came into the wheelhouse and asked if anyone would like a brew.

He looked at Big D, *"yeah"* he grunted, he looked at me, I shook my head, knowing if I had a cup of tea it wouldn't stay in long, the boat was rolling like a pig, looking aft through the open aft door I could see the yacht when it was on top of a wave it was also rolling heavily too.

Knowing we had three to four hours to run before we came into the shelter of Falmouth I wedged myself in the radio seat and concentrated on the clock, passing our position to the Coastguard every half hour, making sure not to transmit in the *'green period'* which I will explain later.

As we passed Coverack, I could see the waves breaking over Carn-Dhu, the only rock visible in the Manacles, a large group of rocks off Lowland Point and just to the east of Coverack Bay.

With the wind in the south east it was going to be pretty lumpy in Coverack, much worse than when we launched that afternoon.

We were approaching Falmouth, Barto called down on the intercom *"standby to shorten the tow"*, I keyed the mike twice to acknowledge the order, Ken went out on deck Trevor made his way down from the flying bridge and Barto eased back on the throttles allowing the boys to begin pulling in the tow rope.

As the yacht got to within one wave of the lifeboat Barto shouted out *"make up there"*, Trevor put a couple more turns on the Sampson post and Ken gave the made fast signal (crossing his arms). There was a big swell in Falmouth Bay so the yacht was around 50 yards astern and towing well. As we approached the Black Rock Buoy at the entrance to Falmouth outer harbour the boys deployed the fenders starboard side, making ready to bring the yacht up alongside. There was no command from the flying bridge, everyone on board knew what to do, Big D and myself went out on deck to help get ready to make up the yacht alongside.

Snowy will have briefed the yacht's crew on what was going to happen. The yacht was going to be fastened firmly to the starboard side of the lifeboat, with around a quarter the length of the lifeboat stern behind the yacht, allowing the lifeboat to steer the joined vessels easily.

The wind was very strong and blowing straight into the harbour. The water was much flatter than in the bay, but with the large superstructure of the lifeboat acting like a sail the wind was blowing us towards the docks at a fair old speed. There was no time to waste, first the *'breast ropes'* (bow and stern) positioning the bow of the yacht almost to the bow of the lifeboat, leaving around 30% of the stern of the lifeboat free, with the stern of the yacht just over half way down the side of the lifeboat. As soon as the breast ropes were made fast, Barto was able to slowly move the two boats into clear water whilst the crew fastened the springs and took up all the slack. The two spring ropes stop the yacht surging alongside the lifeboat when it moves forward and astern.

One rope fixed to the stern of the yacht and made fast on the forward bits of the lifeboat the other on the bow of the yacht to the stern bits of the lifeboat. Once all ropes were tight we were in effect one craft.

Barto had decided to put the yacht on the visitor's pontoon close to the small harbour which is where the lifeboat house is. As we came alongside, Cliff the boarding boat attendant and 3 or 4 of the crew that didn't make the PR visit were ready to take ropes from the yacht, releasing the lifeboat so we could go to the fuel barge to re fuel the lifeboat. I was standing on the aft deck watching the ropes being passed to the boys on the pontoons when two windswept wives emerged from the yachts cabin.

Hair looking like candy floss, the larger of the two wives was not happy "*you bastard*" she screamed at her husband, I began to giggle, I looked at Big D, his face screwed up, his moustache and beard began to move around his face indicating he too was giggling, "*that is the last time you are phucking getting me on a phucking boat!*" she shouted so loud I expect half of Falmouth could hear her, she was absolutely livid. The other wife looked at her husband and screamed in a high pitched voice "*it's not funny John*".... John obviously thought the wife's outburst warranted a smile, this soon disappeared as his wife closed in looking like she was going to '*stick a nut*' on him.

I looked around, the crew were all trying too hard to look serious and busy. We have had many jobs where we have recovered boats of all types, and occasionally when the rescued get ashore a blazing row develops between husbands and wives... the entertainment is priceless.

After putting the lifeboat back on its moorings, signing off with the Coastguard, shutting off the sea cocks and switching off the electrics we all jumped into the boarding boat and Clifford took us ashore.

Cliff looked at me and said "*the wives seemed pretty upset Mr Price*" I said "*yes, looks like they won't be going sailing again*".

We got ashore, walking towards the boat house one of the shore crew said to Barto "*the DLA wants to see you and Pricey up at the Coastguard Station, we heard the effing and blinding on channel zero, there's hell up*".

I looked at Barto, he was absolutely livid, "*you are staying here Chris, I am going to sort this out*" he said.

Barto is a really nice bloke, but not the type to upset. He very rarely gets upset but when he does you had better look out. He is very capable of being very vocal and very violent.

I wasn't going to argue, not out of fear but because he was the boss, I said "*I am very happy to come with you and explain what happened*", he said "*not necessary, I heard every word on the flying bridge, I am not having my radio operator accused of swearing, I'll sort this out my way*".

"*Keep cool*" I said... looking at Barto's face... no chance.

He jumped into his car and tore off up the road to the Coastguard Station situated on Pendennis Point about a mile from the boat house.

I heard later that Barto stormed into the

From the deck of *Elizabeth Ann* at sea.
Photo: Falmouth RNLI Collection

radio room at the Coastguard Station, and before he could say anything or get his hands around the DLA's neck the Chief Coastguard said *"we've played back the tapes and your radio operator behaved perfectly"*, he then apologised for requesting Barto and myself to attend the Coastguard Station.

I suspect one of the Coastguards had pre warned their Chief that Barto would be very angry and diplomacy was going to be needed if he didn't want the Coastguard Station demolished!

I never heard any more about the advice Pedro gave me on channel zero earlier in the day. Perhaps in another life I would have taken it and told the DLA to phuck off!!

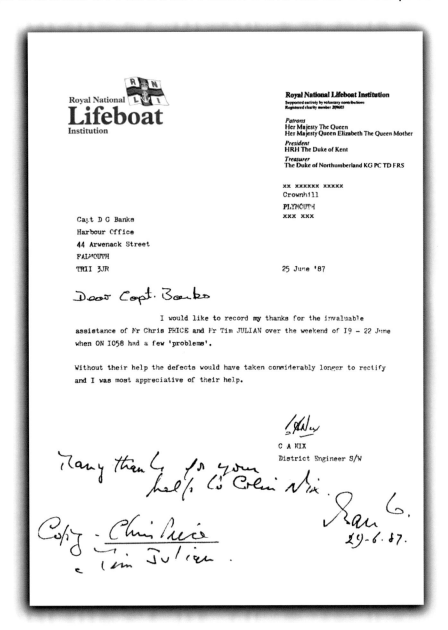

A typical letter of thanks from RNLI personnel who want to put on record their thanks when crew go out of their way to get a lifeboat repaired and back available for service. on this occasion Tim and myself spent three days aboard *Elizabeth Ann* replacing parts on both engines that were down on power to the extent that she was 'off station' and no relief boats were available. When a station has no lifeboat available everyone is holding their breath and praying for good weather and no calls for help.

John Barton on the day he took over as coxswain from Vivian Pentecost. Photo taken on 5 September 1989 on the upper steering postion (flying bridge) of the station's Arun class lifeboat *Elizabeth Ann.*
Photo: Simon Culliford

Plymouth-registered beam trawler *Pescado*. Photo: Plymouth Herald

PESCADO

The *Pescado*, a 55 ton scallop dredger with 6 on board left Falmouth on the 25th February 1991, the weather was southerly 5 to 6, just one of a fair sized fishing fleet that use Falmouth to land fish, re-fuel, repair gear or take shelter.

A few days later word got around the docks that there had been no contact with *Pescado* since she had sailed and ports along the south coast were asked to keep a look out for her.

Saturday 2nd March, early evening in the boathouse a few of us were having a cup of tea and discussing the exercise due the next morning 0800 hours, the weather was building into a full south easterly gale. Then the topic turned to the *Pescado*, the whole of Falmouth was now concerned that she had not been heard from for almost a week. Ports around the south coast were asked to look out for her from as far as Dover to the east round to the south and east of Ireland, nobody was sure where the *Pescado* was bound for.

John Barton 'Barto' was Coxswain, he took over from Viv when he retired, Alan Barns was Second Coxswain, both were extremely accomplished lifeboat men, trained by Viv and just the sort of guys you want around you at sea when the weather is 'marginal'.

"*I reckon we should exercise up to the east, and keep a look out for the Pescado*" grunted 'Big D', the words filtered through the huge beard and moustache, you knew his lips were moving because he was speaking, looking at his face when he spoke brought a vision of big game passing through the jungle, you could see the vegetation moving but not quite see what was causing it.

Graham a true gentlemen and very competent Second Mechanic nodded violently, as did we all in the boathouse.... "*I'll mention it to Barto in the morning but I expect he will want to go east and take a look at the Dodman*".

The area off Dodman Point was popular for the scallop dredgers, but an area of big seas when the wind was in the east to south east.

We decided to get home early that evening as the forecast for Sunday was poor, very poor.

Sunday morning and the forecast was true to form, in the Black Hole the sash windows were rattling, freezing wind finding its way through every gap, the air in the house smelt salty. I thought there was no point in having a large breakfast as there was not much chance of hanging on to it, so a slice of well chewed toast and a cup of tea seemed to be the most sensible.

0730 hours, it was now daylight, I strolled down to the boathouse, there were a couple of cars already parked in the lifeboat parking bays and the boathouse lights were on.

"*Pricey*" Big D grunted, "*Mr Price*" said Graham with his usual grin, "*all right*" said Barto, probably feeling sorry for me as he knows my tummy and big seas are not the best of friends.

Barto called everyone into the crew room situated next to the changing room, Big D, Graham and I shuffled in from the engineer's room.

"Right lads" Barto said "*we are going to do a navigation exercise this morning, up to the east, it's going to be lumpy*" one or two of the crew looked at me and grinned...... the bastards!

Big D looked at me through his thick glasses I had no idea if he was grinning, then the bush moved "*you've got the radio, is that OK?*" "*yes*" I said almost choking to get it out and not trying to look excited.

I knew this was not going to be a routine exercise, we were going to try to find the *Pescado*.

Sunday mornings were the most popular days for daylight exercises for lifeboats, most crew were available and it didn't normally interfere with work. I looked at Graham and said "*I expect most lifeboats and Coastguards are out on exercise along the south coast this morning*", he replied "*yes I was just thinking the same thing*", we were correct, later that morning there was a lot of wireless chatter, on channels sixteen and zero on VHF, and 2182 on MF.

Nearly all the main crew had by now arrived at the boathouse, those that didn't know had guessed we were going to concentrate on practising search patterns up to the east. Our patch extended to Dodman Point where we would normally meet up with our flank station Fowey.

We were lucky at Falmouth to have two good flank stations, Fowey who had a Waveney class lifeboat at the time. The Coxswain was a well-built even chubby guy, Keith Stuart a Geordie who was very difficult to understand when transmitting from the lifeboat on VHF. His crew were made up of what at first glance were a cross between young fit Royal Marines and seasoned criminals, earrings, tattoos, bloody great blokes who were to be taken seriously ...in any weather.

Our flank station to the west was the Lizard Lifeboat, a mixture of all shapes and sizes, and for that matter ages. The Lizard is a desolate windswept village which draws its crew from Cadgwith and the Lizard, all local men who had fishing somewhere in their blood. They had a habit of wearing their lifeboat jumpers back to front, a little weird I thought but it was just typical of a bond a crew has, these guys have been to sea in atrocious weathers, the Lizard having some of the most treacherous seas anywhere around the UK!

Everyone that turned up at the boathouse was going on the exercise, the younger crew and reserves of the inshore lifeboat hadn't turned up as I expect they were advised it wasn't ILB exercise weather.

The wind was whistling down through the harbour accompanied by some pretty noisy squalls. Clifford was in the boarding boat pumping the bilges to get the boat in a fit state to transfer us from shore to the lifeboat moored out in the centre of the harbour.

"*Good morning Mr Price*" he said as I stepped aboard and found somewhere to sit. There were 7 of us in the boat so pretty full. We chugged out towards the Arun with the odd wave just making it over the gunwale and giving everyone a taste of salt water (freezing of course).

As we came alongside the Arun everyone clambered aboard. Big D undid the padlock and the crew moved into the wheelhouse. Mike and Phil made their way up to the flying bridge to remove and stow the covers, Alan went straight to the chart table, waiting for the engines to flash up so he could switch on the radar and navigational aids.

The engines are always difficult to start when cold, they drink the juice out of both battery banks. This would interfere with the delicate electrics of the radar and the Decca if they were switched on before the engines were started.

Everyone in the wheelhouse was waiting for the engines to start up, I stood by the throttles having checked both were in 'detent' (not in gear). Slowly, the engines in turn coughed into life, I brought both into fast tick over and the wheelhouse came to life.

The radar took a couple of minutes to warm up, Alan was discussing with Barto some search pattern exercises we could put into practice once we approached the Dodman area.

The wheelhouse filled with exhaust fumes. This, mixed with salt in the freezing air gave an indication of what my poor old tummy was going to endure for the next 4 to 5 hours.

Mike and Phil had uncovered the flying bridge, Big D and Graham had emerged from the engine room, so everyone was in the wheelhouse ready for the briefing from Barto …..
"Everyone ready?" Barto said, everyone nodding, *"we will head up to the Dodman and run a few search patterns, then a closer inshore run, we are looking for anything that might indicate Pescado has gone down in this area, I expect many stations along the south coast are doing the same"*.

With that said Barto went out onto the aft deck, ready to let go of the mooring and Big D brought the engines back into tick over and engaged the throttles ready to move off.

I opened up with the Coastguard, *"Falmouth Coastguard, this is Falmouth Lifeboat, radio check on channel 16, over"*, they replied *"loud and clear"* I replied *"loud and clear also, channel zero"*…. The reply *"channel zero"*.

"Falmouth Coastguard this is Falmouth Lifeboat, we are launched on exercise in the Dodman area, our crew list is: 1,2,3,4,5,6,8. Total POB 7, request time check, over".

We pass crew list by numbers, me being number 6, this was in the unlikely event the lifeboat was lost at sea there was a record of exactly who was on board.

The Coastguard came back with *"all copied, time 0845 Zulu"*.

By now we had moved off our moorings, Mike and Phil had made their way into the wheelhouse, the boat began to pitch heavily as we passed the docks. There was white water (large waves breaking) on Trefusis Point which was an indicator the weather out in the bay was poor.

We made our way out into open water and motored to the east towards Dodman Point…. *"Falmouth Lifeboat this is Porthscatho Coastguard on channel zero, over"*. I replied, *"Porthscatho Coastguard this is Falmouth Lifeboat, loud and clear, we are exercising off the Dodman for the next four hours, over"*. The wife of the husband and wife team that made up Porthscatho Coastguard replied, *"we are searching the coastline for anything that could relate to the Pescado"*, I replied *"let us know if you see anything, out"*.

Alan had set up a search pattern and began passing courses to the flying bridge. All the lads were on deck keeping a keen look out with the exception of Big D, Alan on the navigation table and myself sat in the wireless seat monitoring the VHF and MF sets, noting down course positions from the chart table as they were passed upstairs.

Bid D sat in the engineer's seat opposite the engine dials, rev counters, oil pressure gauges, and a lot of other gauges that indicated the state of both Caterpillar diesel engines. I looked at the clock which was very accurate, it was coming up to the half hour. We know this as the green zone. On the clock the two positions are coloured in green like two very thin pizza slices.

Radio position on an Arun class all-weather lifeboat. Not *Elizabeth Ann* but *Kenneth Thelwall* 52-37. You can see the lifeboat's clock with the green 'silent period' just after the hour and half hour position. Photo: Royal Bank of Scotland/Rick Tomlinson

As the minute arm approached the green zone, I fiddled with the squelch dial that tuned the MF wireless so that it would pick up the faintest transmission. The 'green zone' actually indicates the internationally recognised "Silence Period" when vessels are not allowed to transmit on the main distress frequency of 2182 MHz, on the hour and half-hour (H00-H03 and H30-H33).

If you are at sea and in trouble, and have very little battery power, you would save all power and make your Pan Pan or Mayday calls in the silence period when you knew all wireless operators at sea would be listening intensely for any transmission. It is regarded as the ultimate sin to transmit on 2182 wave length in the silence period unless you were transmitting or relaying a Pan or Mayday.

Big D and myself listened intensely for the 3 minutes after the half hour, "*bugger all*" Big D grunted, I nodded, very little was said for the next couple of hours.

We were running a lane search from west to east, starting about half a mile off shore working our way seaward, lane widths around 100 metres, with the good visibility 50 metres each side of the lifeboat due to the height we had on the upper deck and flying bridge we could cover each 100 metre strip thoroughly.

The boat worked hard on the legs running into the sea, and surfed down the waves on the return legs as we ran with the sea. The boat rolled heavily as we ran across the sea the 100 meters to the next leg.

I manged to hold on to my morning toast and cup of tea, probably because I was kept busy with the radio log and because the aft wheelhouse door was pinned open with plenty of salty fresh air blowing around.

1225 hours, we were on a leg making our way back to Falmouth. We were around 4 miles seaward of Dodman Point, it was time to make a brew for the crew who had been out on deck for the last 4 hours or so, but first I had to monitor the silence period on 2182.

1230 hours, I kept my ear close to the MF speaker, then at 1231 hours an ear splitting *"Brixham Coastguard, Brixham Coastguard, this is Falmouth Coastguard, Falmouth Coastguard a radio check 2182, over"*….. my eyes bulged, I looked across to the chart table at Alan who was looking at me, I screamed out *"what"*. I couldn't believe the bloody Coastguard was transmitting in the silence period!

I picked up the VHF mike set on channel zero *"you are transmitting on 2182 in the silence period"*…..

I didn't waste time saying who was transmitting (Falmouth Lifeboat) I just hoped the idiot who was transmitting on 2182 would hear my transmission and the urgency and the anger in my voice, or if not anyone else in the Coastguard Station who had 'their ears on' would tell him to shut up. No such luck, I was absolutely livid, the complete knob head started again *"Brixham Coastguard, radio check on 2181, over"*.

No reply from Brixham, I expect they were as shocked as I was that a major Coastguard Station was transmitting on 2182 in the silence period.

I switched to channel 16 and said in a very loud voice, *"stop transmitting on 2182 in the silent period!!"*

There was no reply, but 2182 went silent, the whole coast I am sure was listening intensely, just in case there was a remote possibility *Pescado* would be transmitting….. nothing.

I made a pot of tea and passed the cups around, we were approaching the entrance to Falmouth, the mood was sombre, very little was said, we all thought things were not looking good for the *Pescado*, no sightings, no contact, nothing, we were all thinking the worst.

With the lifeboat tied up on its moorings we had a silent run back in the boarding boat to the boat house, everyone was wrapped up in their own thoughts, where was the *Pescado*? Have they come to grief on our patch? Why is there no wreckage? Where could they be?

Over the next couple of days *Pescado* was on everyone's lips, every port in the country was alerted and asked to keep a look out for her, Irish, French and all the south coast Coastguards were given details of *Pescado* and were asked to keep a look out for her.

First thing, Thursday 7th March Falmouth Coastguard initiated a huge search for the *Pescado*. That evening word was out that part of a wheelhouse had been recovered it had a letter 'P' on the wheelhouse roof, recovered just to the east entrance to Falmouth harbour.

1725 hours Barto rang the main crew, when he got to me he said *"looking for a crew to search off the Dodman a bit of the wheelhouse has been recovered, are you available?"* *"of course"* I replied, *"great, boat house in 30 minutes"* Barto said and rang off.

Wind was in the east and strengthening, I grabbed a quick sandwich and ate it as I walked down to the boathouse, lights were on and plenty of activity inside.

The whole main crew were in the crew room, Barto filled us all in with the info received so far, the parts of the recovered wheelhouse were almost certainly *Pescado*, "*as she had been missing for so long it looks like she went down somewhere off the Dodman and is breaking up on the sea bed*" Barto said, (he knows this area very well).

He then had a chat with Alan, a superb navigator and lifeboat man, between them they agreed a search pattern for us.

Big D rang the Coastguard Station from the boathouse to let them know we were planning a navigation exercise in the area off the Dodman and would keep an eye out for anymore wreckage that may be in the area.

It was pretty obvious to us all this was a disaster that occurred right on our doorstep probably more than a week ago, *Pescado* with a young crew had gone down so quickly with no chance of putting out a mayday call and were lost.

During the launch I don't think a single word was said, the crew got the boat ready, engines started, electrics flashed up, let go moorings and a slow run out of the harbour.

I passed the crew list to the Coastguard on zero, you could tell by the way the duty operator passed the time check and acknowledged our transmission there was an air of gloom within the Coastguard Station.

As we passed Black Rock at exactly 1830 hours, Alan passed the course to get to the first leg of our lane search pattern he had laid out on the chart table.

Both engines pushed up to full speed and we made up towards Dodman Point, short seas, plenty of spray, a reasonably dirty night ahead of us.

Barto called down "*rig both search lights please*", two of the crew went up to the flying bridge to remove the two heavy search lights from their storage and slot them into their respective positions one port side and one starboard, plug them into their sockets ready for use.

The radio burst into life "*Falmouth Lifeboat, Falmouth Lifeboat this is Porthscatho Coastguard, over*".

Porthscatho Coastguard were a husband and wife team, both dedicated Coastguards who knew their patch well, the wife was transmitting, a lovely soft voice, very sophisticated and precise, certainly not the normal Cornish gruff voices we get from the male Coastguard Teams.

"*Loud and clear, we are conducting a search exercise off the Dodman, over*" I replied. "*We are searching the coastline for wreckage*" came the soft reply "*roger, keep safe out*" I replied.

As we moved up to the east I took a look out the port side windows, there were a few blue flashing lights of Coastguard Land Rovers and some search light activity on the beaches. Looks like everyone was out looking for any more signs of *Pescado*.

"*Porthoustock Coastguard, radio check on zero over*", I instantly recognised Henry

Bosustow's dulcet tones, he was obviously checking he was in contact with anyone that could pick up the transmissions from his hand held radio, there are plenty of blind spots along the coastline where there are steep cliffs it is important when its pitch black and windy you keep in touch.

"*Is that you Enery*" I replied on zero, if only just to cheer everyone up who was listening in. Henry always came back with an excited voice "*Yes, yes, who's that, over*"….. normally I would go back and repeat '*is that you Enery*' but tonight was not a night to pull Henry's leg….. "*Chris here, got you loud and clear where are you? Over*"

Henry came back "*down Porthoustock, where are you?*" I replied "*Up off the Dodman, listening 16 and zero*".

The radio transmissions between us were never going to get 10 out of 10 for correct radio procedure, but then no one was going to complain as we were out there in the weather doing jobs. Henry is a legend he has been a very active member of the Coastguard and rescue team for ever, 47 years' service in fact! One of those types you could rely on 100% no weather conditions would stop Henry and his team from working the worst shoreside areas no matter how dangerous!

The weather was now picking up, the lifeboats motion was not very pleasant when running against or abeam the seas, but not so bad surfing with the sea.

Alan passed on the intercom warnings when a course change was imminent. Then the new course followed by '*now*'… the course pattern was very precise, and the boat moving at almost full speed.

The lane distances are chosen so that as we run up one lane and down the next we can be sure to see anything out of the ordinary search lights on wide beam and all eyes peeled.

Operating the search light requires a considerable skill, it needs to be concentrated on the sea's to make sure every inch is covered, also it is essential the beam doesn't catch any part of the boats structure forward of the flying bridge as bright reflection would destroy the Coxswain's night vision which would go down like a lead balloon.

It was now 2030 hours, we had been searching for two hours, my tummy was grumbling, the constant thump of short seas causing heads to roll around, very hard on the neck muscles, it was bloody cold too!

Barto popped his head around the aft wheelhouse door and asked 3 of us in the wheelhouse if we were OK to continue for another two hours, we all gave him the thumbs up.

We had a fair bit of ground to cover to complete Alan's search pattern, I reckon we were all keen to get ashore, but also very keen not to leave a search area until it has been covered properly.

"*Falmouth Coastguard this is Falmouth Lifeboat, over*" the Coastguard came back instantly "*loud and clear, over*" … "*we will be continuing our exercise off the Dodman for another two hours, over*" ….. "*all copied, out*".

The next two hours seemed like four, the strong easterly had been blowing most of the day, the sea was very choppy, not rough but unpleasant enough to produce considerable rolling and pitching of the lifeboat.

After a few hours at sea in lumpy conditions the strength needed to brace for each wave, and the constant holding on as the boat rolls is very wearing. This, coupled with cold and a damp wind whistling around slowly, drags on like what seems forever if there is not much going on.

Alan called up the course change to the flying bridge and advised Barto this was the last leg of the search pattern, it just happened this leg was taking us back to Falmouth, so the search continued all the way back until we reached St Anthony lighthouse and turned to starboard into the entrance of Falmouth.

Big D switched on the wheelhouse lights and the crew began to tidy the boat up, search lights stowed, fuel tank valves opened ready to take on fuel, nav gear put away. We reduced speed as we passed the docks making our way to North Quay for refuelling then back to the moorings.

Barto passed down from the flying bridge, "*I'm finished with engines*", Big D keyed the mike twice to acknowledge, he then pressed two stop buttons and the big diesel shuddered to a stop, all went quiet.

I went below into the tiller flat, opened the door to the engine room and lifted the sea cock flaps, on my knees and spun the two red handles to shut off both sea-cocks, this is standard practice for big lifeboats, the sea-cocks are where the cold sea water is drawn in and circulated around the heat exchangers to keep the engines cool.

Should one of the pipes that carry the sea water fail while on the boat is on its moorings the engine room could fill with water!

As both engine room doors are shut tight when we go ashore, the lifeboat wouldn't sink. Even if they were left open and the water filled the whole boat it wouldn't sink, this is due to the many small compartments around the hull that are filled with ping pong balls, contained in small mesh bags, in effect creating thousands of individual watertight compartments.

The boat filling with sea water is the last thing we would want, it would be completely buggered!

Both sea-cocks shut, the flaps shut then into the engine room to dip the oils, kneeling between both engines, checking both dip sticks to make sure the correct amount of oil is in each sump.

Finally checking the bilges to check they were clean and free from oil or diesel, engine room lights off, and shut the engine room door.

I looked into the wheelhouse from the tiller flat, Big D stuck his head over the stairwell, "*finished with electrics*" I gave him a nod, turned around to the battery bank controls, one hand on each of the two levers. I switched off both batteries, extractor fans whirred down to a stop and the boat was silent.

It was pitch black as I climbed the eight steps up into the wheelhouse, it was empty. The

Elizabeth Ann on a calm morning,on her mooring in Falmouth Harbour. Photo: RNLI Archive

crew were on the after deck waiting for Clifford to arrive with the boarding boat.

We could see him in the distance, yellow gear and his little bobble hat, spray covering him as the bow of the wooden boarding boat ploughed into each wave as he made his way down the harbour.

The boarding boat came alongside starboard side, there was no lee or shelter on either side of the lifeboat as it was pointing seaward and straight into the waves as they rolled in from the bay.

We all climbed aboard, I squeezed in near the stern as I knew those in the bow would get the worst of the spray.

"*Mr Price*" Clifford exclaimed with lips curled in a big smile, I gave him a grunt which was the way we usually exchanged greetings.

A wet run back to the quay, cold and windy and very dark, we all piled into the changing room to get our wet gear off and put them on the large purpose made hangers, I stuck my gear in the Mechanic's room, hoping it would dry before we needed it next …. Nothing worse than putting on cold wet gear to start a shout.

With all the '*see ya latter's*' the crew made for their cars, Big D flashed up his old Land Rover, I could hear it chugging up the road as I made my way up the steep steps to my road, then the 100 yards to the front door of the 'Black Hole', it was almost midnight.

I had no idea how worn out the rest of the crew were, I was cream crackered, straight downstairs, stood next to the bed, trousers and pants down to my ankles, jumper and polo shirt off and placed on top, sit on the bed, socks off and placed on top of the pile, all ready to step straight into if the bleeper goes off.

The bleeper was on the bedside cabinet, approximately 12 inches from my ear when I am asleep, next to that the phone, the bedroom window was rattling in the wind, single glazed and noisy, the rain against the window sounded like a tap dance competition. This, coupled with freezing sleet would normally make it difficult to sleep, I don't remember my head touching the pillow I was that tired.

8th March 0600 hours, Friday morning, still dark, the phone rang... nobody rings at that time in the morning, except... the Launching Authority, Captain Banks... I pick up the phone and said "*yes*", the reply "*Lifeboat launch*", my reply "*OK Captain*" and we both put the phone down simultaneously.

The Coastguard when they want to task the lifeboat have to get permission from the Falmouth RNLI Launching Authority who is our Hon Secretary Captain Banks, he will of course give permission, unless he feels no lives are at risk or the job is not appropriate for a lifeboat, for instance recovering a dinghy being blown out to sea.

As soon as he gives permission for the bleepers to be activated he goes through the phone list to ring the crew, as crewman number 6 I was on the main crew, the first 7 to answer are alerted by Captain Banks, so he knows a full crew will be making their way to the boat house.

No sooner had I put the phone down and started putting on my socks, my heart was beating like mad, mentally I was calm, in fact still half asleep, then off goes the bleeper a high pitched fast Bleep, Bleep, Bleep.

My heart went into overdrive, I grabbed my pants wriggled my toes into what I thought was a leg hole. As I was full of adrenaline I pulled like mad, managing to get my pants to just under the knee where they became stuck, I realised it went through the slit between the leg holes where you pull your willie through when you want a pee. With great effort I managed to retrieve my leg from the willie hole and in slow motion placed each leg slowly into the correct leg holes.

I then concentrated on pulling on my polo shirt and jumper at the same time, when doing it in a hurry it must look like someone trying to punch their way out of a paper bag. Then when both hands see daylight I grabbed the bleeper and begin my way upstairs, doing up the belt. Step into my shoes, shuffle towards the door, unlock it, out into the street, lock the door ready to dash down to the boathouse.

Bang, the first maroon, almost directly overhead, then bang, the second maroon.

The wind was strong and from the east, you could smell and taste the salt in the air... down the steep steps from my street to the street below, I could see the boathouse lights from the steps, and the sound of speeding cars as they came down the high street, obviously crew at that time in the morning.

I was about fifth to arrive in the crew changing room, making my way to the engineer's room to get my gear on, Alan was on the phone to the Coastguard to find out what the job was. It was just dawn, still fairly dark, no sun, just low cloud and heavy rain.

Alan gave the sit rep to Barto, we all listened anxiously to know what we had, whatever it was it must be serious.

"*Considerable wreckage has been seen in the Dodman area, including a large amount of scallop sacks*" Alan said, " *we have been tasked to conduct a search in the area, the Coastguard will pass the coordinates once we are afloat*", Barto nodded his head slowly, looked around and said "*all right*", everyone nodded as they put on their lifejackets. My gear was still wet from the night before, just over 6 hours ago.

It was obviously *Pescado*, giving up wreckage from the sea bed. With the big ground sea, swept up with the strong easterlies over the last few days I expect the trawler was moving violently on the sea bed, spewing out gear and timber from its wheelhouse as it began to break up, the steel hull remaining intact, but everything else that would float making its way to the surface as it broke away.

The boarding boat taking the crew out to *Elizabeth Ann* on a calm day, Bob Monk on the tiller. Photo: David Barnicoat Collection

As we made our way out to the *Elizabeth Ann* I thought '*will any bodies be surfacing*'? Six young crew including a girl who was the *Pescado's* cook, I expect they have been in the water for much more than a week and probably two or three, the prospect of having to recover bodies is daunting but, as I have learnt in my few years on the crew so, so important to the loved ones ashore.. without a body the agony for family and friends must be unbearable.

No time to dwell, back to reality, we were alongside, Big D looked at me "*engines*", I gave a single nod, first into the wheelhouse, down the stairs to the tiller flat, groped around for the two battery switches, as I clicked them on the lights came on and the fans purred into action.

It was bloody cold considering how hot the engine room was only six hours before, engines started I made my way back into the wheelhouse, Big D was on the radio, I made my way out onto the after deck to check we had water coming out of both exhausts, this indicated that the salt water drawn in through the sea-cocks was working its way through the system and being expelled through the exhaust.

The chatter of both engines exhaust covers as the they banged against their stops as the engines were running at fast tick over, when the engines open up and are running at full emergency speed the covers are held wide open by the exhaust blasting out of both pipes with a superb roar.

Everyone on deck and in the wheelhouse was busy, I made my way up to the flying bridge

Launching the Y-boat from *Elizabeth Ann*. Photo: Falmouth RNLI Collection

to keep Barto company, we both kept our eyes fixed on St Anthony light house and Black Rock buoy as we made our way out of the east main entrance into the outer harbour.

The seas were rough, the swell was reasonably high, the day was going to be long, cold and the chance of a good outcome nil, having said that recovering 6 bodies would be a good outcome, but very unlikely.

As soon as we entered the bay and had enough sea room the Arun swung to port and we made our way east on a course of 080 degrees.

It was now daylight, overcast, windy, heavy swell and very cold, we were abeam Gerrans Bay thumping our way eastwards when I could hear traffic on channel zero, I tuned the squelch and turned up the volume on the flying bridge, Barto leaned forward and we both listened, it was Falmouth cliff rescue team who were working their way along the top of the cliffs to the east of *St Anthony Lighthouse*, they had spotted what could be a body amongst the sea weed, plastic, and general rubbish in amongst the rocks but could not be sure due to the surf breaking as the waves washed over the rocks.

Barto called down to the wheelhouse on the intercom *"tell them we are on our way over"*.

We could see far in the distance the blue Coastguard Land Rover with blue light flashing, high on the cliff top, Barto said to me get a dry suit on and take Alan with you, the deck crew were getting the *Y-boat* ready to launch. The covers for the *Y-boat* were already stowed as part of getting the boat ready to leave its mooring, so all they had to do was pay out the cradle that the Y-boat slid down as it made its way over the stern of the lifeboat.

This is a drill that is done by the younger crew and reserves nearly every time we launch on exercise, sometimes if the Coxswain is not happy about the speed or safety of an exercise launch and recovery it can be done several times until it is done right.

For seasoned crew all who have 8 or 10 years under their belts the *Y-boat* can be launched safely in a matter of minutes, this is one of the important drills used to show visiting RNLI District Inspectors (DI's) when they put the crew through its paces on a DI's exercise.

I whizzed down from the flying bridge, on to the aft deck, into the wheelhouse, down the steps by the steering position and into the survivors' cabin towards the bow of the lifeboat. This is where we would normally secure casualties, if we recovered a large number and had to put some below to keep the lifeboat stable. Also here they would be safe and out of the way. Not a pleasant space to spend time in in heavy weather, but this is where the dry suits are stowed.

To get into one it is easiest to sit on the floor, kick off your shoes and climb in, very similar to putting on a boiler suit. As soon as I pushed my head through the neck seal and got a face full of Johnson's baby powder, and the tight grip of the neck seal giving the feelings of being strangled, I felt instantly sea sick. It was a rush to get upright and out onto the after deck for some fresh air before I threw up…. Whilst the crew are used to me '*calling for Hewey*' it was a bit early on into the launch to shoot the cat!

A few gulps of fresh air and tummy sent the brain a signal, '*much happier, keep in the fresh air*'.

The deck crew had the *Y-boat* in the water and was bringing it alongside the starboard quarter (the after end of the starboard side).

As I made my way over to jump in Alan emerged from the aft wheelhouse door strapping on his life jacket,

I leapt into the *Y-boat*, unlocked the engine, lowered the prop into the water, locked it in the down position, took two slow pulls on the chord with the throttle wide open, closed the throttle to the start position, switched the on switch down, took a quick look behind me to make sure no one was in the way when I gave a violent pull on the start chord, (habit, I knew I was the only one in the boat, but an elbow in the kisser from the guy starting the boat is not a good way to win friends).

Elizabeth Ann's Y-boat with Alan Barnes at the helm and crew member Dr Howard 'Sid' Siddal with the handheld radio. Photo: Simon Culliford

Two hard tugs and the little outboard screamed into life, Alan shuffled in and took the bow rope, we were off. I left the shelter of the lifeboat and moved off slowly looking everywhere to get a good gauge of exactly where we were, where we were going, and the size of the sea.

The swells were large, we were only 30 or 40 feet away from the Arun when she dropped into a trough, we were in the next trough, as the large wave approached us.

We all but lost sight of the lifeboat, this gave a good indication to the size of the large waves making their way ashore.

Alan looked around at me and said "*glad you are driving*" ...I smiled and thought '*we will see!*' This trip was not going to be pleasant, I have spent a lot of time at the helm of D-class and Y-class inflatable, the main exercise always being beaching in surf, picking the wave to take you ashore, increasing speed as it rolls towards you, matching the speed so you are just in front of the crest of the wave, and surfing ashore, engine lock off, and lifting the engine just before the skeg and prop grounds.

Normally with two crew, who jump out of the boat just as we are about to ground, to stabilise the boat and spin it round head to sea so it doesn't get swamped.

The next operation to walk the boat into the sea until they are both chest deep, this is deep enough to drop the engine, start it and motor seaward, the two crew holding onto hand holds near the bow are almost swept back into the boat as it moves forward, once in they both lean right over the bow to keep the bow down and make sure we don't climb the wave and get flipped over!

This exercise nearly always takes place on a nice sandy beach with sensible size rollers and surf.

Today was not sensible, and the beach was not sandy. We moved in towards the shore slowly, the Arun was quite a way off by now, completely disappearing in the swells, all the crew on deck watching our progress.

Alan was watching the Coastguards high on the cliff trying to direct us, he had Lifeboat Zulu our handheld radio around his neck, but it was bloody useless, you couldn't hear a thing in the wind, and the noise of the seas breaking on the huge boulders that was the 'beach'.

The water was fairly deep, rising sharply just before the shore line, so the seas were not breaking, just big. Alan pointed to the corner of the small cove we were entering, there was a large amount of netting, plastic sacks, scallop bags, weed and large pieces of wood, we approached looking hard for anything that resembled a body there. Thankfully there was no '*body*'.

To get to this position took us a little too close to the shore, the wave behind us began to grow in height, there was no room to turn the Y-boat head to sea, I screamed hold tight and within seconds we were accelerating towards the big smooth boulders that formed the shore, I flicked the engine into unlock to save smashing it off the stern of the Y-boat, as we were certainly going to be dumped on the shore, as we hit shore the propeller made the familiar clanking sound as the blades made contact with the rocks, the wave broke and swept through the boat, it picked Alan up, I grabbed the back of his lifejacket as he was being swept over the bow of the Y-boat I got a foot hold in the front of the boat and yanked him back in, we both looked back to the sea, the next wave was nowhere near as big and a bit of a way off.

We swung the boat round and I shouted '*oars*', we released an oar each from the top of the sponsons, pushed the boat back into the sea and paddled like mad, as soon as we had 3 or 4 feet under the stern of the Y-boat I spun round gave a yank on the pull chord, the engine started I put it in gear and we roared forward, what a relief.

Well it was until, as we got clear of the immediate shore, we found ourselves in the thick of the floating rubbish that had accumulated in the corner of the cove. The engine was working hard as we still had plenty of water in the boat… the boat slowed to a standstill, engine still revving like mad, I throttled back, lifted the outboard to see a 'birds nest' around the prop, no time to get a knife and try to cut it all off, a large lump of nylon heavy netting!

"*Oars*" I shouted, within two or three seconds we were both paddling frantically towards the lifeboat, '*Hawaii five O*' flashed through my mind, when things are approaching marginal it is surprising how strong we both were.

Barto was a way off but could see we had a problem, he put the Arun head to sea and motored astern, he came in as close as was safe, the crew were lined up on the stern willing us on, as we closed Alan gathered the bow rope of the Y-boat and threw it up to the waiting crew, caught first time, Mike caught the rope took a turn around the stern rail and Barto towed us slowly out to sea, to get far enough away from the shore to safely

Originally stationed at Plymouth, Fowey now had the Waveney class lifeboat *Thomas Forehead and Mary Rowse II* . Photo: Simon Culliford

recover the *Y-boat*.

Back on board I could not get my neck out of the strangling neck seal, and get the '*boil-in-a-bag*' dry suit off.

Big D looked down at me as I was wriggling on the floor fighting with the bloody dry suit to get it off, he grunted "*no body then*" I could tell he was grinning, his thick beard was twitching violently, as if two mice were chasing each other in long grass. "*Bugger all, just a net round the prop*" I replied.

Alan came in the wheelhouse, holding his dry suit, he managed to get it off on the after deck.

"*That was interesting*" he said…"*was it you that pulled me back into the Y-boat?*"… I laughed and said "*there was only the two of us*"…he replied "*all I could see was this bloody great boulder and I was heading straight for it, then I flew back into the boat*".

We grinned at each other, and I thought to myself the Gods were with us on that trip into the cove, it could have gone horribly wrong… not something to dwell on at the time. Big D thanked the Coastguards and confirmed the *Y-boat* had a good look, just rubbish, scallop bags and timber… no need to tell them the Y-boat driver nearly had a bowel movement!

O845 hours, the Y-boat stowed back on top of the lifeboat we resumed our course east towards the search area, Alan was busy on the chart table setting out the search area the

The Lizard Tyne class lifeboat *David Robinson*. Photo: RNLI Archive

Coastguard asked us to cover.

Ahead was unusual white flecks in the breaking seas, as we closed we could see, dozens if not hundreds of white scallop bags, the *Pescado* was certainly on the sea bed and releasing its loose floating gear.

As we approached our first way point Alan passed the course to the flying bridge.

The Coastguard has tasked our two flank stations Fowey and The Lizard lifeboats to join in the search. As our boat was the largest of the three and it was our patch the Falmouth boat was designated '*On Scene Commander*'. This gave us the responsibility of directing the Fowey and The Lizard boats.

Alan suggested to John that the two boats took up positions abeam of us, Fowey on our port side and The Lizard on our starboard, distance off 100 metres.

This gave us the ability to search a much wider strip of sea, the Arun has the ability to cover a fairly wide strips of sea due to the height above sea level of the flying bridge.

There was nothing for me to do in the wheelhouse. Big D was monitoring the engine panel and keeping the Coastguard informed of our progress and Alan had the chart table well covered, so with quite a rough sea I was very pleased to be up on the flying bridge with the rest of the crew keeping a good lookout for anything unusual in the water.

Our lane searches were around six miles long, parallel to the coast, and gradually creeping seaward, as we approached the turns Alan prepared all three Coxswains by advising *"approaching our turning point to starboard (we were on an eastward leg), range 100 metres …. new course starboard steer one, one, zero,… now"*

All three lifeboats turned at exactly the same time, we were making around 15 knots, not full speed but fast enough to keep the boats as stable as possible.

The heavy swell gave us a good hammering on the easterly leg, the next course change for the westerly long leg was very pleasant surfing as we ran with the sea.

The search area was big and going to take it least six hours to cover.

After covering four legs we were all on a run to the east, time approximately 1130 hours, I noticed Fowey on our port side stop, then move off the north. As I pointed to them to alert John, their wireless come on channel zero *"we've spotted something on our starboard beam, just going over to have a look"*. We stopped in the water, Lizard did the same, we wallowed around in the heavy swell, waiting ,….. waiting.

I wondered if it would be a body, with all the wreckage coming to the surface it's about time bodies surfaced.

Bodies that have been in water for a few weeks are difficult to recover… the most important thing for the loved ones at home is that they are recovered.

I expect everyone on the Falmouth and Lizard Lifeboat were having similar thoughts.

"It's only a bit of timber, could be from the wheelhouse on the Pescado but nothing to identify it, we've got it on board ready to resume search, over"

Just after the Fowey passed their find on channel zero Falmouth Coastguard chipped in *"Falmouth Lifeboat, be advised the wreckage retrieved yesterday has now been positively identified as having come from the Pescado, over"* *"all copied"* Big D replied. So now there was no doubt the *Pescado* had gone down, and was several fathoms below us on the sea bed.

We continued the search pattern, ploughing on, into the sea, running with the sea, moving further and further away from the coast.

It was now raining heavily, very cold, very windy, the freezing rain stinging the face, everyone looking through thin slits in the eyes.

I could see a small naval vessel doing her own thing a few miles to the south east of the Dodman, and further inshore a Sea King running its own search pattern along the coastline.

1720 hours it was now getting dark, we were nearing the end of our search pattern *"all stations, all stations, this is Falmouth Coastguard, Falmouth Coastguard, sit rep, the body of a fisherman has been found on Duporth beach, the Police are in attendance, over"* *"all copied"* Big D replied, both other lifeboats and the Coastguard Cliff Rescue Team also acknowledged.

The crew had a tough day, poor sea conditions, freezing rain, found nothing of significance and then to hear the *Pescado* was beginning to release crew.

The body was later identified as the young female cook aboard the *Pescado*. Nobody spoke, the expressionless faces said it all.

I went below to see what was going on in the wheelhouse, and see if anyone wanted a brew.

We had just turned on our last leg to the west at 1755 hours, when the Coastguard came on *"Lizard Lifeboat due to the day light fading you are released can return to station"* *"roger they replied"*.

All three lifeboats were still running abreast on a westward leg, Lizard increased speed and left the search pattern, making for home, it was now dark and very little visibility, low cloud and still raining heavily.

Within a few minutes Fowey lifeboat was released from the search, *"Falmouth lifeboat, this is Fowey lifeboat, pleasure working with you, safe trip home, over"* *"you too"* Big D replied.

I was getting almost excited, it was our turn to be released and told to return to station, I was shattered, the last few days had been tough, cold, feeling sick most of the time, little sleep, thinking 'come on Falmouth Coastguard get a move on, you can't have forgotten us'.

"Falmouth Lifeboat, Falmouth Lifeboat this is Falmouth Coastguard on channel zero, over" yes, yes I thought..... *"loud and clear"* Big D replied...

"We have a new search area for you, are you ready to take down the co-ordinates, over" what! I thought, they must be kidding, Alan shouted out *"what!"*... Big D replied to the Coastguard *"ready"*.

The Coastguard passed the 4 corners of the box they wanted covered by latitude and longitude, Big D and Alan took down the positions.

Barto shouted down on the intercom *"they must be joking don't they realise it's pitch black out here,"*..... I said to Big D *"I'll nip up top and help rig the search lights"* *"roger"* he grunted.

Up on the flying bridge Barto looked at me shook his head, and shrugged his shoulders, he didn't need to use words to express his disbelief.

I started to remove the cover off the searchlight stowed on the port side of the flying bridge, Alan came through on the intercom *"I've just laid out the box search on the chart the Coastguard gave us, it reached from St Austell bay down to Coverack, they have to be kidding!"*

I looked at Barto, he was grinning like a cheshire cat, as he reached towards the intercom mike to reply to Alan the Coastguard came on channel zero *"Falmouth Lifeboat this is Falmouth Coastguard, we are calling off the search you can return to station, over"* Big D replied, *"roger, returning to station"*

We were heading west anyway, Barto picked up speed, turned the lifeboat to starboard onto a course that took us past the Dodman across Gerrans Bay and towards Falmouth. I lashed down the cover to the searchlight, *"time for a brew Mr Price"* Barto shouted (it

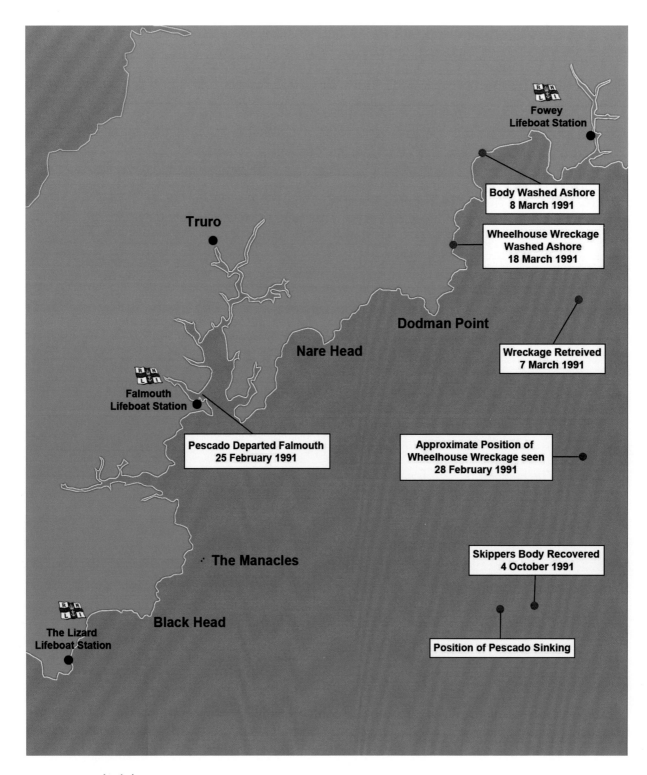

was very windy).

I made my way below to the wheelhouse, the rest of the crew were now inside, Barto called down on the intercom "*take the wheel Al, I'm coming down*" Alan keyed the mike twice to acknowledge, they gave the steering wheel a kick to port then starboard to indicate to the flying bridge he had control of the boat.

Barto stepped in through the aft wheelhouse door, we were all now in the wheelhouse trying to warm up.

The small heater situated on the floor under the MF wireless set was blowing full speed, it was bloody useless, just blowing cold air around.

The wheelhouse is constructed of thin sheet aluminium, with a dark fleck material sprayed onto the inside to stop condensation. There was no insulation, so if it's below zero degrees outside, it's below zero degrees inside! The only good thing about being in the wheelhouse was that you weren't being blast frozen and soaked with sea spray and rain.

1850 hours we were rounding the lighthouse and entering the entrance to Falmouth, making our way to the docks. Alan reduced speed so we didn't drag our wash into the harbour itself, also of course to observe the speed limit!

As the crew were all 'main crew' with ten to fifteen years under their belts no orders were required. Everyone knew what to do to get the boat re-fuelled, get all the kit properly stowed and ready for the next shout.

With the boat re-fuelled, we left the quay to make our way to the mooring, Barto gave the boat to Mike to put us back on the mooring, this was typical of all the Coxswains I have served under at Falmouth, everyone on the main crew had to be competent to undertake all the jobs, drive the boat, navigate, operate the wireless, rig for firefighting, emergency steering, and of course work the deck, which involved rigging for tow, dropping anchor and so on.

It was not unknown on a 'District Inspectors' exercise that the Coxswain and Mechanics were told to sit in the wheelhouse and do and say nothing while the younger crew ran the boat. I looked astern as we slowly made our way to the moorings, I could just make out the boarding boat which was following us, spray coming off the bow as it cut its way through the short waves running through the harbour and Clifford in his yellows at its stern.

With the lifeboat put to bed and the engines on tick over, I could hear the clanging of the exhaust flaps, then the engines stop, silence, the wheelhouse lights went out as Big D switched off the battery banks, I stood by the aft door holding the padlock, ready to snap it on and lock the back door as soon as Big D emerged from the black interior of the wheelhouse. It was a cold and wet run back from the lifeboat to the quay, nobody spoke. This was a shout nobody enjoyed, not because of the foul weather, but the outcome couldn't have been worse.

Confirmation the *Pescado* had sunk on our door step, just to the east of Falmouth 13 miles south of the Dodman, the whole crew lost, all youngsters without a chance to call for help. If they had called for help we could have been there within half an hour, Fowey could have been there too with a similar time to run as us.

Two more bodies were recovered from the sea many months later, the wreck of the *Pescado* was recovered from the sea bed more than 2 years after she went down, on 20th September 1993 and taken to a dry Dock at Devonport Royal Dockyard.

This tragedy was a reminder to all on the south coast how dangerous the occupation of fishing is, no matter what size boat. I remember those weeks when we were looking for the *Pescado*, then finding it just outside Falmouth as if it was yesterday, one of the many shouts you never forget.

Foot note: a few weeks later at The Annual *Lifeboat Dinner the* Branch Chairman announced during the dinner, *"I have a special award to make, will Chris Price please step forward"*. I was awarded the Y-boat prop from the *Pescado* job, complete with the dings from the rocks ashore when we made violent contact .... A round of applause from the crews of both boats, from me, no speech just a red face!

The damaged propeller that was presented to the author at the Falmouth Lifeboat Dinner and Dance. Photo: Simon Culliford

The *Pescado* being raised. Photo: Fishing News

Falmouth Packet

Incorporating the PENRYN PACKET and FALMOUTH GAZETTE

No. 7002/38 | Established 1855 | THURSDAY, SEPTEMBER 23, 1993 | Telephone (0326) 373791 | 30p

Mums in a Million — *Read their stories on the centre pages*

Queen and Duke to visit Cornwall

by **Staff Reporter**

THE Queen and the Duke of Edinburgh are to distribute the famous Maundy money in Truro next year.

The announcement came on Monday and although no other details have been released, it is known she will be present at the Maundy Service at Truro Cathedral where the distribution of the money will take place.

Time for the service on March 31 has not been made known but everyone at the cathedral this week was delighted with the news.

A spokesman for the Bishop of Truro, the Rt Rev Michael Ball, said it was a great honour for any cathedral to have the Queen visit and Truro was looking forward to it.

There would be a meeting later in the year to discuss arrangements.

The Queen was last in Cornwall in 1992 for the Royal Cornwall Show at Wadebridge. But on that occasion she did not come to West Cornwall.

The last major visit by a Royal was earlier this year when Prince Charles officially opened the new Tate Gallery at St Ives.

Princess Diana was in West Cornwall in October last year when she opened a factory in Falmouth and visited the Freshfields Drug Counselling Centre in Truro.

UP SHE RISES!

But Pescado sails into new storm

AT long last, the fishing vessel Pescado was pulled to the surface by salvors this week...bringing to an end a relentless campaign by its owner and families of the crew lost when she went down.

But as the Pescado was taken to Devonport, a new controversy broke out over who should have access to the stricken vessel while police try to unravel the riddle of her sinking in February, 1991, after leaving Falmouth.

THIS dramatic picture by David Brenchley shows the long-awaited moment when the stricken trawler Pescado broke the surface of the sea after being hauled from a watery grave off Dodman Point. The vessel went down mysteriously, with the loss of six lives, after leaving Falmouth bound for Plymouth nearly three years ago.

● See the full story on Page 13 and Opinion on Page 12

Driver 'lost control' in death crash

A YOUNG naval rating who crashed a car in which three of his pals died, may well have been travelling too fast and lost control, a resumed inquest was told this week.

Three Royal Navy ratings were killed in the two-car pile-up in March on Stickenbridge Hill, 100 yards from the Tavbowall Roundabout.

Martin Delmer, 21, had hired a high-powered Vauxhall Cavalier SRI and was on his way to Plymouth for a burger with four of his friends.

He was 10 miles from Coldrose when the accident happened and he smashed into an oncoming car whose driver had little chance to take evasive action.

That car was driven by a Falmouth hotelier, Mr Andreas Townson, who was seriously injured. His wife, Teresa, is still in hospital receiving intensive therapy treatment.

Still nursing his wounds, Mr Townson, 48, said after the inquest: "My wife is coming along but it has been a long time. She is still very poorly."

● *Full story Page 15*

Hundreds of cars for sale – INSIDE

Elizabeth Ann on exercise off the Dodman. Taken from the Fowey Lifeboat *Thomas Forehead and Mary Rowse II*.
Photo: Simon Culliford

SHEAR PIN CHANGING EXERCISE

Elizabeth Ann makes her way out into the bay on exercise with Coxswain Alan Barnes at the helm.
Photo: Royal Bank of Scotland/Rick Tomlinson

Alan has been the Coxswain for about a year or so,... the crew have settled down since John resigned, '*a story in itself*'. John was a superb Coxswain, but the pressure ashore,... paperwork, general problems that come with the running of the station, liaising with launching authorities, branch, Coastguards etc etc... began to affect home and social life. John, with great sorrow, decided to resign. Needless to say, he is still held in very high esteem by the lifeboat's crew in Falmouth and stations all around the Cornish coast.

Alan did well to hold the team together during those trying times, a lot of the crew have left or retired over the last two to three years, Donald the Mechanic, Graham the Second Mechanic, John (Viv's successor), John Bobbin Deputy Coxswain, and quite a few lower down '*the list*'.

There are now only three of us left from the *St Simeon* job of 1985. At 43 years of age I'm the second oldest in the crew!!!, I'm looked upon as one of the steady experienced, seasoned main crew. Blimey, it seems like only yesterday I was shy, reserved wet behind the ears, and with lots to learn.

We have a lot of new crew and trainees on the station. Tim took over from Donald as station Mechanic, he came up '*through the ranks*' very quickly following the big change due to retirements etc., Tim has grown into the job well and does a good job looking after both boats, the 52 foot Arun '*Elizabeth Ann*' and the Atlantic 21, a high speed twin engine rigid inflatable.

John Murray took over the job of Second Mechanic from Graham, Steve Datsun became Second Coxswain, Mike Wilson deputy Second Coxswain, and with the young crew and trainees there was a lot of new blood to train.

Exercises were normally once a fortnight… every other Sunday morning, with the odd night exercise thrown in.

This little story is just a part of one of those exercises, not particularly extraordinary, except that it is recalled from time to time as years go by as one of those *'marginal close shaves'*.

Elizabeth Ann's Y-boat with Miichael Wilson at the helm.
Photo: Falmouth RNLI Collection

We have a *Y-boat* on top of the wheelhouse of the Arun, it's a small inflatable boat fitted with a 15 horsepower outboard engine, able to carry up to four persons… at a push. For its size, it's fast and very manoeuvrable.

I used to be a D-class helmsman on the crew of the inshore lifeboat at Coverack, it gave me four years valuable experience in small boat handling, It was a fast very manoeuvrable machine… as youngsters we would thrash around in the surf , and many times in the sea conditions that we shouldn't,… when the Coverack boat was withdrawn from service I moved to Falmouth to join the Falmouth crew, I was very lucky to be accepted.

Over the years I have been given some of the sticky jobs that have needed to be done with the *Y-boat*. I love the freedom, speed and danger it instils… but I must point out whilst I'm happy to take calculated chances, I'm not too reckless…. Well….

SUNDAY EXERCISE

Sunday morning 0830 hours, the lads roll in through the boathouse door, hangovers, the odd fag dangling out of the corner of the mouth of a face, white, blood shot eyes, what a sight... young men, Saturday nights… I suppose it's to be expected.

It was cold, fresh, windy, lumpy sea conditions; we were off for an exercise with the Fowey Lifeboat off the Dodman… from our moorings about an hour's steam up to the east, that should sober some of them up!!!!

Our crew for the morning consisted of seven or eight new lads, for some of them this was the first exercise they will have been on when there was a bit of sea running. I expect one or two will decide today that life-boating is not quite what they thought it was.

We left the moorings at around 0850 hours which gave us thirty to 40 minutes to run through a few drills before we met up with the Fowey Lifeboat. We moved out into the bay, there was a heavy swell, we made our way east, running about half a mile off shore, I made my way from the wheelhouse up to the flying bridge to have a chat with Alan, to see what he had in mind …"*good sea running*", I said.. "*ideal for a Y-boat exercise*"… Alan looked at me and grinned, he knew if I took the *Y-boat*, that whoever came with me would get a '*good ride*'. "*Take young Keith, see if he's got any bottle*"… "*OK*"… I said nodding… "*who else*?" Alan thought for a second or two "*Tim*" he said… I continued to nod… with a big grin on my face.

I went back into the wheelhouse and advised young Keith and Tim that we were going for a spin on the *Y-boat*, and asked them to put on a dry suit each. We carry four dry suits on the boat,… a rubber suit with wellingtons sealed onto the legs, and a rubber seal on the end of each arm and one on the neck, it has a water proof zip across the back, this allows you to put the suit on… a bit like a

Steps down to the Arun's survivor cabin, situated under the foredeck. One of the liveliest places to be when motoring in heavy weather!
Photo: Gulf Group Marine Brokers Ltd

boiler suit, but waterproof,… in theory it should keep your clothes dry and you warm.

With the boat pitching as it rode the waves, and the bow gently slamming, it was difficult getting the dry suits on, Tim, Keith and myself were in the forward compartment, a small area under the foredeck where survivors can be 'stowed' (should we have a lot on board), this part of the boat is the worst to ride in, as it rises and falls more than any other part of the boat.

Keith tried to get into his dry suit standing up, he soon ended up on his bum, and had to get the suit on, on the floor, wiggling like a worm in an effort to get his arms and legs into their respected 'tubes'.

Tim and myself who have both done this before, when the boat's motion is far from comfortable, were sat on the survivors' benches, swaying with the boat's movements and occasionally steadying ourselves as the boat dipped into a trough…. eventually all three of us were dressed, we made our way to the after deck where the *Y-boat* was being prepared for us.

Crash hats, lifejackets the hand held radio, we were all ready to go… Alan brought the lifeboat to a halt and turned her head to sea, ready to launch the *Y-boat* into the water, off

Launching the Y-boat from the stern of *Elizabeth Ann* on a calmer day. Photo: Simon Culliford

the gantry arrangement on the stern of the lifeboat.

Y-BOAT 'AWAY'

We were off, Tim and Keith in the bow, myself on the engine, we were about 100 yards from the shore, the lifeboat was drifting, rolling heavily, some of the lads were on the after deck, watching us... We rode the waves, plenty of spray… the two in the bow were hanging on, wondering what I had in mind…. Tim knew it would be something interesting, his eyes were full of trepidation, Keith hadn't a clue what was in store… I was still to make my mind up.

The big decision was, were we going to go for a beaching, this consists of a flat out dash for the shore on the back of the biggest wave we can find, in the hope we get dumped as high up the beach as possible giving the crew time to jump out, steady the boat and prepare to take the next wave.

Alan was expecting a beaching; it was a process that would definitely test the nerve of young Keith. I circled around, studying the beach, and the way the seas were breaking, the larger of the waves were curling and breaking before they hit the shore. Occasionally there was a very big one that would run up the beach without breaking, that was the type of wave we had to pick.

The small bay we were heading for was very rocky, no sand. It was surrounded by high cliffs, and was only accessible from the sea... To the west of the bay was a large group of rocks, the tide was in, these rocks were surrounded by water, as the waves broke against them, the spray rose some fifteen to twenty feet in the air.

I leaned forward and shouted out, "*we are going for a beach landing*".... Tim's eyes bulged, I smiled at him,... It was a mischievous type of smile that did not help to reassure him that all would be well,. Keith's face was expressionless. I had the impression that he was going to turn out to be a '*dead weight*', anyway... the briefing.

"*We are going to ride in on the back of a big wave, when we hit the beach, I will be busy raising the outboard engine and switching it off,... you two jump out and steady the boat, in readiness for the next wave........ OK?*"... two nodding heads was the reply.

We were fairly close to the lifeboat, Alan and Mike were looking down at us from the flying bridge,... I gestured that we were going ashore... Alan smiled and nodded his head.

We moved off towards the shore, then stood off, circling, about fifty yards off, looking for the '*big one*'.

I could the see the wave we wanted, just out beyond the lifeboat, it was a beauty, it ran towards us, the lifeboat lifted and rolled heavily as it passed underneath. I grinned at Tim and nodded towards our wave... he nodded back... he was not smiling... this was the moment of no return, we began to run before the wave, the idea is to run before the wave top starts to break,... letting the *Y-boat* rise as the wave comes underneath, then flat out to keep on top.....'*surfing*' till we hit shore.

This monster wave was by now right behind us, and '*building*', I had my eyes on the shore and then back to the wave, then back to the shore again... I was aware that Keith glanced round to see what was happening … his face was a sight to behold, he looked at me the expression on his face said '*you must be nuts*', or something like that... I gave a laugh... perhaps I was... anyway…. If Keith was going to have a bowel movement, this was the time for it.

We were now close to shore, it was time for want of a better expression to mount the wave... as we came up on top, it was curling... at this time I noticed for the first time the size of the rocks we were heading for... they looked quite small from out to sea,... they were in fact boulders.. all round, smooth, and varying from about one foot across to say three or four feet across, we had about a six or seven seconds to run before '*touch down*',... I positioned myself to raise the engine... just before grounding. The wave was now breaking…we were amongst the surf... we hit hard, the boat was enveloped in spray, I didn't have time to see if my two crew had made a successful exit of the boat, I was too busy trying to switch off the engine and secure it in a raised position, before getting out of the boat myself.

It was too late, the next wave was on top of us before I could get out... I had cut the engine and just tuned to face the bow and climb out, when the wave broke over my head and crashed down on top of me and the boat, I noticed Tim and Keith trying to gain a foothold on the beach, this proved to be almost impossible due to the size of the boulders... The boat was completely full, I was washed out, the boat turned sideways, we all hung on to the sides, then the waves fell away to nothing… running back into the sea, to make way for the next wave. In the hope that it would be easier to control,... all three of us were grunting away, trying to move the boat, keeping an eye on the next wave as it steamed towards us….. it was hopeless, the inflatable rubber tube that surrounded the boat held the water from the first wave level to the top… it must have contained about one hundred gallons, or to put it another way approaching half a ton of water. Add the weight of the boat to that, it was no wonder we couldn't shift it,… we hung on as the next wave broke,… it lifted the boat as it ran in around us, (up to around waist height)…for a few seconds I felt that we had a big problem,… what on earth were we going to do!

ASHORE (NOT A PRETTY LANDING)

It was pretty obvious we were going to be unable to relaunch from this position,… we needed shelter from the sea's this would give us a chance to bail out the water and prepare to get back to the lifeboat.

To the west end of this little cove was the group of large rocks, they stood off shore by approximately 40 feet. The waves broke against them, sending a plume of spray high into the air… the sea between the rocks and the shore looked pretty calm from where we were.

Time for another 'briefing'… *"We are going to drag the Y-boat to the calmer water behind the rocks,… each time a wave lifts the boat we can pull it along …OK?"*… they both nodded,…. The idea worked, after a fashion, we stumbled and grunted and swore… and eventually ended up floating the boat to relatively calm water behind the shelter of the large rocks. As the waves ran ashore, they would curl around behind our shelter... the force having been absorbed… the *Y-boat* would rise and fall as the waves came and went.

I called up the lifeboat: *"Falmouth Lifeboat this is Lifeboat Yankee, radio check on channel six please"*… *"Lifeboat Yankee this is Falmouth Lifeboat, loud and clear"*… Roger replied … although our hand held radio got soaked when we beached it was still working….

"Falmouth Lifeboat, this is Falmouth Lifeboat Yankee, we are just going to get ourselves organised, then run back out to you, should take about 5 minutes, over"…. *"All copied"* was the reply.

Tim and Keith were both very quiet; they looked at me both wondering what the plan of action was... I watched the waves rolling in for a while… the chances of a successful run back out to sea were pretty slim… we needed a calm patch for at least a minute to give us a chance to get deep enough out to sea to escape the breaking waves… if one broke onto us as we ran out it would flip us over… what would happen then would be in the lap of the Gods.

As I watched I thought to myself…'if there is not a period that presents itself that gives us a good chance then we will stay here, if necessary for as long as it takes… even if it meant a few hours',… that would mean missing the exercise with Fowey… then, it happened, three of four waves in succession rolled in, all of them small and certainly negotiable by the *Y-boat*… this meant that there would be a chance to get back out.

"We need to get the boat bailed out and prepare ourselves for the run out… any ideas?"… Tim noticed an old plastic bucket just above the tide line, in amongst the seaweed and bits of wood etc... *"we can use that"*… he said pointing … *"good idea"* I said. Keith and I steadied the boat as Tim stumbled up the beach to get the bucket… it had a big split in it,

but it did the trick… a few minutes hard bailing and the boat was empty…

I jumped in and lowered the engine, we were in four feet of water. Tim and Keith were standing in the water holding the boat steady… water rising from the waists, up to just under the necks as the waves rolled in. The engines started first pull… I gave it a few revs… I gave them both a big grin, I was now full of confidence… Tim tried a smile, Keith's face was expressionless… this must have been his fourth or fifth exercise as a trainee… I wonder what was going through his mind… did he think… *'is Price'y balmy?'* … is this sort of thing normal on an exercise when the weather was lumpy? … *'should I take up golf instead?'*

Knowing that the lifeboat was standing off, and waiting with great interest to hear of our intentions, I gave them a call…

"Falmouth lifeboat, we are going to make our dash for freedom shortly, over"… reply… *"good luck… we are all watching"*… I bet they were!!

It was time to let my crew know what we were going to do… I gestured that we were going to have a chat… they both leaned into the boat and listened, not wanting to miss a single word…

"We will stay here until we hit a calm patch, then we are going to go for it… when I open her up you two jump in… then up to the bow… get as far forward as you can, to hold the nose down, OK?"… two nodding heads was my reply… I revved the engine… watching the waves… the idea was to open her up as soon as

Mr Price at the helm of a Y-boat in fine weather.

the opportunity arose, come out from the shelter of rock we were hiding behind, and run as fast as we could for deep water.

'BUGGER ALL'

"Now" I screamed, put the engine in gear, revved up…. Tim and Keith pulled themselves into the boat,… bugger all…. The engine was screaming,…. We hadn't moved an inch… we all looked at each other in amazement… I throttled back, checked we were in gear… nothing… *"back in the water"* I shouted…. The lads rolled back out of the boat into the water.

I switched the engine off, lifted it up, spun the prop in gear,… as I suspected the shear pin had gone… I must have hit the prop on the beaching, (not unusual for me),… there were a couple of respectable dings on the blades, I've done in my share of props over the years. The shear pin is a small bar that engages in two slots in the propeller,…

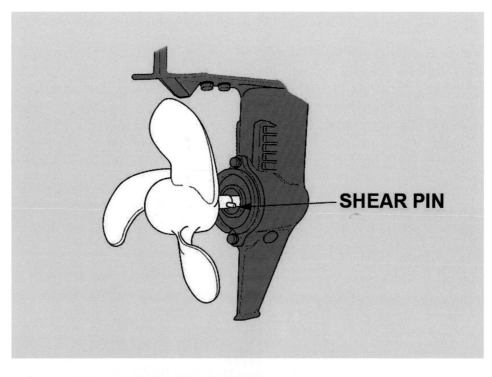

SHEAR PIN

it's made from fairly soft metal.. the idea is that if the prop hits something hard (like the shore) the pin breaks,… this is easily replaced. It saves doing severe damage to the blades of the propeller, or worse busting the gearbox.

"Falmouth Lifeboat this is Lifeboat Yankee, over"…*"go ahead Yankee"*… *"Shouldn't be to long now, we are just doing a shear pin changing exercise"*… there was a pause… then as Roger pressed the key on his mike to speak to us, we could hear the roars of laugher in the background…. *"all copied Yankee"*….

We changed the pin, taking great care not to drop the pliers, or other tools necessary to do the job… we were now ready for our second attempt…. *"same as before"* I said,… we waited and waited…. engine revving… 3 or 4 minutes must have passed… things were looking good.

Once again I screamed *"now"*… this time we were off….Tim rolled in over the sponson, Keith got half way in, he was struggling, I leaned forward with my spare hand caught hold of the strap on the back of his lifejacket and pulled him in,… this was great, we were running well, good speed, up over each wave that came at us… it was too good to be true.

There ahead of us about five waves, distance about fifty yards… a whopper … it rolled in under the lifeboat, growing as it came towards us... it looked like two or three waves joined together,… I glanced back to the shore... we weren't going to be able to turn and out run it… it would run straight over us,… we had no choice but to run on...

I eased back a bit,, by now Tim and Keith had seen it... if only I could see their faces… *"forward I screamed"*…. they wriggled forward,… hanging almost right over the bow,…. I leaned forward as far as I could,… one more wave to pass under us before we hit this wall of water… as it approached we lost sight of the horizon and the lifeboat which was only about 40 yards ahead of us, all we could see was this bloody great wave…I didn't think we had a hope in hell of getting through this one,… there was no time left to think, I wound the throttle up,… and drove straight at it,… as we ran into it, the bow lifted, we

Launching a D class inshore lifeboat off a beach. The D class is the big brother to the Y-boats carried on top of the Arun liofeboat. Photo: Stephen Duncombe/RNLI Archive

ran straight up it… we were now vertical… and being carried backwards towards the shore,…. our bow broke through the top of the wave, just at the exact moment that the wave itself 'broke' … we sort of emerged through the top…. the engine dug in and carried us off the surf on top of the wave and down its back… I couldn't believe it!

Tim and Keith looked back at me and smiled,… relief, I suppose,… we came up alongside the lifeboat… Steve the Second Coxswain looked down at us, smiled… shaking his head… he said "*nice one*", I looked up at Alan on the flying bridge, he was smiling and shaking his head too….

If I had to describe that last big wave in one word, it would be '*marginal*'… Tim never forgot that exercise, he spoke of it regularly for years to come.. I've overheard him say "*If I had to go on in the Y-boat in rough weather, I'd want Price'y driving, he knows how to handle it*".

I didn't have the heart to tell him that I nearly crapped myself… anyway modesty wouldn't permit it.

Keith stayed on as a trainee for a few months after this particular exercise… he sort of lost interest… shame really, he had the makings of a good crewman.

We've had many hairy trips in the *Y-boat* since… but none that I would describe as '*marginal*'.

Elizabeth Ann at sea. Photo: Falmouth RNLI Collection

MEDIVAC

Medical evacuation in lifeboat terms usually means removing a sick or injured person from a vessel, or structure and returning them to shore to receive treatment. Casualties sometimes require evacuating from rocks or beaches that are not easily accessible by land ... The seriousness of the case and the state of the sea will determine whether the job is pleasant or not. It's usual to have a few "medivacs" each year, ... They can be pleasant and rewarding ... especially when the *emergency* turns out to be less serious than first thought, they can also be sad and distressing ... you never know what the next *'shout'* will bring.

The call to Falmouth Coastguard by the Captain of *M.V. Lexington*, advised them that his Chief Engineer was unwell and required medical attention. The Coastguard advised Alan the Coxswain by telephone that the lifeboat would be requested to perform the evacuation from *Lexington* to Falmouth, and requested the lifeboat took a Doctor.

All this started early in the evening on February the 8th 1993.

The *Lexington* was steaming in from the Western Approaches, she was due off the Lizard at 2030 hours, Alan rang around the crew at 1900 hours and advised us all that we had a job on... Medivac ... boathouse 2000 hours. This gave us time for a bite to eat and a cup of tea. The forecast was lumpy and I had no idea how long the job would last, I always chew my food well when I know we could be in for a rough ride, just in case I had to *'shoot the cat'* or plant a *'pavement pizza'* on the after deck ... nothing worse than a lump of grub lodging in ones beak!

I arrived at the boathouse 1950 hours, ... it was windy, due east, ... the sea was lumpy with a reasonable swell running, it was a very dark February night, ... not too cold. By the time I had my kit on, the rest of the *'A team'* had arrived, Alan the Coxswain (who was already there) Steve, Second Coxswain... Mike Deputy Second cox ... Tim Mechanic, John Second Mechanic ... Roger, crew ... and myself, wireless operator.

Alan was itching to get on board the lifeboat, ... He didn't have much information, ... the briefing from the Coastguard was patchy, anyway we had plenty of time to ascertain the details on the run out.

The port Doctor was away, his stand in for this evening was a local man who, to be fair, should remain nameless, I can say he was young fit and spoke with a broad Scots accent. Anyway, he has been briefed to arrive at the boathouse at 2030 hours. We left the boathouse at 2015 hours. Cliff, the boarding boat attendant ran us out to the lifeboat. Cliff was a small jolly retired chap, good company always good morning or good evening to me, tonight was no exception *"good evening Mr Price ... looks a bit lumpy out there"* ..., he grinned, knowing full well we were going to get a soaking in the boarding boat.

The boarding boat was a fine craft, 16 foot long, heavily built and sat fairly low in the water, put seven crew on board and the free board was near bugger all. The crewmen sitting aft would start cranking the hand pump lever as soon as we left the quayside to make sure we didn't sink on the way out to the lifeboat!

START MAIN ENGINES

Everything was ticking over nicely. The crew settled down and we slowly moved off our mooring, no panic, the Doc wasn't due for another 10 minutes or so. The plan was to bring the lifeboat alongside Custom House Quay, pick up the Doc, then run out into the bay and rendezvous with the *Lexington*.

Tim the Mechanic went below, turned on the battery bank, and then undid the sea cocks before heating the glow plugs on both Caterpillar turbo charged ginners ... (engines for the land lubbers). Meanwhile up in the wheelhouse, I checked that the throttles were in detent (neutral) and set at around one third revs, as soon as both lumps had finished coughing and spluttering into life the wheelhouse got busy.

Two of the crew were on deck ready to slip the mooring on the Coxswain's instruction. Mike flashed up the radar and began to set the MFDF a monster piece of kit that was quite difficult to get right. (Medium Frequency Direction Finder).

Very little is said in the wheelhouse when the A team are on board, everyone knows exactly what to do having trained and worked together for years. Tim checked the engineer's panel to make sure we had oil pressure on both Cats, alternators were charging and as soon as he was satisfied he moved forward to the steering position pulled both throttles back to tick over where they jumped out of '*detent*' and were ready for use. "*Ready to go Al*" Tim said on the intercom… two presses of the mike on the flying bridge which gave two short crackles in the wheelhouse was Alan's acknowledgement.

The deck crew were ready to let go the mooring, they were both looking at the flying bridge anticipating the let go signal, normally only a few seconds after the engines go to tick over ... Alan held out his arm with his hand outstretched and gestured upwards as if tossing a ball in the air ... A tug on the mooring chain release rope and we were ready to go.

We slipped our moorings at 2025 hours it was time to open up with the Coastguard ... I made a note of the time on my pad, 2028 hours, channel 16, "*Falmouth Coastguard, this is Falmouth Lifeboat, over*" . "*Falmouth Lifeboat this is Falmouth Coastguard go to channel Zero, over*" ... I replied, "*Roger, channel zero*" . . the Coastguard on duty tonight was sharp, snappy almost curt ... for me it was going to be one of those evenings, perhaps he had a row with his '*missus*' ... who knows.

Channel zero… 2029 hours, "*Falmouth Coastguard this is Falmouth Lifeboat, good evening, may we have the casualty position, sit rep and time check please*"…I threw the pleasantries in to try and be friendly, ,… a waste of time, back came old '*sour puss*' . . "*The vessel is called Lexington, the pilots are working on her radio on channel 9, the Chief Engineer has high blood pressure and a headache, the Captain wants him to be seen by a Doctor, he is willing to land him, time check 2029 local, what is your crew list please*" … well, a good sit rep, and he did say please when asking for a crew list, ... all was not lost, however as always... I never get the information in the order requested, and of this occasion never even got the *Lexington's* position.

I replied immediately… "*I will pass my crew list shortly, please advise casualty position*"... reply, "*The Lexington is making for the 2D Buoy*"… "*Thank you*" I replied… with a little starch added just to let him know I was not impressed (still no position for the *Lexington* not that it was too important at this time).

The idea of asking for position, sit rep, time check in that order is simple ... On service, as we drop our mooring, the wheelhouse is preparing itself for a few minutes of intense action, one of the lads is warming up the radar… the navigator is stood by the chart table desperate for the casualty's position so that he can put a fix on the chart. The first thing the Coxswain needs to know is the casualty's position, if he doesn't get it pretty quickly things can become 'tense' in no time at all. ... Everybody needs various information instantly so that they can begin to function. For instance if we have a short distance to run, the Coxswain will need to know where we are going, how long before we are on scene and what the job is exactly. ... He can then steer the best course, and prepare in his mind the most likely plan of action. He will brief his second, who will advise the rest of the crew what our intentions are; the engineer wants to know what the Cox'n has in mind, so that he can prepare all necessary boat's equipment.... ropes, stretchers, searchlights, tow ropes, etc. etc.

The navigator needs to know where the casualty is. This allows him to select the correct chart and have the information required by everyone as soon as possible.

If the reply to my initial request for position, sit rep and time check, came in the correct order, I would write down the position on the first page of my pad, rip it off and slap it on the chart table. Then I would proceed to write down the essential parts of the situation report, and finally glance at the clock when the time check came. By the time the initial information had been passed, if necessary, I would ask for any additional information I think we could do with,… the estimated time of arrival with the casualty would come back to me from the chart table, ... this is one of the first things the Coastguard wants to know, ... it looks good if we have the answers all ready.

Normally as I am preparing to advise the Coastguard of our eta and crew list, the navigator is passing the course and eta to the flying bridge via the intercom.

It really is very handy to get all this done quickly, especially if the weather is poor... for the first few minutes of a 'shout' we are generally in reasonably calm waters, protected from the open sea by the docks, ... as soon as we enter the bay, chartwork, writing… even standing in one position becomes a little more difficult.

Luckily this evening, we were in no great hurry, and the weather was reasonable if just a bit windy and choppy.

The 2 D buoy was about 15 minutes run for us at full speed... as soon as we picked up the Doctor, we could be on our way ... 2030 hours, I called the Coastguard, "our crew list is, 1, 2, 3, 4, 5, 6, 9" ... the reply "Roger".

We were standing off Custom House Quay, ... waiting ... waiting, it seemed like hours, . . then at last the Coastguard broke the silence 2039 hours, "The Doctor is on route to the boathouse",, ... I replied "thank you for informing us, that will save us mooring up alongside, we will advise you as soon as the Doctor arrives and we are departing Custom House Quay", ... reply "Roger" still no hint of humanity in the Coastguard's voice.

We waited and waited... come on Doc, we want to get going ... I'm sure we were all thinking the same.

Alan was holding our position about twenty yards off the quay, then at last, a pair of headlights appeared at the top of the hill... it was the Doctor.... we made our way into the quay, Alan put the bow against the quay, a couple of the lads helped the Doc aboard and we were away.

THE DOCTOR ARRIVES

2054 hours, *"Falmouth Coastguard this is Falmouth Lifeboat, we have the Doctor on board, we are now proceeding into the bay"* ... reply *"Roger"*.

3 minutes later we received a call from the *L K Mitchell*, a pilot cutter that works Falmouth. She is similar to the lifeboat in size, power and colour... she was responsible for putting the pilot aboard the *Lexington* this evening. In fact the *L K M* had put the pilot aboard the *Lexington* and he was calling us from the bridge of the ship using *L K Mitchell* as his call sign, ... on channel 16 (the call up and distress channel) ... *"Falmouth Lifeboat, this is the L K Mitchell over"* *"loud and clear"* I replied, *"go to channel 9"* ... my reply *"Channel 9"*, the *L K M* called us on channel 9 ... *"what are your intentions?"*...I replied *"stand by please"*... I now had to inform the Coastguard officially that we intended to work channel 9, I expect they had already copied us down anyway, however, it was right and proper that I informed them properly ... 2058 hours, *"Falmouth Coastguard, this is Falmouth Lifeboat, we are switching to channel 9 and will be working from now on on channel 9 over"* ... reply from Coastguard *"Roger, listening 16 and 9"* ... my reply *"Roger thank you"*.

Back to the L K M 2059 hours, *"we are leaving harbour now and making for your position over"* ... L K M 's reply *"Are you happy with pilot ladder on our starboard side? It will take us sometime to rig the accommodation ladder"* ... I thought for a second ... Alan was pretty busy sorting the boat out, we were by now steaming past the docks, some 5 minutes had passed since we had left Custom House Quay, ... I knew from experience that the Coxswain wouldn't be able to make his decision on how he was going to transfer the casualty at this time, ... we had no idea of the sea conditions or the ship's size or anything ... anyway my response was as follows: *"we will wait until we arrive on scene and assess the conditions and then decide how to transfer the Doctor to Lexington, and the casualty to the lifeboat"*, ... L K M's reply *"Roger"* ... my reply *"What is your position please"* ... answer ... *"One and a half miles off Rose Mullion Head"* ... I replied *"Thank you"*.

I passed all I had said up to the flying bridge together with *Lexington's* position... Alan said *"thanks"*.

ENTERING FALMOUTH BAY

We were now entering the bay, there was a fair old lump running... this was my first time to look around the wheelhouse,... my pen had been writing furiously, the radio log needed the gaps filling in. ... Each message is written down with the time and bare facts then as soon as there is a little lull in the radio traffic, I fill in all the important words, so that the transmissions make sense.

The Doc was hanging onto a centre pole in the wheelhouse, he was swaying as the boat rolled and pitched. We were travelling at *'full emergency speed'* ... 18 knots, ... at this speed in choppy seas it is a fairly violent ride for someone who is not used to it, ... the poor old Doc was definitely not used to boating ... his face was a picture ... full of concern and anxiety.

The chart table and radar were busy, the rest of the lads were up on the flying bridge with Alan, looking out for the *Lexington*.

Coxswain Alan Barnes with Mr Price affording the photographer some resect! Note the 'hands free' communicator we are wearing, a brilliant piece of kit but it never really caught on. We trialed this after trying to wear hevy crash helmets fitted with plug in intercom bungee cords. The helmets were too heavy to wear and if you forgot to unplug and left your post, you would feel a tug, look around and see the plug hurtling towards you at high speed!   Photo: Falmouth RNLI Collection

2103 hours, the Coastguard called us on channel 9 and asked us to go to channel zero, ... how odd I thought ... I wondered what on earth could they have wanted to say that couldn't be said on our working channel, ... *"Falmouth Lifeboat, this is Falmouth Coastguard over"* ... *"Falmouth Coastguard this is Falmouth Lifeboat, you are loud and clear on channel zero over"*.... *"Falmouth Lifeboat, this is Falmouth Coastguard, we are not happy about the transfer of the Doctor to Lexington because of the weather conditions"* ... I couldn't believe my ears... bloody cheek... who the hell do they think they are... they have the audacity to infer we are incapable of making such basic decisions concerning safety at sea... Well if I had broadcast what I thought, I would have been arrested upon our return...I knew exactly what I was going to say in reply ... and the tone in which I was to say it! ... there would be no doubt ashore that I on behalf of my Coxswain was not in the least bit amused!!!

Just as I was to begin my reply I noticed Steve enter the wheelhouse... he had come down from the flying bridge... no doubt with the Coxswain's instructions for a reply ... (They had monitored the incoming message from the Coastguard on the flying bridge radio).

I put my hand up to Steve indicating I was not in a position to receive instructions from him as I was transmitting, ... I then began my reply ... *"Falmouth Coastguard this is Falmouth Lifeboat, be advised under no circumstances will we be putting the Doctor, our crew or the casualty at risk, we will assess the situation when we arrive on scene, we will keep you closely advised"* ... I didn't say *'over'* as I felt no need to invite a reply ... all at the Coastguard station must have now been aware they had insulted us ... my manner and tone of voice will have certainly relayed that sentiment! ... well we did get a reply ... it was a muted *"Thank you"*.

I looked at Steve, ... I was still fuming ...he smiled, nodded his head in approval of my transmission and disappeared back up to the flying bridge ...Alan called down over the intercom *"Thanks for that Chris"* ...that meant he was happy with my reply...phew...I felt quite pleased with myself.

As I carefully wrote up the last *'exchange'* with the Coastguard I noticed the Doc's face ... greenish… he was having a bit of a rough ride. I gave him a smile and suggested he stood near the aft wheelhouse door where he could get some fresh air ... he staggered over, hanging onto anything he could use to steady himself with as the boat rolled from side to side, ... there at the door he gulped in the fresh air ... he nodded towards me as if to say ... that's a bit better… but not a lot…he was certainly suffering… I felt for him.

LEXINGTON DEAD AHEAD

Looking through the wheelhouse windows I could see a large ship dead ahead of us, ... range about 2 miles, it was the *Lexington*, she was well lit. We would be alongside in about 5 minutes, we were approximately two miles off land. There was a heavy swell with a very stiff breeze still blowing, the Doctor had now stepped out onto the after deck still looking for relief from the lifeboats motion.

All of the lads with the exception of Mike were out on deck, Mike sat at the radar position, looking ahead through the window, ... I joined him, leaning over the steering position, ... wondering what condition the casualty would be in, ... and how the transfer would go.

At 2108 hours, the *Lexington* called us, *"The weather is moderating, we are reducing speed, we have six cables to run, the pilot ladder is two thirds down to the water line, under the aft Sampson posts"*…I replied *"Roger, all copied"* ... I checked with Alan on the intercom that he had received the complete message,… we were now alongside the *Lexington* and steaming in toward her anchoring position with her, ... she was travelling at around 6 knots. Just as our searchlight went on, the pilot aboard *Lexington* called up again *"you can come alongside now, we have our searchlight on the pilot ladder"*, ... my reply *"Roger thank you"*.

The pilot ladder is a rope ladder with wooden rungs, every third rung is thicker than the other two, this helps hold the rope off the side of the ship, allowing you to grab the rungs as you climb the ladder, and stops your fingers from being pinched between the ladder and the ship's side.

Alan made a run in alongside the ship, to see what it would be like for the transfer, ... the ship's side was flat, and sheer ... It towered above us, ... we bumped into the side of the ship a few times, our heavy fenders that were deployed along the starboard side absorbed the impact and saved the lifeboat from damage... Alan called down *"Get the Doctor up on the bow, ready for transfer"*... you should have seen the Doctor's face... what a sight... *"I will not be going up that ladder"* he said with a broad Scots accent ... Mike looked at me, I smiled and relayed to Alan via the intercom *"The Doctor is not happy about going up the ladder, over"*…Alan replied *"Neither am I, it's a bit too lumpy to transfer, we will look at her when she comes to anchor"* … I replied *"OK I'll advise Lexington".*

2113 hours, to Lexington *"Our Doctor and our Coxswain are not happy with the transfer of the Doctor by pilot ladder, we will wait until you have come to anchor and have a look at you then"*, the pilots reply *"Roger good decision"*, He obviously thought it was a bit lumpy for the Doc to try and ascend the ladder too.

I thought I had better call the Coastguard, as I had promised to keep them *'closely informed'*… rather than pass a complete sit rep of our last exchange of transmissions with the *Lexington* I decided to ask them if they copied our last with her, …they replied *"Yes all copied"*. They were no doubt listening to every word.

We shadowed *Lexington* in towards her anchoring position, she was slowing all the time, we were now approximately one mile off shore, there was a bit of shelter from the land, the sea conditions were improving but there was still a good swell running… as the Lexington almost stopped, she came over the radio *"We are coming astern now, dropping anchor"*… I replied *"Roger, thank you"*. Alan stood the lifeboat off, about 20 yards, where we waited until Lexington got herself sorted out.

A call came down from the bridge *"Ask the Doctor if he would like to find out how the patient is"*… *"OK"* I replied… I waved to the Doc and beckoned him into the wheelhouse, I advised him Alan would like him to talk to *Lexington* and find out how the patient is…. he nodded.

2122 hours, I called Lexington *"Can our Doctor talk to your Captain please"* … reply *"Yes, stand by"* … *"This is the Captain"*, … I handed the mike to the Doctor and showed him how it worked … *"How is the patient?"* the Doctor said, … *"He has taken pills for blood pressure, when he stands up he is 190 when he lies down 160"* … The Captain's voice was very professional, he was Greek or similar with an accent to match… Mike said to the Doc *"Ask him what sort of stretcher they have to lower him down in"* … the Doctor did this… the pilot on board *Lexington* replied *"The Captain would prefer your Doctor to see him on board the ship before transferring"*. The Doctor passed me the mike… he was busy hanging on to his tea and not really in a fit state to carry on the conversation…(we were rolling heavily, hove too alongside the ship), … I replied *"Our Doctor is not happy to use the pilot ladder"*, the pilot replied *"The casualty should be able to make it on board by the accommodation ladder"* … The accommodation ladder is a staircase lowered down by the ship's side at an angle of about 45 degree's almost to the water line. This is a much safer way of transferring, but requires utmost skill from the Coxswain when manoeuvring alongside, as the metal structure of the ladder can easily damage the lifeboat.

Alan called down over the intercom, *"Tell him we can pass a life jacket if necessary"*… *"Roger"* … to *Lexington* *"We can pass a lifejacket to you if you wish"* . . *"Yes if you pass one up, we will send him down, it will take a short time to prepare the ladder"*… I replied *"We will stand off and await your call"* … reply *"Roger"*.

To make sure the Coastguards were fully aware of what was going on, and to make sure they had no cause to criticise us in any way I once again asked for confirmation that our last had been copied… to the Coastguard *"confirm you have received our recent conversation with Lexington and are aware of our situation"*… the reply *"Yes all received"*… the tone was now improving. I expect the operator realised that he was well out of order

The Arun lifeboat alongside a ship on a different medical evacuation on which the pilot ladder was used to put the lifeboat doctor on board. Dr Richard James is climbing the ladder while the lifeboat crew assist. Photo: Falmouth RNLI Collection

in phrasing his earlier transmission in the way he did. He was certainly aware of the offence it caused by my abrupt and unfriendly reply.

We continued to stand off, *Lexington* was well lit. I looked out through the wheelhouse windows, watching her roll slowly from side to side. Our searchlight played on her starboard side, waiting for the accommodation ladder to be lowered into place. The crew of the lifeboat were watching from the after deck and the flying bridge, I was alone in the wheelhouse.

Lexington began to lower her accommodation ladder, it was 2131 hours... she called us up ... "*You see our accommodation ladder, please advise what height your require it,*" ... Alan called down on the intercom tell him we will come in, our bow to his stern and let him know" ... I acknowledged ... "*We will come along side you, our bow to your stern and advise*" ... the pilot aboard Lexington replied, "*Yes it's never easy ... will you take this opportunity to transfer the lifejacket?*" ... I replied "*Yes*"... all was going smoothly. I caught a glimpse of the Doc through the aft wheelhouse door, the poor old soul was looking washed out.

It was time to pass a formal sit rep to the Coastguard, I noted our position from the Decca navigator, (a piece of electronic equipment that gives us our position in latitude and longitude) ... very useful.

2137 hours "*Falmouth Coastguard this is Falmouth Lifeboat, I have a sit rep for you over*"... "*Pass your sit rep*", was the reply ..."*Our sit rep, we are standing by Lexington awaiting the transfer of the casualty, our position is 50 degrees 07 50 north, 05 degrees 03 93 west, over*"... they replied "*Roger, what is the E.T.A. of the casualty?*" ... how the hell should I know I thought, still I had better give them some sort of reply ... "*We are waiting for Lexington to call us in, I do not expect it will be long,*"...the Coastguard replied "*Roger*"... As all the transmissions were on channel 67, the *Lexington* heard my reply to the Coastguard. It had the desired effect of prompting the pilot to give us a sit rep on the casualties' ETA at the companion ladder.

Within a few seconds of my completion with the Coastguard the *Lexington* called us, 2138 hours "*our Captain has just been called to the radio room to take a link call, when he has finished we will be able to transfer, I will advise*"...I replied "*Roger thank you*" ... then on the intercom to the flying bridge "*Did you copy all that Al?*"... Alan replied, "*Yes, all copied*" ...the link call the Captain was receiving was a telephone call from the shore that was being '*linked*' to the ship by Lands' End Radio station I expect. As soon as he was finished with it, the transfer would begin.

By now, we had passed the lifejacket up to the *Lexington* via a rope lowered down to the lifeboat. Alan was running up to the ladder and holding the bow of the lifeboat onto the side of the ship ... it wasn't easy, ... we had fenders out all along our starboard side, we were rising and falling about ten feet on the waves, as the waves rolled along the ships side occasionally the rise and fall fell to four or five feet. It was one of those calmer patches that Alan was going to have to choose to make his run up to the ladder. Then with no warning the sick man appeared at the top of the ladder, . . it was obviously him, as he was wearing a lifeboat lifejacket... one of the *Lexington's* crew began helping him down the ladder.   Alan stood the boat off a few feet watching the waves, waiting for the precise moment to run in. By now the casualty was on the bottom of the ladder, holding on to the hand rail, his crew mate behind steadying him. The ladder was about fifteen feet from the sea... the waves were rolling alongside the ship, the tops of the waves ran under the ladder, just missing the bottom rung, then as the trough passed under, the gap increased at times to almost twelve feet or so, it must have been pretty frightening for the sick man, as he stood at the bottom of the 'staircase' watching the lifeboat bobbing up and down, and rolling from side to side.

TIME TO COLLECT THE CASUALTY

Alan waited and waited...he was not going to rush, it was a matter of picking just the right moment ... the foredeck of the lifeboat looked pretty crowded, four of the crew were positioning themselves for the run in... two near the edge of the bow the other two behind holding them in position, to make sure they couldn't slip over the edge and get squashed between the ship and the lifeboat. Then for a moment we stopped rolling... this was the moment... the engines picked up revs, we moved in... bang ... as the bow of the lifeboat made contact with the ship's side... we moved forward ten or so feet, up to the ladder, the patient held his arms forward, the lads on the bow grabbed him, Alan came astern ... full revs ... we had him, it was all over in a flash ... Perfect!

2144 hours, the pilot on board the *Lexington* called up "*The casualty is ready to transfer to you now*"... they obviously couldn't see what was happening on the ladder from their bridge ... I replied "*Thank you, he has just stepped aboard the lifeboat, we are now departing for Falmouth, please advise the Captain that our Doctor is now examining the patient, we will take good care of him, over*" ... the pilot replied "*Roger thank you*".

I then called the Coastguard *"Did you copy our last?"* they replied *"yes"*... my reply *"I will advise you of our ETA. Falmouth as soon as we have decided upon our cruising speed"* the reply *"Roger"*.

The wheelhouse was now very busy indeed. We were slowly making for Falmouth... I had a quick look around, Mike was helping the patient onto the bunk on the starboard side just behind the chart table... the Doc was hanging onto the central pole in the wheelhouse in an effort to stop himself being thrown around as the boat rolled heavily from side to side... I called up to the bridge, ... *"They are getting the casualty into the bunk and making him comfortable... as soon as the Doc has had a look at him and says full speed is OK I'll let you know"*... *"OK thanks"* Alan said.... the next few minutes should have been filmed ... it was so funny.

The same medivac as the previous photo and the ship's accomdation ladder was used to transfer the casualty to the lifeboat.
Photo: Falmouth RNLI Collection

THE DOCTOR'S WORST MOMENTS WERE IMMINENT

We were steaming slowly towards Falmouth... across the bay. We were out of the Lee of the *Lexington*...and so we were unable to make use of her size to protect us from the sea. The lifeboat was rolling heavily ... the motion was very unpredictable, and unpleasant ... the patient was a short red faced jolly looking little man, thick rimmed glasses, and a little *'beer belly'*... he didn't look that ill... he was half sat up in the bunk watching the Doctor, who looked dreadful. Mike looked at the Doc, he was obviously concerned. I was sat in the radio seat and, having swivelled it around to face the three of them, folded my arms and proceeded to watch the *'examination'*.

The wheelhouse was fairly well lit.... I had turned the inside lights from red to white... (we use red lights at night to help preserve the night vision of any of the crew who may have to come into the wheelhouse from outside). The Doc wrestled with his little black bag, and like a magician plucked from its '*bowel*s' a stethoscope... he dropped the bag ... and held onto the stethoscope as if it was a live wriggling poisonous snake... at arm's length!

The other hand made a desperate grab for the safety of the wheelhouse pole.... we rolled heavily to port... the Doc swung around the pole almost a full 360 degrees and sank to his knees, ... I had to smile... the look on the patient's face... he was horrified, ... contemplating being examined by a man who it appeared was fighting for his life!!

By now Mike had gathered the black bag and put it into a convenient corner where it would be safe... he then helped the Doc to his feet... the Doc was delirious... eyes rolling, green face… boy did he look ill. He let go of the pole and attempted to plug the stethoscope into his ears, ... he was now staggering uncontrollably ... bouncing off the chart table ... toward the patient... who by now was looking positively frightened. It looked for an awful moment that the Doc was going to lunge at the patient and end up lying on top of him... then by chance we hit a fairly large wave that sent the Doc into reverse, ... he staggered back and ended up sitting in the spare crewman's seat right next to me. He looked at me through his glazed eyes, . . I gave him a smile. He then stood and made another attempt to get to the patient.

I looked over to Mike, who by now had a bucket in his hand. Mike took up position behind the Doc holding the bucket up at shoulder height. I thought to myself what on earth is he doing with that bucket? ... Then ...it happened! The Doctor spun around, facing away from the patient, grabbed the bucket, put his head right into it and ... whoosh ... splat!!! ... out came what was obviously a strong curry ... what an awful stink ...I had to turn away, the scene was more than I could bear ... I could feel tears in my eyes ... there was no doubt this was a job the Doctor was never going to forget!

Enough time had passed for a decision on cruising speed ... I made my way over to the patient, ... who was watching Mike attend to the Doc...*"How are you feeling?"*, I asked ... *"I'm all right, you had better look after him"*, he replied, as he nodded towards the Doc and Mike who were still staggering around the wheelhouse together clutching this bucket of steaming curry! ... I caught Mike's eye ... *"OK for full speed?"* ...he nodded and said *"yes"*, it was obvious that the sooner we reached the shelter of the docks the better for all!

FULL SPEED FOR FALMOUTH

"Bridge, wheelhouse, OK for full speed"... Alan didn't reply with words, he just pushed both throttles forward, we were off.

I could see the lighthouse ahead of us through the forward wheelhouse windows, we only had ten or 15 minutes to run before we were back in the harbour... the Coastguard called ... *"Do you require an ambulance?"*...I replied *"Stand by please"*... I looked over to Mike, who by now had sat the Doctor down, jettisoned his dinner over the stern rail and was getting things back in order, ... *"What's the Doctors intentions?"*, I said... Mike looked at the Doctor who appeared barely conscious, and said *"we had better wait until we get ashore before the Doc examines him"*... I nodded ... I then prepared my message for the Coastguard... *"From the Doctor, our intentions are to take the casualty to the boat house and examine him properly there, could you advise the boathouse of our intentions and confirm?"* … reply *"Yes"* ...I replied *"Thank you"*.

I relayed the message I had passed to the Coastguard up to the bridge... Alan said thanks, then asked me to ask *Lexington* what her intentions were, was she going to wait or sail?... This information was going to be of interest to the casualty too, ...I don't expect he was all that keen on being left all alone in a strange country.

2155 hours to *Lexington*, "*What are your intentions?, do you intend to sail or stay in Falmouth for a few days?*" ... There was a pause ... the Captain of the *Lexington* replied, "*We will wait your Doctors examination and contact our owners*", I replied "*We will contact you as soon as the Doctor has examined him properly*"... the Captain replied "*Roger*".

We were now rounding Pendennis Point, the seas were improving, the Doc was back on his feet... as the boat's motion eased the Doctor's condition improved, one or two of the lads came into the wheelhouse to see how things were going... Steve the Second Cox put his head through the door... "Chris, Alan says can you ask the Coastguard to get someone from the boathouse to collect the casualty from the south steps by car and run him round to the boathouse. We wouldn't have enough water to land at Custom House Quay", I nodded... 2159 hours, to the Coastguard, "*Our ETA Custom House Quay is 5 minutes, could you please phone the boathouse and ask for a crewman to collect our Doctor and patient from south steps by car and take them round to the lifeboat house?*" ...reply "*Yes will do*"... I replied "*Much appreciated, thank you*"... the Coastguard sounded almost human...

As the lifeboat rounded the docks, we could see activity ashore, the boathouse was well lit, plenty of crew moving around... Tim came into the wheelhouse, put the deck lights on, then disappeared below to check the engines. Ropes and fender were made ready for coming alongside... the Doctor had made what looked like a complete recovery... he was now grey in colour, instead of green... a vast improvement!

We drew alongside south steps at 2205 hours, I walked over to the patient, who looked remarkably well... gave him a big smile and a handshake and wished him luck... I then turned to the Doc, shook his hand... I couldn't think of anything appropriate to say... so I gave him a big smile ... the corners of his lips made an effort to smile back ... I must say, he put on a good show... I don't expect he will attend another patient at sea if he can possibly avoid it... but if he had to, I'll bet he's got the guts to give it a go!!

2207 hours, to the Coastguard ... "*We have just transferred the Doctor and patient, I expect the Doctor will contact you by telephone in due course, we will refuel and close down when we are back on our moorings, over*"... reply "*Roger, thank you*".

Half an hour later at 2236 I closed down with the Coastguard... tongue in cheek I wished them a pleasant evening'.

I expect by now the Coastguard who had the audacity to question our competence earlier on, was by now suitably embarrassed. The job went well indeed, Alan handled the boat superbly. Only those in the wheelhouse knew how things went in the wheelhouse... until now of course.

I expect the *Lexington's Chief Engineer* (who made a complete recovery), has '*dined out*' on the story of his '*rescue*' many times since that night in February '93.

ROYAL NATIONAL LIFE-BOAT INSTITUTION
RADIO TELEPHONY MESSAGES

STATION FALMOUTH O.N. 1058

Name of Casualty (if any) LEXINGTON Date 8/2/92

M.F. Freq. or V.H.F. Channel	Local Time	To	From	Text of Message
16/0	2028	C/G	L/B	May we have the casualty position, sit rep and time check
				please. R/ The vessel is called Lexington, the pilots are
				working with her on channel 9, the chief engineer has high
				blood pressure and a headache, the Captain wants him to be
				seen by a doctor, he is willing to land him. Time check
				2029 local, what is your crew list please.
				R/ I will pass my crew list shortly, please advise casulty
				position. R/ The Lexington is making for the 2 D buoy.
				R/ Roger Thank you.
0	2030	C/G	L/B	Our crew list is: 1) 2) 3) 4) 5) 6) 9. R/ Roger.
0	2039	L/B	C/G	Doctor Magee is on route to the boat house. R/ Thank you
				for informing us, that will save us mooring up alongside,
				we will advise you as soon as the Doctor arrives and we
				are departing Custom House Quay. R/ Roger.
0	2054	C/G	L/B	We have the Doctor on board, we are now proceeding into the
				bay. R/ Roger.
16/9	2057	L/B	L/K MITCHELL	What are your intentions? R/ Stand by please. R/ Roger.
0	2058	C/G	L/B	We are switching to channel 9 and will be working from now
				on on channel 9. R/ Roger, listening 16 and 9. R/ Roger
				Thank you.
9	2059	L/K MITCHELL	L/B	We are leaving harbour now and making for your position.
				R/ Are you happy with a pilot ladder on our starboard side?
				It will take us some time to rig the accommodation ladder.
				R/ We will wait until we arrive on scene and assess the
				conditions and then decide how to transfer the Doctor to
				Lexington, and the casulty to the Lifeboat, R/ Roger,
				R/ What is your position please. R/ 1½ Miles off Rosemullion

Note—This form MUST be submitted to Head Office IMMEDIATELY after a service

---

RADIO TELEPHONY MESSAGES—Cont.

M.F. Freq. or V.H.F. Channel	Local Time	To	From	Text of Message
				Head.
9	2103	L/B	C/G	Go to channel zero. R/ Roger.
0	2103	L/B	C/G	We are not happy about the transfer of the Doctor to
				Lexington because of the weather conditions. R/ Be
				advised under no circumstances will we be putting the
				Doctor, our crew or the casualty at risk, we will assess
				the situation when we arrive on scene, we will keep you
				closely advised. R/ Thank you.
9	2110	L/B	Lex-ington	The weather is moderating, we are reducing speed, we have
				6 cables to run, the pilot ladder is 2/3 down to the water
				line, under the after samson posts R/Roger all copied.
9	2111	L/B	Lex-ington	You can come along side now, you have your search light on
				our pilot ladder.
				R/ Roger Thank you.
9	2112	Lex-ington	L/B	Our Doctor and our Coxwain are not happy with the transfer
				of the Doctor by pilot ladder, we will wait until you
				have come to anchor and have a look at you then.
				R/ Roger good decision
9	2113	C/G	L/B	Have you copied our last with Lexington?
				R/ Yes all copied.
9	2119	L/B	Lex-ington	Coming astern now, dropping anchor. R/ Roger Thank you
9	2122	Lex-ington	L/B	Can our Doctor talk to your Captain R/ Yes stand by....
				this is the Captain R/ How is the patient? R/ He has
				taken pills for blood pressure, when he stands up he is
				190, when he lie down 160 R/ What sort of stretchers do
				you have for lowering him down to us? R/ (Pilot speaking)
				The Captain would prefer your doctor to see him on board
				the ship before transferring. R/ Our doctor is not
				happy to use the pilot ladder. R/ The Casualty should
				be able to make it on board by the companion ladder. R/
				we can pass a lifejacket to you. R/ Yes if you pass one

ROYAL NATIONAL LIFE-BOAT INSTITUTION
RADIO TELEPHONY MESSAGES

STATION FALMOUTH O.N. 1058

Name of Casualty (if any) LEXINGTON Date 8/2/92

M.F. Freq. or V.H.F. Channel	Local Time	To	From	Text of Message
				up we will send him down, it will take a short while to
				prepare the ladder. R/ We will stand off and await your
				call. R/ Roger.
9	2127	C/G	L/B	Confirm you have received our recent conversation with
				Lexington and are aware of our situation.
				R/ Yes all received.
9	2131	L/B	Lex-ington	You see our accommodation ladder, please advise what height
				you require it. R/ We will come along side you, our bow to
				your stern and advise. R/ Yes it's never easy.... will you
				take this opportunity to transfer the lifejacket? R/ Yes
				R/ Roger.
9	2137	C/G	L/B	Our sit rep, we are standing by Lexington awaiting the
				transfer of the casualty, our position is 50° 0750N, 05°
				0393W, R/ Roger what is the ETA of the casualty?
				R/ We are waiting for Lexington to call us in, I do not
				expect it will be long. R/ Roger
9	2138	L/B	Lex-ington	Our Captain has just been called to the radio room to take
				a link call, when he has finished we will be able to
				transfer, I will advise R/ Roger Thank you
9	2144	L/B	Lex-ington	The casualty is ready to transfer to you now. R/ Thank you
				he has just stepped aboard the lifeboat, we are now departing
				for Falmouth, please advise the Captain that our doctor is
				now examining the patient. R/ Thank you
9	2145	C/G	L/B	Did you copy our last? R/ Yes. R/ I will advise you of our
				ETA Falmouth as soon as we have decided upon our cruising
				speed R/ Roger.
9/0	2150	L/B	C/G	Do you require an ambulance? R/ From the doctor, intentions

Note—This form MUST be submitted to Head Office IMMEDIATELY after a service

---

RADIO TELEPHONY MESSAGES—Cont.

M.F. Freq. or V.H.F. Channel	Local Time	To	From	Text of Message
				are to take the casualty to the boat house and examine
				him properly there, could you advise the boat house of
				our intentions and confirm? R/ Yes R/ Thank you.
9	2155	Lex-ington	L/B	What are your intentions? do you intend to sail or stay
				in Falmouth for a few days? R/ We will await you doctors
				examination and contact our owners R/We will contact you as
				soon as the doctor has examined him properly. R/ Roger
0	2159	C/G	L/B	Our ETA Custom House Quay is 5 minutes, could you please
				phone them and ask for a crewman to collect our doctor
				and patient from South Steps by car and take him round to
				the lifeboat house? R/ Yes will do R/ Much appreciated
				thank you .
0	2207	C/G	L/B	We have just transferred the doctor and patient, I expect
				the doctor will contact you by telephone in due course,
				we will re-fuel and close down when we are on our moorings
				R/ Roger thank you
0	2236	C/G	L/B	We are now back on moorings, ready for service, switching
				off the wireless and going ashore, we wish you a pleasant
				evening R/ Roger thanks for all your help.
				Signed [signature] C.D. Price 9/2/92
				Boarding Boat Attendant Cliff Atherton
				Casualty
				Alimos
				Athens
				Greece Tel:

Radio log from this service.

Two men die as fishing boat goes down

Tragedy of the Karen Marie

MARINE investigators were this week trying to piece together the final hours of the Helford fishing boat Karen Marie, which plunged to the bottom of Falmouth Bay last Friday with the loss of two lives.

by
Stephen Ivall

The 21-foot vessel is lying in 112 feet of water with the skipper's dog trapped in the wheelhouse. But there is still no sign of the lost crew.

Families of the dead men were left devastated by the tragedy. The wife of one of them is expecting her first child.

As marine accident investigators arrived in Cornwall to talk to rescuers and others involved in the search for Peter Williams, 27, and Tony Culmer, 38, questions were once again being raised about safety on board fishing boats.

Mr Williams' wife Denise raised the alarm when the boat was overdue.

The Karen Marie lies off The Manacles, where she was found by a Culdrose diver at the weekend. Lobster pots were seen on both sides of the vessel and Mr Williams' dog was still in the wheelhouse, indicating the vessel went down very suddenly and with no chance for the crew, who were dressed in oilskins.

Mr Williams, a Falmouth man who went to live in Ruan Minor, where he married a local girl, was the owner of the Cygnus Marine-built boat he bought second hand for his fishing business.

On board with him was Mr Culmer, of Coastguard Cottages, Cadgwith, an experienced deep-sea fishermen who gave up his job on large trawlers because he feared a lack of safety.

The Karen Marie went missing on Friday after leaving her berth in the Helford and heading into Falmouth Bay and on towards Cadgwith.

She was seen at sea on Friday but relatives later reported her overdue. A search was immediately carried out. The Falmouth lifeboat was launched and remained on service for 17 hours.

Coxswain Alan Barnes took the Arun class vessel through the notorious Manacles passage in adverse conditions using parachute flares to illuminate the scene.

The search was then widened using a helicopter from Culdrose and more lifeboats, including The Lizard and Fowey boats. Even the Plymouth lifeboat went to sea and searched off the Eddystone.

Seventy-five auxiliary coastguards, with sector officer Edward Davies in charge, searched the coastline from The Lizard to Dodman Point in an effort to find the men or clues as to what might have happened. Auxiliaries from Mevagissey also joined the search.

Later Mr John Sheppard and his team, assisted by station officers Geoff Stout and Steve Huxley, called for a Nimrod aircraft from Kinloss to carry out a radar search on Saturday.

Senior watch officer Mr Simon Rabett took over the watch at the height of the incident, which had the eight-man team at the coastguard headquarters working flat out co-ordinating the units. The search was scaled down when oil and wreckage was finally discovered.

The boat was then spotted lying in an upright position on the seabed without apparent damage. Two fishermen, one of them George Mitchell, skipper of the Silver Queen, had found her.

A Culdrose diver then dropped into the sea and walked round the vessel in murky conditions but found no trace of any bodies except for a dog owned by Mr Williams which was still shut inside the wheelhouse.

Newspaper cutting from the Helston Packet.

KAREN MARIE

Friday evening 4th March 1994, leave work 1800 hours, pop into the supermarket on the way home; arrive at the 'Black Hole' 1900 hours.

The wind was picking up, around force 6 south-westerly not bad enough for me to consider eating something that I could eject later if we went afloat, so it was Fray Bentos, mash and peas, hot bath and down to the Chain Locker for a pint of orange squash.

Having drunk my share during my teen years, since joining the crew I gave up drinking - the thought of turning up for a shout smelling of booze and being left behind was not an option.

2230 hours, walking back up to the Black Hole I noticed the wind had increased and was now blowing a full gale, in the door, down stairs to the bedroom, undressed next to the bed letting the clothes fall in a careful heap, pants and socks off last, because they would be the first on if there was a shout - clean the gnashers, into bed and within probably thirty seconds asleep... but not for long, 2345 hours one ring… "*yes*" … "*big boat Chris*" ... "*thanks Captain*"... slam the phone down, switch on the light, check the time, pull on the clothes, shirt and jumper came off as one, and went on as one!

The pager starts bleeping, activated by the Coastguard as soon as possible after Captain Banks gave permission for the Arun to be launched.

Within 4 minutes I was in the lifeboat house, panting like anyone who has run flat out for around 300 yards.

I went into the engineer's room, Tim the lifeboat Mechanic had just put the phone down, Alan the Coxswain was next to him waiting anxiously to find out what the job was.

 "*Fishing boat overdue, due back in the Helford at 1800 hours, 2 POB (persons on board) the wives were very concerned, they have been unable to make contact and expected their husbands to be home before 2000 hours*".

Alan went into the crew room there were plenty to choose from to top up the 'A' team. Looking at those of the 'A' team who were kitted up, Alan took a reserve and one of the inshore lifeboat crew to bring us up to eight.

A few quivering bottom lips from those not chosen to come on the shout. I felt their pain, having been there like all the young reserves, desperately wishing a few from the main crew had sprained an ankle, or were at home with the flu!

Tim our Mechanic came out of the Mechanic's room he handed me a pack of hot cans, to take on board with us, "*I slung the old cans away, they were well out of date, forgot to put these on board this afternoon*" he chirped, I detected a slight smile on his lips, he knew instantly how impressed I would be if anyone heated one up in the wheelhouse in heavy weather! The stink of sausage, bacon and baked beans was bad enough, but then watching someone enjoying scoffing it would send me sprinting for the back door to puke all over the deck.

Hot cans were the size of small buckets with an inner tin a bit bigger than a baked bean can. Surrounding the inner tin containing the stinking grub was a compartment that contained chemical material that would heat up when poked with a skewer (supplied with each tin).

The hole between the inner and outer tins required constant poking to get the heat up; eventually the grub was steaming, giving off the deadly gas of boiling baked beans... For me this was worse than the smell of diesel or heavy oil fumes often encountered on bad shouts.

As we made our way down the gang plank to the lifeboat, tied up on the pontoon just outside the boat house, I could have easily jettisoned the hot cans into the drink, but to be fair to those who have cast iron stomachs, a hot meal after 10 or 12 hours boosts the energy, and morale. As a 'wheelhouse wallah' it made sense to keep everyone on their top game, whilst I could be down to 70% physically but still do my job, although I always needed to be 100% mentally.

Tim was like a racing whippet in the engine room, he was a time served boat builder having served his apprenticeship with Cygnus Marine, one of the larger boat builders in Falmouth. He knew modern boat diesel inside out, and better still enjoyed bad weather, swinging through the wheelhouse like a monkey through the trees, always grinning... I hated the bastard… not really.

As the engines started everything in the wheelhouse came alive. I was busy checking the current crew list and was noting everyone's crew number on the radio log, ready to pass to the Coastguard.

With all ropes let go, Alan took the boat off from the alongside the pontoon and we made our way out of the harbour, passing the docks.

The sea state in the harbour was slight, but the wind was ferocious, blowing from the south west. We were heading west which meant we were going to the see some big seas if we couldn't find the fishing boat on its moorings in the Helford.

Saturday very early morning, 0010 hours, channel zero *"Falmouth Coastguard this is Falmouth Lifeboat, we are launched and proceeding, request sit rep, time check and job number"*.

The Coastguard replied *"the vessel is a 21 foot fishing boat, red hull, blue wheelhouse, white top, it left Porthkerris from Helford at 0700 yesterday morning, due back at 2000 hours last night, time check 0010 UCT"*.

Having got the gist of the message onto my notepad I asked *"please advise the name of the vessel and number of persons on board"* Coastguard reply *"2 persons on board, the vessel name Karen Marie, FH 199"*.

FH 199 being the official registration of the vessel, registered in Falmouth.

Tim said *"that's Peter's boat, Peter Williams and his mate Tony"*.

One or two of the crew knew the *Karen Marie*; she fished the Falmouth area waters and was from our patch. I called up the Coastguard to confirm the wish for us to work channel zero, the Coastguard came back *"yes zero, Porthoustock Mobile is in the Helford by the Shipwrights, FMRC are on their way, Rescue 193 has been alerted, over"* I replied *"Roger I will pass my crew list shortly"*.

We had just passed Black Rock Buoy at the entrance to Falmouth harbour, and feeling the full force of the gale, the seas close to shore were not too bad, the bay up to the Helford benefiting from the protection of the land. The seas outside will be considerable as the gale has been blowing for some hours now.

Alan swung into the wheelhouse to discuss his plans and listen to any thoughts from the crew. He said "*I reckon we can get the ILB to do the Helford, the sea conditions aren't too bad here. If the fishing boat has gear off Porthkerris she is working down to the west. I think we should work west, through the Manacles, Coverack bay down to Blackhead, any thoughts?*"

The crew including myself all nodded, Alan had a sixth sense about these things, it all made sense, a small fishing boat normally works inshore close to its base, if they begin their day's work to the west it would make sense this is the direction they would work in.

Alan said to me "*Can you get hold of Captain Banks and ask him to task the ILB to the Helford, advise him the sea conditions will be OK for them if they keep inshore*", "*no probs*" I replied.

0015 hours "*Falmouth Coastguard this is Falmouth Lifeboat I have our crew list for you*" … "*pass your crew list,*" I replied "*1,2,3,4,5,6, 10 and 3i, total P.O.B. 8, over*" the Coastguard replied "*all copied, will do out*".

This was a seasoned crew. Alan is a brilliant Coxswain, looks after the crew, makes sure everyone is capable of doing all the jobs required, everyone gets a chance to drive. Tonight's crew included

Coxswain Alan Barnes on *Elizabeth Ann*.
Photo: Falmouth RNLI Collection

the Mechanic, John Second Mechanic, me Deputy Second Coxswain (number 5), Pete Deputy Second Coxswain, Alan Rowe number 10 (I gauged Alan up when he joined the crew some years ago, a sensible head, a guy you could rely on 100%) and one from ILB, Glen crew member 3i (ILB crew), another good hand.

I prepared the message the Coxswain wanted passed to the Coastguard.

0020 hours, to the Coastguard "*our intentions are to search from the mouth of the Helford, down through the Manacles to Coverack, our ETA abeam the Helford is 14 minutes over*" the Coastguard replied "*all copied, we have your Launching Authority in the OPS room with us, over*". That was lucky I thought, I replied "*can I talk to our Launching Authority please*" the reply "*this is Captain Banks, over*", "*Captain, Alan has asked me to advise*" *you that the sea conditions from Falmouth to Helford are safe for the ILB to get to the Helford and make a detailed search up to Karen Marie's moorings"*. Captain's reply *"Chris can you advise Alan I will launch the ILB, Rescue 193 will be airborne shortly they can also search the Helford area"* … I replied *"thank you Captain, I will advise Alan"*.

Before I had a chance to pick up the intercom mike to advise Alan he piped down the intercom *"all copied"*.

John, Alan and crew upstairs keeping a look out, Pete and Tim were in the wheelhouse with me, as every minute passed I thought to myself *'this job is not going to end well'*. Every year we get a few jobs looking for overdue fishing boats. They usually turn up either late after hauling their gear, or stopped off in the pub on the way home for a quick pint…. which develops into a piss-up and ended with a good verbal thrashing when they crawled through the door, comments like *'where the hell have you been? The police, Coastguards and lifeboat are out looking for you, you bloody idiot!'*

Crew member Alan Rowe. Photo: Jon Crane

This job was not one of those typical *'over dues'*… small open boat, big seas, full gale, more than four hours overdue, approaching 1 o'clock in the morning.

I looked at Tim, he was not grinning, he had big eyes, and looked the way we all felt…. this is going to be a long night and as every minute passed the more the outcome was not going to be good.

We were making full speed towards the Helford. Tim was filling in his engine log, noting down engine temperatures, oil pressures, engine revs, etc. Pete was on the radar trying to tune it to give a clear outline of the coast; it was difficult due to the sea conditions. The sea was coming at us from the west; the boat was pitching heavily as we pushed into each oncoming wave.

0034 hours, I decided to call *Karen Marie* on channel 16, the call up channel, also two of the fisherman's working channels, 8 and 6, just on the off chance they were at anchor somewhere safe but couldn't get ashore, or raise the Coastguard, *"Karen Marie, Karen Marie, Karen Marie, this is Falmouth Lifeboat on channel 16 over"* … no reply, then again on 8 and 6, all with no luck.

0035 hours Alan called down "*Chris, can you ask Tim to fire one white para off the after deck now, and advise the Coastguard*", I replied "*Roger*".

Tim went to the flare box situated at the rear of the wheelhouse door just to the port side and close to the aft wheelhouse door. Para (parachute) flares are kept in a big red wood box marked 'explosives!'

The aft wheelhouse door was fastened in the open position. Tim staggered out onto the after deck clutching the flare, he was staggering around getting the flare ready to fire, for one terrible moment I had this image of him falling forward towards the wheelhouse and popping off the flare at the same time, with the flare flying around the wheelhouse out of control.

Luckily, or through Tim's skills, as soon as he had got the bottom cap off the flare and the trigger dropped down, he wedged himself against the tow rope drum, pointed the flare skywards and fired it off.

As it whooshed off into the sky I advised the Coastguard. The cloud base was low with thick driving rain and gale force winds, the flare naturally flew into the wind up through the low cloud base and illuminated, as it slowly floated down it lit the inside of the cloud, having very little effect on the coastline close by or the sea, then as is passed through the cloud it fizzled out and dropped into the sea.

I always have the comforting thought that when we are out searching for someone, if they are alive and conscious and see our flares, they will work hard to stay alive if they know someone is out looking for them.

0038 hours "*Falmouth Lifeboat this is Porthoustock Mobile we are at the Shipwrights, searching the shore line, nothing found yet Chris, we are working channel zero, over*"

I replied "*Thank you Henry we are currently searching from Gillan to Nare Point*"… reply "*roger*".

Henry is a well-seasoned Coastguard who knows his patch like the back of his hand; he has been over every inch of it, man and boy. It is always comforting to the crew to know Henry is out taking care of the shoreside search.

0040 hours, we were slowly making our way past Nare Point, the search light was deployed on our starboard side; Roger was up on the Flying Bridge fanning shoreside for any sign of wreckage. The chances of finding any in areas protected by the coast from the westerly gale were slim, but there is a possibility *Karen Marie* had a problem, sprung a leak and been steamed ashore.

Alan came down to the wheelhouse, he knew Tim knew the *Karen Marie*. We chatted about the boat, Tim mentioned it was a Cygnus 21. The Cygnus 21 is a big boat for its length, a lot of deck space. "*What type of fishing do they do?*" Alan asked Tim… "*don't know*" he replied. Alan looked at me, "*see if Henry has any idea*" … I gave a single nod.

0050 hours "*Porthoustock mobile, this is Falmouth Lifeboat are you there Henry?*"

Henry came back "*loud and clear Chris*"

"*Do you have any relatives of the fisherman with you?*"

"*Yes*" Henry replied.

"*Please ask them what type of fishing the Karen Marie are engaged in*"

There was a pause, the Henry came back,

"*They have gone out to look at pots and set some nets*"

"*How many nets are they fishing?*"

"*Ten tiers of nets*"

"*How many pots could they have on board?*"

Reply "*thirty pots*"

Alan chipped in to the conversation "*where are they setting?*"

I asked Henry, he replied

"*Blackhead area, they will have been steering towards Blackhead in the morning*"

"*Thanks Henry*"

Not good news, ten tiers of nets, thirty pots, you do not set pots off Blackhead in a gale, you pick them up and set in a quieter area, pots and nets are not cheap to buy, and time consuming to repair, when big tides are coming and bad weather is forecast it is normal for inshore fishing boats to get their gear in, rather than risk leaving it set and possibly losing it.

The weight of ten tiers of nets or thirty pots will bring the boat low in the water, just one good wave over the transom (stern) and she will go down, with no time for a '*May Day*' or putting on a life jacket.

0057 hours, the Coastguard called up "*Falmouth Lifeboat this is Falmouth Coastguard continue to search as far as Falmouth Bay area*".

"*Roger*" I replied …. Alan was still in the wheelhouse, I looked at him and smiled, he looked to the floor and shook his head.

What a waste of words I thought, continue to search as far as Falmouth Bay area, what the hell does that mean? There was no point asking, we were going to make our way down towards Blackhead where the worst of the weather had been for the last 24 hours, and where the *Karen Marie* was known to have been working.

We could hear a bit of chatter on zero between Porthoustock Mobile and Rescue 193, a mighty Sea King helicopter from 771 Squadron based at RNAS Culdrose just ten miles away, she was beginning her search of the Helford River. Alan went back up to the flying bridge, as he left the wheelhouse he turned and asked Tim "*rig the search light on the foredeck we will take a look through the Manacles on our way down to Blackhead*".

I looked Tim in the eye "*you are going to get wet*" then a big smile …engineers like to keep in the wheelhouse, nice and dry… on this job we were all going to get wet, eyes are no good in the wheelhouse during a search.

0104 hours, we were entering the inside channel through the Manacles, just off Porthoustock, large short seas, in each trough the bow digs in sending the top of the wave up over the flying bridge, Alan on the intercom, "*where is the helo?*".... I replied "*still up the Helford spotting each boat with its searchlight*".

"*Let everyone know we are firing a white para off Porthoustock*".

I replied "*roger*".

0105 hours, "*all stations, all stations, this is Falmouth Lifeboat, we are firing one white para off Porthoustock now*".

Up went the flare, it lit up the area reasonably well even though the flare was burning above the low cloud base.

We were moving slowly, the boat was pitching heavily.

0110 hours, we could hear the chatter between Rescue 193 and Porthoustock Mobile, the helo was making her way towards the entrance of the Helford, Alan advised he was going to pop off another white para, I called Rescue 193, "*Rescue 193 this is Falmouth Lifeboat we are just off Porthoustock, we want to put up another para is that OK with you?*"

The reply "*OK with us*", I replied "*roger*".

Alan called down on the intercom "*thanks Chris, firing white para now*".

We would never fire a white parachute flare at night when a helicopter is in the area without first getting permission, the pilot and crew rely on their night vision, a white parachute flare illuminating the area would blind the helo crew for several minutes if they were not warned and had no time to flip their sun visors down to protect their night vision eyes.... worst case would be if we hit a helicopter with a parachute flare, I've never heard of this happening, that could be a disaster.

Mike picked up the intercom from his position on the radar, "*Alan I've got no radar picture*", after a moment or two Alan called down "*Chris, come up to the flying bridge now*"... "*roger*" I replied. Clipping my life jacket on as I stepped out of the aft wheelhouse door onto the after deck, as I climbed the steps to the top of the lifeboat I got a wave right in the kisser, nothing wakes you up more than a bucket full of freezing salt water!

I squeezed in next to Alan who was on the wheel young Alan was on the starboard search light, Glen was keeping a look out on the port side. John was preparing a white para. I knew the rocks in the area well, one of the submerged rocks a little too well but that's another story.

Alan also knew the area well, but all the marks to check where we were couldn't be seen. We had '*Sharks Fin*' close on our starboard beam, one of the landmarks for '*Main Land*' rocks was not visible, this was St Keverne church steeple at the end of the valley in line with a big clump of trees, easy to see in day light but no bloody good in the dark.

With no radar this is not the best place to be, I shouted to Alan "*knowing where Sharks Fin is, all we need to do is spot Carn Du and we can steam out into plenty of sea room*" he nodded, we all strained our eyes for *Carn Du,* the tide was high, there wouldn't be much showing.

Carn-du Rocks. Photo: Falmouth RNLI Collection

Up went the next white para, there were some big waves coming at us, then a monster gusher, the bow dipped in and up came the wave, we all instinctively leaned forward to get the protection of the perspex flying bridge windscreen, not such a clever idea, the RNLI jacket has a big collar, this acts like a funnel, half a bucket of water down the back of the jacket reaching down beneath both cheeks of the bum and absolutely freezing. Everybody groaned, Alan and myself looked over the windscreen to see Tim clinging onto the foredeck railings, he was on the deck operating a searchlight, I expected that last wave must have knocked him off his feet.

"*Get in the wheelhouse*" Alan screamed at Tim who was looking up awaiting instructions…. like a whippet he was gone, down the starboard side of the boat and into the wheelhouse… "*is he in*" Alan barked down the intercom, "*yes*" Pete replied. "*Rocks*" Glen screamed pointing with his outstretched arm somewhere off the port bow we all strained, we could see it clearly in the next trough, "*Carn Du*" I screamed, we were in a good position, I gave an arm signal move straight ahead, "*run Carn Du down our port side and we are into Coverack bay*".

Alan put on some more power, we have deep water right up to *Carn Du* on our port side, we could cut it as close as we liked, we would be safe. If we left too much room we would need to worry about the *Little Wrea*, a group of rocks stretching out from *Lowland Point.*

As we passed *Carn Du* motoring into clear water the rolling seas spread out, although bigger seas the lifeboat handled them well.

I made my way back down into the wheelhouse, Tim was soaked to the bone and shivering, I threw him a blanket from the stretcher which is located on the aft starboard side of the wheelhouse.

Alan called down, "*advise the Coastguard we are going to fire another white flare*" …. "*roger*".

0135 hours, *"all stations, this is Falmouth Lifeboat we are just west of Coverack Bay, moving down to Blackhead, firing one white para now, out"*.

We moved slowly down to Blackhead, making around 6 knots, we fired off a couple more white flares, completing our shore line search.

Alan came down to the wheelhouse, *"ask the Coastguard what search area they would like us to cover next please"*.

0154 hours, *"Falmouth Coastguard this is Falmouth Lifeboat, we have completed out shoreline search from Helford down to Blackhead have you a new search area for us?"* The Coastguard replied *"a new search area is being prepared for you now"*.

0200 hours, *"Falmouth Lifeboat search the Helford River as far as Helford Ferry"*… I replied *"roger"*.

Alan said *"we will work our way up to the Helford, searching on the way"*.

We took a slow run up towards the Helford firing off white illuminating paras on the way, this time searching seaward side of the Manacles.

0235 hours, Glen called out *"dark object port bow"* Alan relayed to the wheelhouse, three of us left the wheelhouse, Pete and John went up on the bow, I stayed on the after deck to keep an ear on the wireless, Tim was now warming up and drying out, still cocooned in blankets.

We motored slowly over to the *'object'*, I was expecting a body, it was a large dark plastic sheet, Pete recovered it with the lifeboat hook, the longest boat hook you have ever seen, and not easy to use.

The boys on the foredeck checked it to see if there were any markings to indicate where it came from…. none.

I was hoping we might find *Karen Marie* anchored off in the Helford, but realistically more than six hours overdue with a full westerly gale blowing, no contact, it was increasingly looking like the boat had gone down, the chances of surviving in these seas are slim.

But slim is good enough for everyone in the Falmouth crew, or for that matter any RNLI crew.

No one said as much but I felt we were looking for bodies and hoping for them to be alive.

0240 hours from the Coastguard *"have you searched the Helford yet?"* I replied *"negative we have just investigated a dark object in the water, it was a tarpaulin, no markings to suggest it was from Karen Marie, we are making our way to the Helford, firing one white para now, over"* reply *"roger"*.

0300 hours to the Coastguard *"we are at the mouth of the Helford now, beginning our search of the river now, over"*.

After a minute or so the Coastguard came back *"you are looking for a punt with the name Luewin, I spell, lima, uniform, echo, whiskey, india, november… Luewin, how copied? Over"* I replied *"all copied"*, the Coastguard came back *"Falmouth mobile is at the Helford*

Elizabeth Ann's Y-boat was used to search among the moorings in the Helford River. Photo: Simon Culliford

Passage", I replied "*roger*".

We went to anchor in the Helford and launched the *Y-boat*, we worked with the *Y-boat* on a private channel 'P1' this enabled general chit chat without clogging the Coastguard's working channel, zero.

The *Y-boat* with its hand held torch moved around in amongst the boats on their moorings looking for the *Karen Marie's* punt. The ILB with its more powerful searchlight was also searching off the Shipwrights (pub) and the area south of Durgan, to do a thorough job takes time, the *Y-boat* searched for over 30 minutes, this gave a chance for the rest of the crew to come into the wheelhouse, out of the freezing wind blowing across the river, and for the majority who could keep it down I made a brew, strong tea with powdered milk, yuck!

Out came the McVities biscuits, I opened the packet at the top, there were a few takers, so I put them on the small table space between the engineers panel and the MF wireless where I write the radio messages on my pad.

0340 hours Alan said to the crew "*the Y-boat has had a good look around, lets go and have a look up towards the Dodman*", I called up the *Y-boat* on P1 "*if you have completed your search for the punt we are ready to recover you and search up towards the Dodman*". Glen who was in the *Y-boat* replied "*we have searched everywhere no sign of the punt we are returning to you now*".

I had a quick tidy around in the wheelhouse with Tim, getting everything stowed or tied down, getting ready to leave the shelter of the Helford and back out into the rougher seas past Falmouth and off up towards the Dodman.

0342 hours I advised the Coastguard "*we are recovering the Y-boat having completed its search of the area*", they replied "*roger*".

0408 hours with the *Y-boat* stowed securely Glen came into the wheelhouse and passed Tim 'Lifeboat Zulu' the handheld radio, Tim stowed it in its charger.

I called the Coastguard "*We are just leaving the mouth of the Helford river, making our way towards the Dodman, searching inshore as best as we can*", the Coastguards reply "*roger*".

0415 hours the Coastguard called up "*be prepared to return to the station, and resume the search at 0700 to 0730*".

Alan piped down to the wheelhouse on the intercom "*we are going to search inshore up to the Dodman*". My job was to dress the message up and relay it to the Coastguard.

0418 hours to the Coastguard "*we are able to do an inshore search from Zone Point to the Dodman, as we are out here, we have plenty of fuel, we can do a close inshore search*".

Their reply "*roger do a close inshore search up to the Dodman then return to station*" I replied "*roger*", they came back "*we are tasking a Nimrod for a search of the area 5 nautical miles offshore at first light*". I replied "*roger*".

Whilst it's the Coastguards job to co-ordinate sea searches, they are not in charge of the lifeboats movement, this is entirely the responsibility of the Coxswain, Alan like all Coxswains decides what happens, he will consult with the crew and as a team we decide when it is time to abandon a search.

We all knew that the chances of finding the *Karen Marie* were very slim, as was the chance of finding its two crew, but like all searches we will continue until we are satisfied there are no lives to be saved.

Searching for survivors or bodies in the water is difficult enough, but in big seas the only way we had a chance of spotting someone is if we nearly run over them.

A lifeboat is not the best platform for searching the sea, darkness makes things much worse; the best chance of spotting people in the water or on shore is in daylight, and from the air. A Nimrod or helicopter will cover a search area in a much shorter time than surface vessels, normally we will search until daylight then much better search platforms can take over.

0425 hours, the Coastguard called up "*do you require fuel and food when you return to Falmouth?*" I replied "*yes please*".

0428 hours we heard Fowey Lifeboat call up Brixham Coastguard for a radio check on channel zero; once they completed comms with the Coastguard I called them for a radio check, "*Fowey Lifeboat radio check on zero*" they replied "*loud and clear, we are searching east of Dodman, nothing sighted yet*". I replied "*we are doing a shore search from St Anthony to the Dodman*".

0451 hours Falmouth Coastguard called up "*there is hot food for you at the boat house when you have refuelled*".

I replied "*thank you, we are to the east of Gerrans Bay continuing our search, we will advise when we reach the Dodman and make our way for Falmouth*", the Coastguard replied "*roger*".

0530 hours, to the Coastguard "*we are at the Dodman, making our way back to Falmouth, our ETA 0605 hours*" they replied "*roger*".

A half hour's pounding as we steamed at full speed into the sea, having searched down to the Dodman, we were abeam St Anthony lighthouse, I sat in the radio seat resting the back of my neck on my life jacket to take the strain off my neck muscles, the constant slamming into the waves saps the strength out of all muscles as they strain to keep you in the seat.

Keeping one eye on the wheelhouse clock and looking out for the lighthouse light I caught what was now an empty packet of McVities rolling backwards and forwards between the engineer's panel and MF wireless set.

As we rounded the lighthouse Tim switched to the wheelhouse lights from dim red to bright white … I looked at my radio log, it was covered in the dust of the McVities, from a full packet! All over the table, what a mess, reddish brown dust everywhere, the lesson learnt, put the bloody biscuits in the draw in bad weather!

0604 hours I had advised our ETA as 0605 hours so I decided to wait a minute before calling the coastguard to advise them we were entering Falmouth, just to show them how brilliant we were at estimating ETA's.

0605 hours, we had just passed the light house making our way to the docks. "*Falmouth Coastguard this is Falmouth Lifeboat we are abeam the lighthouse, over*" they replied "*roger*".

We pulled alongside Custom House Quay, there were four or five reserve crew and ILB crew ready to take our ropes and refuel us. What a brilliant sight, they like us had been up all night, in the boathouse, tuned in on channel zero, plotting our progress and knowing that if we had no luck we would have to come back to refuel and get ready for a daylight search, and of course hoping there was room for them on board if any of the crew were going ashore.

We refuelled by 0645 hours and into the boathouse, Ken the Tea Pot looked at me as last off the boat and said "*all right mate? You go in and have a cuppa, I'll put the hose away and catch up in a minute*"... I replied "*thanks mate!*"

Ken like 'Big D' was a guy you could rely on, a real '*gor blimey*' Londoner, reminded me of my youth, the dulcet tones of Londoners gassing away in shops and on the streets, often punctuated with swear words and corny rhyming slang.

Ken looked like he had been towed backwards through a hundred hedges but as always grinning and giggling.

Heather Nicoll was busy making tea and coffee, a big heap of bacon sandwiches were wrapped in tin foil on the crew room table, it was like Christmas but without the decorations

Falmouth's Atlantic 21 inshore lifeboat *Elizabeth Bestwick* was also involved in the search for the *Karen Marie*. Seen here on exercise alongside *Elizabeth Ann* off Dodman Point. Photo: Simon Culliford

…. "*tea Chris*?" Heather said, looking up at me and giving a smile, similar to my Mum's.

Heather height wise came up to my chin, not big in size but huge joy when you are coming in from a crap job, or a long uncomfortable search or tow, just knowing there is a big welcome and to be looked after by the whole crew's second Mum.

The bacon sandwiches went down well with the crew, I would have loved to have scoffed one, but knew it wouldn't get to my stomach and I would be saying farewell to it within the hour, the wind was still gale force westerly, big seas, great when you are surfing with it, but not so pleasant when you are ploughing into it, or rolling your guts out with sea on your beam.

Snowy, and Dave (Heather's son) were in the crew room, they had searched the Helford in the ILB with two other ILB crew and were getting ready to go out again, Alan was tasking them to do a close inshore search from the lighthouse up to the Dodman.

0715 hours, not quite daylight but it was on its way, Alan stood up, the rest of the crew stood up as one within two seconds, he said "*anyone want relieving*?" ... I looked around and thought what a stupid question… he must have thought the same, "*let's go then*" he said. Alan looked at 'Tea Pot' who also stood up, he nodded to him "*get your kit on*", Kens eyes lit up, he grabbed his kit and caught us up as we reached the door, we filed out of the crew room, doing up our lifejackets. *Elizabeth Ann* was on tick over, bobbing up and down as she was tied alongside.

Everyone went to their stations, deck crew recovered the fenders that were protecting the lifeboat as she was rubbing against the quayside, stowing them well for the lumpy journey ahead.

0725 hours, a cup of tea in my tummy, but not for long I thought as we slipped our mooring and left Custom House Quay. I called up the Coastguard *"we are refuelled and leaving Custom House Quay for our search area, our crew list, 1,2,3,4,5,6,10,11, and 3i, I total POB '9', over"*, Coastguard replied *"roger"*. Ken the Tea Pot being No 11 was by now an experienced reserve crew member. If you needed anything on the boat doing, you only had to ask Tea Pot, rig for anchor, deploy port side search light, dip the fuel tanks, Ken was there, a most useful hand.

0731 hours, Alan briefed me of his intended daylight search area, we were searching to the east up to 5 miles off shore, he suggested we tasked the ILB on zero at the same time, I knew this was to let the Coastguard know we were not waiting for them to give us a ridiculous search area, which to be fair was not always ridiculous, but most of the them have little knowledge of setting out sensible search area's …. The tide for the last few hours was moving east, so was anything on or just below the surface. We have in the past been tasked with searching up tide of a sensible estimate for a datum, which of course we ignore!

I called up the ILB on zero, *"our search area is from St Anthony to Dodman up to 5 miles off shore, request you do a close inshore search from St Anthony to the Dodman, over"* ILB reply *"roger"*.

Having the ILB in our area made sense. The crew were all very accomplished helmsmen, but the ILB in lumpy weather is definitely a young man's game. The heavy constant slamming would be enough to compress an older man's spine by many inches!

As both boats made to the east we could hear chatter between the Coastguard and *Rescue 193* the search and rescue helicopter from RNAS Culdrose. The air crew like us wanted to be searching at first light.

0758 hours, *Rescue 193* called up the Coastguard *"we have sighted light oil in position 50 degrees 07 north, 005 degrees 01 west, the oil appears to be coming from under the water"*.

Alan called down *"copied that, give me a course for that position please"*.

Pete was on the navigation table, working out the position, Alan came back on the intercom *"I can see Rescue 193, making our way over now"*.

Pete gave two clicks on the intercom button to acknowledge. The lifeboat went to full speed, turning into the sea as we made our way down to *Rescue 193*'s position.

0800 hours from the Coastguard *"did you copy our last with Rescue 193?"* I replied *"yes"* they came back *"go to the datum and investigate, we require a closer look at the oil slick"*.

Pete looked up from the chart table, *"our ETA datum 13 minutes"*.

I relayed this to the Coastguard.

We were half way to the datum when a local fishing boat out searching called us up *"Falmouth Lifeboat this is fishing vessel Sovereign, I will go to the helicopter marker, put my sounder on, then go to the west of there, over*", I replied "*roger, many thanks, we will be with you shortly*".

0816 hours from the Coastguard "*any fishing vessels offering you assistance, accept their offer and assume on scene commander*", I replied "*roger*".

Pete having listened to the Coastguard's transmission, looked up and shook his head, I just smiled. We arrived at the datum, the shine from the oil slick was easy to spot. Alan followed it down to the 2D buoy. I called up the Coastguard to keep them up to speed on what was a fast moving development, we moved up to the datum.

From *Rescue 193* "*request water depth at the datum*", Pete looked at the echo sounder and called out 66 feet, I relayed this to *Rescue 193*.

Alan called Tim out from the wheelhouse and asked him to take a look at the oil slick. I stood at the aft wheelhouse door to listen to the conversation on the after deck, Tim said to Alan "*that's not diesel that's light oil, diesel has its own shimmer and you would be able to smell it too*".

Alan and Ken nodded; Alan looked over to me and said "*relay that to the Coastguard please*". I gave a single nod and went back to my seat "*Falmouth Coastguard this is Falmouth Lifeboat, we have two engineers on board, we are of the opinion that the oil is light oil and not diesel oil, and there is no shimmer in the water normally found with diesel oil, over*" they replied "*roger all copied*".

0826 hours, *Rescue 193* came on zero immediately "*we copied your last to the Coastguard, we are off to investigate other sightings*" I replied "*all copied*".

0829 hours, fishing vessel *Sovereign* called us up "*can you give me the most westerly point of the slick, I think the source will be at the most westerly point*".

I replied "*we followed the slick up to the datum from 2D buoy, we are of the opinion it is light oil not diesel*".

Sovereign replied "*understood, can you give me instructions?*" I asked them "*do you know of Karen Marie's fishing area?*" Sovereign replied "*no, I know of the boat but not her fishing area or where she works her gear*".

I replied "*roger stand by on 67 please*" they replied "*OK 67*".

0832 hours I called up the Coastguard to update them on the slick "*the slick is very large and light oil not diesel oil, stretching from the 2D buoy up to the datum, over*".

4 minutes later 0836 hours the ILB called up "*at Pendower, negative result proceeding*", Alan clicked twice to acknowledge that he heard OK.

It was the ILB busy doing its own thing; they didn't need any instructions from us.

0837 hours the Coastguard called up "*when the helo returns to you they are willing to put a diver down your anchor rope to do a sea bed search, the sector officer suggests you go to a position at the start of the slick*" I replied "*roger, we will go to the 2D buoy*".

Alan called down, "*you could release Sovereign and thank them for their help*" I replied "*will do*".

0840 hours to fishing vessel *Sovereign* on channel 67, "*we are going to liaise with the helo, for his diver to do a search, if you can carry on about your business and keep a sharp eye out, and from the Coxswain thank you very much for your help*" they replied "*our pleasure, good luck with the search, we will be working up to the east and listening on channel 8*" I replied "*roger thank you sir, it is very much appreciated, out*".

We hung around the 2D buoy waiting for *Rescue 193* to appear, we knew they went west down towards Blackhead, the most likely place *Karen Marie* came to grief… if she did.

0910 hours we copied *Rescue 193's* transmission to the Coastguard "*suggest you send Falmouth Lifeboat around to Blackhead to assist our search, we have spotted some wreckage*"

0911 hours, I chipped in "*Coastguard, copied your last with Rescue 193, we are proceeding to Blackhead, we have our Y-boat that is able to recover any wreckage close to shore*", they replied "*stand by … yes if you are happy with the conditions please proceed down to Mullion mobile*".

0915 hours from the Coastguard "*fresh oil has been sighted on the surface in position 50° degrees north 005 degrees 08 west, Rescue 193 is on scene.*"

This was just west of Blackhead, where we expect the seas were worse yesterday afternoon/ evening.

0917 hours to the Coastguard "*our ETA on scene 0945 hours*" the Coastguard acknowledged "*all copied*".

It was a long punchy run down to Blackhead, everyone piles into the wheelhouse, Pete took the wheel from the steering position, we all hung on wherever we could for the 30 minute flat out full speed run. We rounded Blackhead and made our way towards the helicopter that was hovering low close to shore.

Mullion mobile, the local Coastguard for the area called up 0945 hours "*are you aware the Jay Rock is ahead of you, some way off?*"

We were aware of the Jay, it sticks out of nowhere some way off the shore and not where you would expect it, visible at low tide, I replied "*yes we are aware, but thank you for mentioning it, we have our Y-boat available if you want it, over*" Mullion mobile replied "*roger, we will let you know*".

We slowed down in the area the helicopter was working, the wheelhouse emptied, I was the only one left, the wireless was red hot, the Arun cruising at tick over, around 6 knots, beam to the sea was rolling like a pig, fresh air would have been great, but no chance.

By now Falmouth Cliff Rescue had arrived opposite the search area, their blue flashing light on their Land Rover prominent on the track at the top of the cliffs.

1009 hours, Falmouth Zulu (their call sign) called us up on channel zero "*move inshore we are in a position 10 o'clock from you, there is wreckage, please investigate*".

I replied "*will do*", Alan turned the boat towards the shore and moved in slowly towards some old net floating on the surface, John recovered it onto the after deck.

I relayed to Falmouth Zulu, "*it is some old netting, we have recovered it, over*" they replied "*roger*".

1010 hours from Falmouth Zulu "*Rescue 193 asks for an accurate depth reading at the datum for their divers*" I replied "*roger, we will make our way over to the datum and take a sounding, do you have an accurate position?*"

Zulu replied "*49 degrees 59.70 north, 005 degrees 08.15 west*". I replied "*roger*".

1026 hours, the Coastguard called "*can we have the sea temperature at the datum please*".

We don't carry a thermometer for measuring sea temperature, except the one in the medical kit, I guess we could have lowered it into the sea somehow but we don't have time to bugger about, I called Alan on the intercom "*what do you think?*" He replied "*tell them we estimate between 6 and 7 degrees*".

I called the Coastguard and gave them our best estimate. By now *Rescue 193* was on route back to refuel and pick up 2 divers.

We arrived at the datum, on the echo sounder we could see clearly what looked like a wreck on the sea bed, it must be the *Karen Marie*, we passed over it a couple of times and recorded the depths, also on paper print out from the sounder so we could be accurate.

1029 hours to the Coastguard "*we are now over the datum, we have a steady 116 feet rising sharply to 88 feet when we go over the top of the marker, over*" reply "*roger I will pass to Culdrose*".

1032 hours dive boat *Patrice II* called us up on 16, I replied "*go to channel 12*", "on 12 from *Patrice II* "*are you on the marker? over*" I replied "*yes*", *Patrice II* came back "*we will come over to you*". Channel zero, to the Coastguard "*Patrice II will be on scene in 10 minutes, over*", the Coastguard replied "*roger, does she intend to dive?*" I replied "*I will confirm*".

1033 hours channel 12 to *Patrice II* "*what are your intentions? over*" their reply "*we will put two divers down, they have 12 minutes at the bottom at that depth without de-compression, over*".

Alan chipped in on the intercom "*mention there is a good chance nets will be in the water*".

My reply to *Practice II*, "*be advised that the vessel Karen Marie had up to ten tiers of nets on board when she went to sea, there is a strong possibility of nets in the area, over*" their reply "*nets are no problem for my divers, they are very experienced*", I replied "*roger*".

1035 hours I called the Coastguard on zero "*the Patrice will put two divers down, they have 12 minutes without de-compression, over*", the Coastguard replied "*roger*".

1044 hours to the Coastguard "*the Patrice has arrived on scene*", they replied "*are they aware of the nets*" I replied "*yes the Coxswain has made them very aware of the nets, they are quite happy about that*", Coastguards reply "*thank you*" my reply "*I will keep you closely informed of the dive*". Reply "*thank you*".

The Lizard Lifeboat Station at Kilcobben Cove in 2009 with the relief Tyne class lifeboat *The Lady Rank* 47-011 on the slipway, standing in for the station Tyne *David Robinson* 47-030. Photo: RNLI/Nigel Millard

1051 hours, from the Coastguard *"please advise Patrice that Culdrose would like them to wait until Rescue 193 arrives on scene"*, my reply *"roger"*.

1052 hours, to Patrice on channel 12 *"Culdrose request you stand by until they arrive before diving"* Patrice replied *"my divers have already gone down, my only way of recalling them is with a thunder flash, we have our diving officer on board and all safety measures are observed, I am happy to wait until they return to the surface, it will not be long now"* I replied *"roger"*.

1053 hours, to the Coastguard on channel zero *"the divers are already down, the Patrice has advised she has a diving instructor on board, all safety measures are taken and the divers will be returning to the surface soon"* the Coastguard replied *"roger"*.

We were standing off the datum to give the dive boat *Patrice II* plenty of room. The Lizard Lifeboat joined us after completing their shore search from Kilcobben Cove round to Cadgwith and up to us, the wind was easing slightly and the lifeboat was rolling heavily in the Atlantic swell, as were my guts. I thought I'd pop out and jettison the cup of tea I had some three and a half hours ago, the Lizard was right alongside our port side. *"Mr Price"* one of the crew screamed out, I looked at him, gave him a big grin and said I won't be a moment. I scuttled round to the starboard side and produced a mini tea slick on the water, regained my composure, wiped my chops and moved round the foredeck and back along the port side. I shook hands with three or four of the crew and Phil Burgess the Coxswain, he was chatting with Alan. We had no doubt we had found the *Karen Marie*, we were anxious to find out if there was any sign of their crew.

We were drifting slowly towards the datum, both lifeboats moved off slowly to the West to give the dive boat more sea room.

1059 hours, from *Patrice II* on channel 12 *"How long before Culdrose arrive? We are worried about losing slack water"* I replied *"I'll find out, stand by."* To the Coastguard *"how long before Culdrose arrive? Patrice is concerned about losing slack water, over"* the Coastguard replied *"Culdrose will be airborne at 11.30, over."* I replied *"roger."*

1103 hours, from the Coastguard *"as we understand the Patrice is concerned about losing slack water, we do not want them to stop diving, the decision is entirely theirs"* I replied *"I will relay this now."*

1104 hours, to Patrice *"the Coastguard does not want to stop you diving, the decision is entirely yours"* they replied *"I will wait until my two divers come up and then we will have a chat about it."* I replied *"roger."*

I smiled to myself, the Coastguard *'didn't want to stop Patrice diving, the decision was entirely theirs'*… As if Patrice would ask the Coastguard's advice about diving matters. The divers on board weren't beginners or holiday makers down for a weekends dive, these guys were qualified instructors who knew their stuff. Falmouth area is one of the most popular diving areas in the UK, spring and summer there are dozens of dive boats. We have had lots of shouts for missing divers over the years, some do not end well, and it's usually the inexperienced that get into trouble with spring tides, we can get tides running off the Lizard and Blackhead at 6 to 7 knots, that's about the speed of a small boat running flat out.

On the odd occasion when I have been west of Blackhead fishing in my 21 foot Cygnus fishing boat called 'The African Queen' I've had to go seaward of Blackhead when the tide is running to make any headway.

The African Queen was a good boat; I purchased the hull from Cygnus in Falmouth and fitted it out myself with a Ford diesel lorry engine. It was a heavy boat, the Harbour Master at Coverack was a miserable git, so just to cheer him up I painted large jaws on the bow, it looked great, the Harbour Master didn't think so… which was perfect as far as I was concerned.

The tide at the datum was now on the turn.

1109 hours, from Patrice *"do you want to come over, a bit closer?"* I replied *"roger, coming over now."*

1110 hours a local boat *St Ruan* came up on channel 16 *"Falmouth Lifeboat this is St Ruan on 16 over"* I replied *"go to channel 12, over."* St Ruan came back of 12 *"we are in the area is there anything we can do to help?"* I replied *"not at the moment Sir, from the Coxswain thank you for your offer, can you keep a sharp eye out for any floating wreckage? Over"* they replied *"roger will do."*

We came alongside Patrice II for an update of the dive, they obviously wanted to speak

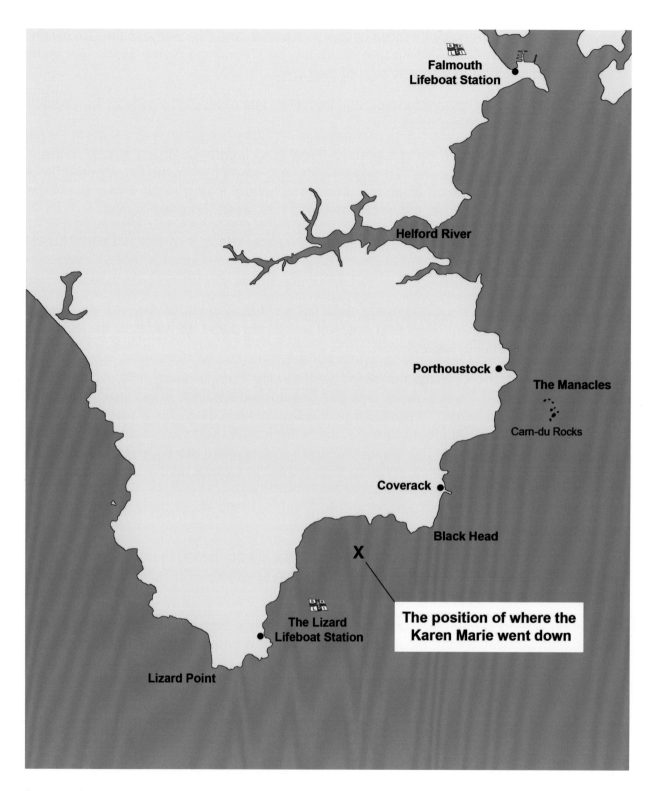

Falmouth
Lifeboat Station

Helford River

Porthoustock ●

The Manacles

Carn-du Rocks

Coverack ●

Black Head

X

The Lizard
Lifeboat Station

Lizard Point

**The position of where the
Karen Marie went down**

face to face rather than over the airwaves.

The skipper of *Patrice II* said to Alan *"my two divers have had a good look around the wreck, it is the boat you are looking for, Red hulled fishing boat, no one on board, no gear on board, we have buoyed the wreck off for Culdrose".*

The mood was sombre, bad news that *Karen Marie* had gone down, no bodies, the seas were big to the east of Blackhead last night, a small 21 foot boat in big seas only takes one or two exceptional waves to fill the boat and she's under water… Too quick for a 'May Day' or to put up a flare, the water is very cold, it doesn't bear thinking about …imagining those moments.

At least we could now plan a search area, looking at the tides and having a datum gives us the start point. The same for the shore parties.

1112 hours to the Coastguard "*the two divers have returned to Patrice, they confirm the wreck is a red hulled fishing boat, there are no persons in the wheelhouse, they have buoyed off the wreck for Culdrose, over*". The Coastguard replied "*will you thank Patrice for us, and will you remain on scene until Culdrose arrive, over*" I replied "*will do*".

1115 hours to Patrice "*go to channel 67*" reply "*channel 67*" "*from the Coastguard and my Coxswain thank you very much for all your help today, it is very much appreciated, over*". Reply "*that's OK, the boat is buoyed off, the buoy is made off to a cleat, there are no nets on board, and there is no gear on board*". I replied "*many thanks for all your help, out*".

1131 hours from the Coastguard "*can we have the depth of water at the datum please*" I replied "*111 feet*".

1140 hours from Rescue 193 to the Coastguard on zero "*we have left Culdrose on route to the datum, our intentions are to drop 2 divers and a Gemini, then return to Culdrose to collect a further two divers, we expect to dive at 1215 local time*".

1153 hours from the Coastguard "*remain on scene until the helicopter arrives, then we will have another task for you*" reply "*roger*".

1155 hours from *St Even* on channel 16 "*Falmouth Lifeboat this is St Evan on channel 16, over*" reply "*go to 67*" reply "*roger, 67*" St Evan to lifeboat on channel 67 "*is there anything we can do before we go in?*" I replied "*negative, thank you very much for your help, it's very much appreciated, the Coxswain sends his regards and thanks, and wishes you a safe journey*" they replied "*we felt we had to do something*" I replied "*roger, we know the feeling well, your presence is very much appreciated*" they replied "*thank you*".

1158 hours from the Coastguard "*we can arrange some food for you if you wish, to collect at Coverack, over*" … Alan chipped in on the intercom "*will this be in the area of our next task?*" … I relayed this to the Coastguard, they replied "*yes*"… I replied "*that would be most welcome*".

Blimey, what a perfect gesture from the Coastguard, to be fair they have teams all along the coast searching, so they know how exhausting the day has been …. So far!

We could see Mullion Mobiles Land Rover on the cliff top, and the search team working the shoreline.

1210 hours from Mullion Mobile on channel zero "*we have spotted an object approximately 400 yards off the shore from our position can you investigate please*" I replied "*roger, will do*".

The area he was talking about was just ahead of us, all eyes on the flying bridge were peeled, the lifeboat took a turn to starboard and slowed, Alan called down "*just 2 dans, heavily weeded*" I relayed, they replied "*roger*".

1225 hours *St Ruan* was a few hundred yards ahead of us, making her way slowly up to Blackhead, she called us up on 16, I sent her to channel 8 *"there is something big and red on the shore close to our position, the Coastguard may not be able to see it from their position, over"* I replied *"I will contact them"*.

1226 hours to Mullion Mobile *"St Ruan has spotted a large red object on the shore just below you, over"*… they replied *"it's a big rusty drum"*.

1226 hours to *St Ruan* *"it's a big rusty drum, Mullion Mobile are aware of it, thanks for calling it in"* St Ruan replied *"roger"*.

1230 hours from the Coastguard *"your next task with Lizard Lifeboat is to search an area as follows… North latitude 50 degrees 05 north, south latitude 49 degrees 58 north, the western edge of the box 4 degrees 55 west, search to the coastline, search half mile tracking"* I replied *"roger"*.

1255 hours to the Coastguard *"we are able to depart the datum now, Rescue 193 is recovering his divers, we can make for Coverack now, over"*.

1330 hours we arrived in Coverack bay, sheltered from the west the sea was slight, we saw nothing on the way down from the datum, the deck crew deployed the anchor and prepared the *Y-boat* to go ashore and collect the pasties from the Coastguard, I was on the afterdeck, Alan said *"Chris take Glen and pick up the pasties, I expect that is what the Coastguard have for us"* …. I could see the Coastguard's Land Rover outside the Paris Hotel; I expect they ordered them from the pub.

Ken the Tea Pot had the *Y-boat* up alongside the lifeboat, Glen and myself jumped in, I set the throttle to half throttle, pulled out the choke, two slow pulls, quick check there was plenty of room for a violent pull without elbowing Glen in the gob, one pull the engine burst into life, Tim was hanging over the rail, gave me a wink and a grin, I gave him a couple of nods to say impressed with the way he looks after the lifeboat kit, with only one 15 horsepower outboard engine it needs to be super reliable.

We motored into the harbour, Glen climbed the ladder onto the quay and walked up to the Paris door, out came the Coastguard clutching a big cardboard box, it contained pasties and cans of coke.

Back to the boat and into the wheelhouse, two or three from The Lizard boat were inside, (The Lizard Lifeboat was tied up alongside).

Glen handed out the pasties, leaving Lizard's pasties in the box. I took one and stashed it in the radio log drawer, there was no way I was going to eat it, we had a big search ahead of us and it was still lumpy out there, eating a whole pasty and then planting it on the afterdeck an hour later was not an option, I much prefer to just feel rough and get on with it.

The new search area was mapped out on the chart, the Lizard Lifeboat were happy to take the western side of the box, Falmouth to take the east, we would work up into Falmouth bay area. Pete and Alan agreed that to cover the search area will take just under two hours, we all shook hands with the Lizard crew and prepared the boats to leave the shelter of Coverack bay and make our way out to the search area.

1415 hours to the Coastguard " *We are in Coverack bay with Lizard lifeboat, just organising how we are going to tackle the search area, we should begin in about 5 minutes, over*" reply "*roger*".

1425 hours, to the Coastguard "*we are starting our search now, leaving Coverack bay, steering 095 degrees, we will take the box to the east, Lizard to the west*" reply "*roger*".

Both boats steamed out of Coverack bay, when it was time to go our separate ways to begin the first leg we all waved to each other. There is rivalry between stations but when we are working together we are all brothers with a common cause.

We surfed up our first leg to the west, running with the sea, it was bloody cold, the wind was whistling into the wheelhouse due to the aft wheelhouse door being pinned opened, cold air with a hint of exhaust fumes, something you get used to over the years.

1500 hours, to the Coastguard "*sit rep, we are on the second leg of our search, entering the Manacles, over*" reply "*roger*".

All eyes on the flying bridge and top of the lifeboat were peeled, looking for anything unusual, the state of the sea was slowly improving, there were no smooth patches so no chances of seeing anything just below the surface, so very little chance of spotting a body… and not smooth enough for me to scoff my pasty!

1525 hours, to the Coastguard "*we are on the perimeter of our box running north, getting ready to take our last leg west to Nare Point, over*" reply "*roger*".

Our last leg from Falmouth to Nare Point revealed nothing, listening to the updates from The Lizard Lifeboat to the Coastguard, they had the same luck as us… None.

1542 hours, Alan called down from the flying bridge, "*Chris, we are nearly at the end of our search pattern, the light will be fading soon, advise the Coastguard we have completed our search and returning to station*" I replied "*will do*".

1545 hours, to the Coastguard "*we have completed our search pattern, returning to the station*" they replied "*roger, many thanks for your help throughout the night*" they were nice words I thought, I replied with "*it's been a pleasure to work with you and the shore parties, you have done an excellent job*" the Coastguard replied "*thank you*".

To be fair the last 16 odd hours have been tough for everyone. A horrible night weather wise, and a job that after the first two or three hours looked like it was not going to end well.

The loss of two young fishermen is not uncommon off the shores of Devon and Cornwall, winter seas can grow quickly and catch small craft out, their need to set and recover gear is driven by living costs as well as the cost of keeping a small boat running, and of course gear wears out and gets lost.

The run back to Falmouth was quiet, apart from the roar of the Caterpillar diesels.

I looked out of the forward port window, I could see a Coastguard Land Rover with its blue light flashing on the cliffs and two or three Coastguards clambering over the rocks, I expect Henry was there looking after his boys, they too had been out for over 14 hours, right through the night, freezing rain, big winds, they will be as knackered as I felt.

As we turned slowly into Falmouth, under the Coastguard station I noticed a Coastguard standing on a fire escape door at the top of the station building waving at us, I piped up to the flying bridge on the intercoms, "*Coastguard waving*" Alan came back "*we see him*".

I looked through the aft wheelhouse door, three of the crew were waving from the after deck, I knew Alan and those on the flying bridge would be waving too, Alan gave them a blast on the lifeboat fog horn.

Alan came into the wheelhouse and said "*check with the boathouse and see if we can refuel at Falmouth Oil Services*" this made sense as the tide was right out and handling the fuel line is more difficult from our supply tank when the lifeboat is well below the top of the quay.

The boat house came back to advise "*they are waiting for you*".

1656 hours to the Coastguard "*we are alongside Falmouth Oil Services in the docks, refuelling*" reply "*roger*".

Tim was whizzing around the deck opening the fuel caps on both sides, then down below to open the valves between port and starboard tanks, this allows both tanks to fill from one side.

As soon as he was happy we were full he indicated to Glen on the fuel hose to stop pumping by using the gesture where one cuts one's own throat.

With all valves closed Tim came into the wheelhouse "*finished fuelling*", Alan nodded and went up to the flying bridge and took us back to our moorings.

"*Finished with main engines*" from the flying bridge. The boys put the covers on, stowed the fenders and generally tidied up the deck, I swept up the remaining crumbs of the McVities from the radio table, made a note of the shut down time on my log and called up the Coastguard… and retrieved my pasty from the radio log drawer.

1715 hours on channel zero, "*back on our moorings, switching off the wireless, it's been a pleasure working with you, we are all sorry we didn't get a good result, wish you a better evening, over*". They replied "*roger, thank you for all you have done*".

That last transmission brought a lump up into my throat; it had been a shit day with a shit outcome.

After around 17 hours at sea we mustered on the aft deck waiting for Clifford to arrive with the boarding boat. I thought what must it be like back in the homes of the lost fisherman Tony and Peter, I wish we could have found them, they are out there somewhere.

Most overdue fishing boats shouts end well, the crew are in the local pub and have not bothered or forgotten to phone home.

The search for the missing crew from small vessels that have sunk in bad weather is always going to be a long job. In the winter immersion in the sea without appropriate clothing and life jacket, the chances of lasting more than a few minutes is slim.

At the time of this shout fishermen didn't often wear lifejackets, they're cumbersome and interfered with their work, luckily times have moved on, lifejacket technology has improved considerably and fishermen have been educated, they know the occupation is the most dangerous there is, and most have lost good friends to the sea.

At least with a lifejacket that functions there is a chance we will find the wearer alive, and if not a very good chance we will find the body.

For those left behind the loss is horrendous, but no body to bury more than doubles the grief.

I have been to several memorial services for fisherman that have been lost at the sea, the grief is tangible and cuts you in half, not what you join the RNLI for, but it comes with the territory.

Just returned from the shout, Clifford sat in the chair having tied the boarding boat alongside the lifeboat, Tim recording the engine oil pressures and filling in the engines record, myself closing down with the Coastguard. Tim and me both wearing our "Ted Tuckerman's". Note the curtain by Cliffords head, this can be drawn at night time to maintain night vision in the wheel house when lights are required in the aft of the wheel house, for instance when the lifeboat doctor is attending to a patient.
Photo: Falmouth RNLI Collection

Elizabeth Ann berthed at her pontoon at Falmouth's new lifeboat station which opened in 1994. The station's boarding boat is also tied up alongside the pontoon. Photos: Falmouth RNLI Collection

DI'S EXERCISE

Late September, the silly season is nearly over, holiday makers and fine weather yachtsmen laying up their speed boats and yachts, clocks go back in 4 weeks. Winter brings with it a different type of lifeboat shout, typical shouts are commercial vessels getting into trouble, or smaller fishing boats desperate to retrieve gear as a gale approaches, often leaving it to the last minute.

The phone rang at work mid Monday afternoon, it was Alan "*DI's exercise Thursday 1730 hours at the boathouse, we are looking to give the boat a run tomorrow 1730 hours can you make it*"?... "*of course, see you tomorrow*" I replied.

The DI's exercise is a pretty important event at a lifeboat station. The gear, the boat, boathouse and crew get a thorough examination. The RNLI invests public money, on larger stations like Falmouth it runs into millions of pounds! They have an obligation to ensure everything is top notch!

Over the years that I was on the lifeboat the South West region has had a few District Inspectors (now known as Divisional Inspectors). They come in all shapes and sizes, all very skilled at their jobs and know everything about lifeboats of all types, all equipment and, most importantly, how to interface with the Coxswain and crew who are a complete spectrum of types and temperaments!... Our DI Captain Hugh Fogarty was no exception, a big bloke, full beard, big hands, a firm handshake.

He would only be happy if everything at the Falmouth station was perfect, it was our job to make sure it was so!

All Coxswains and crews have learnt that there is no way you can get anything past a DI. Hugh is a man of the sea, having started boating on Lake

Captain Hugh Fogerty, not an easy face to read, his job as DI is to make sure the lifeboat and crew are perfect and ready to face any situation. A smile at the end of a DI's exercise means we have passed!
Photo: Nathan Williams

Victoria as a boy. On leaving school he joined a General Cargo company and worked his way through a Merchant Navy apprenticeship and the various ranks of Deck Officer until he was made Master (Captain) at the age of 30. As a Master Mariner with command experience he then joined the RNLI's Operations Department as a Lifeboat Inspector.

We were lucky to have Hugh as our DI, as was every station in the South West. On a DI exercise he observes and coaches, setting scenarios or advising the Coxswain as to what he wants to happen. He puts the Coxswain and crew under extreme pressure, often he will ask the Coxswain to take a back seat and put one of the crew in charge, watching carefully how the team adapts and functions when things are turned upside down.

In Falmouth we have been so lucky. Every Coxswain I have served under requires and expects every main crew member to be able to do every job on the boat, including being in command and making decisions as circumstances dictate. Just as on a shout, on an exercise nobody knows what is going to happen.

Tuesday late afternoon I left work early to get to the boathouse by 1700 hours. Tim had spent all day checking the boathouse records, stores, machinery, crew kit including the lifejackets, all inflated to check they hold air. The gear on the boat has to be checked, first aid kits, firefighting equipment, extinguishers 'in test date', ropes, charts, tools, just about everything you could think of, it all had to be in the right place and in perfect working order, lives depended on it. A lot of responsibility considering the gear could be put to test at any time in any weather!

"Alright Tim"? He replied with a smile *"so far"* , *"there is nothing I haven't looked at, tested and inspected, just need to make sure it's perfect for Thursday's DI's exercise"*.

"Need a hand with anything"? I said *"no everything in the boathouse is OK, I just need to run the salvage pump and Y-boat this evening, I'll ask Al if we can fit those in with the exercise"*.

The rest of the crew began to arrive, John the 2nd Mechanic, Alan, Roger, Pete and Mark.

Alan called everyone together *"we are going to run out into the bay and run all the boats gear, I've no idea what Hugh has got in store for us on Thursday, I just want to make sure everything is working, Tim wants the Y-boat and bilge pump run, I'm looking at anchoring, emergency steering and fire in the engine room, if we have time for anything else we can fit it in, I want to be back by eight"*.

We all nodded in agreement and went down to the changing room to kit up.

The new boathouse was great, the Arun was on the pontoon right next to the boathouse, much faster for a shout… out of the boathouse, down the gang plank and on board, no run out in the boarding boat, into the wheelhouse nice and dry!

Normal routine to flash the boat up, Roger took the wheel and took us into Falmouth Bay. As we passed the docks, Alan briefed the crew, *"as soon as we get out into the bay I want to do a fire in the engine room, and rig for emergency steering, everyone happy"*?

"Yes" everyone replied.

Tim had passed the crew list and advised the Coastguard we were on exercise in Falmouth Bay for the next couple of hours, and available if required.

I went up to the *Y-boat* with Mark to prepare it for launching, we took the cover off and stowed it behind the steering position and removed the lashings, just leaving a couple of straps in place to hold it in position until we were ready to rig the gantry so we could get it into the water.

Everything else in the wheelhouse was running smoothly, radar, navigation gear, wireless; both engines were purring away, the boat was in tip top condition.

1830 hours, we had plenty of sea room, Alan said to Roger *"this will do us, stop engines, fire in the engine room please"*.

Roger put the throttles into neutral, Tim pressed both stop buttons and engines went silent, then he pressed the fire alarm, the alarm was a noisy bell, no mistaking what it meant!

First thing to happen, the Mechanic (Tim) calls out *'fire in the engine room'* at the top of his voice. The crew leap into action, into the tiller flat, electrics off, then back up into the wheelhouse, first job is to starve the fire of oxygen, so shut all doors and inlets. Outside on deck there are a series of flaps that have to be shut and vents that have to be plugged up. The air is drawn in through air intakes out on deck. They are designed to close or seal automatically in the unlikely event of a capsize, but they are also designed to only take in air and not salt water, of which there is plenty when large waves break over the boat when running at full speed into a big sea.

Air intakes have weighted flaps that shut when the boat is upside down, so they have to be shut manually as we are the right way up. Some of the intakes have large ping pong balls that seal the holes when under water, others need specially shaped bungs put into the intake holes to seal them and deny the fire the oxygen it requires to keep it going.

Engine room view leading through to the tiller flat. Photo: Gulf Group Marine Brokers Ltd

In the wheelhouse wooden plugs for port and starboard are kept in a special locker, each plug numbered to identify its respective hole. There are also a couple of air intakes in the foredeck rope lockers that must not be forgotten to be closed.

The whole crew know exactly where everything goes, if two of the crew undertake to 'close vents' one walks up the port side and the other the starboard, then go down the side they didn't plug to check his crewmate's work.

As the deck crew deal with closing off all sources of oxygen for the fire the Mechanics rig the breathing apparatus for a volunteer to descend into the tiller flat.

By now we have had a head count, and usually for the exercise one crewman is missing.

The breathing apparatus is a cumbersome contraption, but it actually works. The 'volunteer' puts on the face mask, similar to a scuba mask but with a hole to plug in the air hose, a long heavy rubber hose with a valve that allows you to breath in air from the pipe but not to blow air back out though the pipe.

Lifeboat jacket done up, leather gloves on, handheld torch on, face mask on, hose connected, in position at the top of the steps to the tiller flat, now already to go.

First the Mechanic runs through the signalling drill, along with the air hose there is a rope

Exercise at Poole with a casualty in a Neil Robertson stretcher Photo: RNLI/Nigel Millard

to signal the crew in the wheelhouse what you need: 1 tug for more hose, 2 tugs for more air, and 3 tugs for "get me out". Once the volunteer has heard the three signals he gives the thumbs up and is ready to go.

Tiller flat hatch is opened, total darkness below, down goes the crewman, the Mechanics feed the rope and airline down, the other end of the airline is fed through a small gap in the aft wheelhouse door so there is plenty of fresh air for the airline. It would be no good breathing in smoky air that might be in the wheelhouse. We can see the torch light is now being shone through the engine room door window.

While this is going on one of the crew kinks the hose to starve the volunteer of air, two sharp tugs on the rope soon occurs, the hose is unkinked and the air supply is restored.

"Fire is out, crewman unconscious in the engine room" is shouted from below.

Tim goes down into the tiller flat, switches on the electrics, the fans start up, he helps the volunteer remove his breathing apparatus and checks through the engine room door that it is clear to open the door and check the casualty.

For the exercise the crewman is unconscious and must be retrieved using the Neil Robertson stretcher.

This is a great bit of kit, but not if you are in it! A canvas and wooden slat contraption, a full length re-enforced straight jacket when it is wrapped around the casualty and the buckles are buckled up! You literally cannot move, even worse if your arms are by your side when it's wrapped around you, the good thing is that the wooden slats protect you and keep your back from bending.

It allows you to be lifted in a horizontal position just like an ordinary stretcher or, for use in confined spaces like an engine room in a boat, you can be lifted vertically through a small hatch. A very clever design and one of the essential stretchers an off shore lifeboat carries, the other being a 'scoop stretcher', more like a conventional stretcher but with sides to stop you from sliding out. The hard plastic material means it can be used to float under a casualty in the water. They can then be lifted out of the water in a horizontal position should their condition require this type of handling.

The fire in the engine room exercise stopped short of actually deploying the Neil Robertson, partly due to a lot more kit needing to be tested, and partly because the casualty was John (the winch) a huge man, solid muscle, 6 foot odd tall and probably 16 stone if he was an ounce, I'm not sure if the Neil Robertson would actually go around him!

The next job was to rig for emergency steering. The two rudders, situated below the water (obviously) and just behind the propellers are linked together and normally moved with a hydraulic ram. When this fails for whatever reason, the hydraulic link is uncoupled and a Mechanical arm is rigged.

To do this the hatch on the after deck is unlocked and lifted, Tim goes down into the small steering gear compartment and pushes up the 'emergency tiller arm', a steel contraption that has a shaft attached. Directly above the rudder stock is a hole in the deck, normally sealed with a big brass screw plug, with the plug removed the emergency tiller arm can be connected to the rudder. A threaded screw collar on the contraption stops sea water getting into the compartment.

On deck the arm attached to the shaft, which is about three feet long, is lying just above the deck, pointing towards the aft wheelhouse door. When in line with the boat (fore and aft) the rudders are central, or 'mid ships', where they need to be for the boat to steer in a straight line.

Two ropes are attached, one held by a crewman on the after deck port side, and the other by a crewman on the starboard side.

To turn the boat to starboard when under way, the crewman on the portside pulls the emergency steering arm to his side, and to turn to port the starboard man pulls.

With the lifeboat under way at full speed the Coxswain can call 10 degrees to port, midships, 10 degrees to starboard and so on, a Heath Robinson contraption, but it works and gives the Coxswain full control.

With proper steering restored, the last two jobs before returning to the boathouse were to run the Y-boat and salvage pump.

The salvage pump is a petrol engine with a pump attached, stowed in a big watertight orange drum, situated just outside the aft wheelhouse door.

We have used it countless times to help pump out flooded boats, it's a great bit of kit. It can be passed to a vessel in most sea conditions. If it is too rough to go alongside a casualty to pass directly across it can be floated, in the big orange watertight drum, with a heaving line and the casualty pulls it across to themselves and brings it on board.

Members of Falmouth lifeboat crew 1998. Left to right: John Murray; Carl Beardmore; Nick Lewis; Ben Rowe; Alan Rowe; Coxswain Alan Barnes; Snowy Angove; Chris Price; David Proud; Alan Blakely; Jonathon Blakeston, Ken Avis, Geoff Gill; Dr Richard James. Photo: Jon Crane

It's easy to use, noisy, but very effective. A large pipe is attached with a big filter attached to the end, full of small holes to make sure if a trawler is pumping out its flooded bilge, that it does not suck up a pile of floating cloth or other pieces of rubbish that could be sucked into the pump and bugger it up.

On one occasion, a year or two ago we were tasked to a small speed boat that was taking in water, they put out a mayday for a lifeboat to help them. It was mid-afternoon in the summer, they had hit a submerged rock just off the Helford river. We came alongside and took the two occupants off the speed boat. Tim had the salvage pump all ready, he leapt into the half submerged boat which had a small open cabin at the front and an aft seating area with the cushions floating in the water as the boat was half full.

Two of us passed the bilge pump across, Tim placed the pump on the flat section at the stern of the speedboat, tugged on the starting cord and the pump roared into life. He put the pipe with the filter into the water that was now more than half way full up the inside of the speed boat.

A few minutes went by, the water from the pump was pouring over the stern, but not fast enough to keep up with the water coming in.

Tim was up to his waist in water in the speed boat, I was keeping an eye on the sea that was lapping against the stern of the boat, we had it held alongside the lifeboat with one rope from the bow and the other from the stern.

I was watching the stern getting lower in the water, I noticed as the waves were almost about to lap over the stern of the boat it was about to go under.

I shouted out "*Tim*", we were only about four feet from each other, me on the side deck of the lifeboat and Tim up to his waist in the speed boat "*get out now*" I shouted, looking him straight in the eyes, "*what about the salvage pump?*" he shouted back. I looked at the wave that was just about to roll right over the stern, I screamed "*Now! "*. As he clambered aboard the lifeboat the stern of the speed boat went under and the boat flipped over. Tim looked back just in time to see the salvage pump disappear into the drink, I grabbed the strap at the back of his lifejacket to help him over the lifeboat rail, as he looked at me I said "*bugger the salvage pump, you nearly went down with it*"!

We don't make a habit of losing valuable gear, but sometimes you don't have the luxury of time, you have to know when to move, to dither can be fatal!

Over the years we have lost two or three salvage pumps. Normally when they are used in an emergency things are critical, our focus is on saving lives first, boats second... always in that order.

Anyway, back to the exercise! Whilst the mechanics prepared the salvage pump for a run on the after deck, it got a little crowded as three of us prepared to launch the *Y-boat*. We pulled the frame out from under the *Y-boat* on top of the wheelhouse, the frame slides out to its stop, the end is lowered to the after deck railing and forms a slide for the *Y-boat* to slide down to the back end of the lifeboat. A second smaller frame is locked on to the stern rail of the lifeboat and lowered into the sea, we now have a ramp from the top of the wheelhouse right down over the after deck and into the sea.

Time to lower the *Y-boat* down and get it ready for a spin, as expected everything flashed up perfectly. A quick run around and the Y-boat was recovered. Meanwhile the salvage pump had worked perfectly, Tim carefully stowed it, he was happy it was going to work equally perfectly when it was next needed whether it be that night to pump out a boat or Thursday on the DI's exercise, if it was asked for.

With everything checked and tested correctly, Tim flashed up the main engines and we made our way slowly back into the harbour while all the kit was wiped dry and carefully stowed, ready for Thursday.

With the lifeboat refuelled and ready for service it was 2030 hours exactly, perfect timing, back into the boat house, all the kit neatly hung up, boots upside down in their slots, Tim came into the Kit room when everyone had sloped off for a beer, adjusting hangers, getting everything perfectly inline. The DI, Hugh, was due at the boathouse in the morning to look at boathouse records to make sure everything was up to date, and check all the boathouse kit like lifejackets, Personal Protective Equipment, spares etc . Once the boathouse was declared in good order, all focus was on the lifeboat.

When Hugh got on board the boat absolutely everything was checked, flares in date, ropes removed from lockers and inspected from end to end to make sure they were in perfect order, every single thing has to be perfect, Hugh is fussy, very fussy, "OK" is not acceptable, it has to be perfect!

Thursday afternoon soon arrived; I arrived at the boathouse early, 1700 hours, better to be half an hour early than one minute late!

Hugh stood in the door way to the Mechanics room, "*Mr Price*" out came a huge hand, when I shake hands with a firm hand shaker I look carefully at the hand, then like lightening I plunge my hand forward to ensure we lock in a good handshake. I squeeze as hard as I can, it's a bit of a squeezing competition, a couple of seconds then break free, hand survived! The worst thing is to put your hand forward slowly and the vice grip of the greeter grasps the four fingers and squeezes them, leaving you sinking to your knees in agony.

Well, having survived each other's squeezing contest, and eye contact, I looked past Hugh's shoulder to Tim at the back of the room. I gave him my question mark look to receive both thumbs up, a signal that normally indicated we have water coming out of both lifeboat engines…. Obviously not the case this time but with both thumbs up and a beaming face it meant Tim has had a good day and Hugh was impressed.

The main crew began arriving, getting their kit on and preparing for the exercise, no one having any idea what the DI had planned.

It was a perfect evening, reasonably warm, almost flat calm sea, one thing for sure; everyone will be working flat out for the next two and a half hours!

Hugh and Alan were having a chat upstairs in the crew room, the rest of us now all kitted up made our way down the gangway onto the pontoon, and onto the lifeboat.

Tim flashed up the engines, the rest of us moved around the boat to make sure everything was perfect, eventually Hugh and Alan came down the pontoon, onto the lifeboat and into the wheelhouse.

We all gathered around Alan to find out what Hugh had in store for us, "*Pete you're in charge of the boat, we need to make our way into the bay, Hugh will let us know what he wants, everyone happy*"? Alan said, everyone nodded and went to their stations, three of us went on deck and let go the ropes that held the lifeboat alongside the pontoon, then the bow and stern ropes, Pete took the boat away from the pontoon and then out past the docks and into the open sea.

Once clear of the docks Pete put the throttles down and we were away. I looked in through the aft wheelhouse door and noticed Hugh was alongside the stretcher position, getting his dry suit on, we all knew this would happen. On every daylight DI exercise in reasonable weather one thing you can bank on is that Hugh will put on a dry suit. He stepped out onto the after deck just like Jo Cool, "*I'll just wander around the boat, just ignore me*" he said… As if we didn't all know that as soon as Hugh thinks no one is looking he would catapult himself over board to see if we noticed he was no longer on board.

To help pick a moment we would all look busy, with eyes looking forward, I went into the wheelhouse, crouched down by the tea urn and kept an eye on the after deck…within a minute or so Hugh dashed across the after deck and like an Olympian flew over the stern, to disappear in the wake of the lifeboat.

I rushed out of the wheelhouse and screamed *"man overboard"* pointing with arm outstretched, at the same time two of the crew up on the flying bridge did exactly the same *"man overboard"*.

As soon as the Coxswain hears these dreaded words he instinctively looks towards the *'shouter'* for the direction of the man in the water... obviously astern as we were at full speed of 18 knots!

To turn any vessel around and retrace one's path on the original course line one needs to execute a *'Williamson's Turn'*. The helm is put hard over one way and held there until the boat's heading has changed by 60° and then turn the helm hard over the other way and keep it there until the boat comes round to the reciprocal of the original course. All things being equal you will find yourself heading directly along the line of your own wake.

There he is, life jacket inflated bobbing around, Hugh thought he caught us out... no chance. Years later Hugh actually told me that he always alerted one crew member to his intentions just in case he did manage to catch the rest of the crew out. Some years earlier one of his colleagues had spent two progressively more anxious hours bobbing around in the English Channel after slipping unnoticed over the side. When he was eventually missed by the crew a full scale Search & Rescue operation was instigated - red faces all round!

Pete brought the Arun alongside Hugh as we rigged the gantry on the port side, getting ready to recover him. As expected Hugh did nothing to help us, he just lay there, we had to get a lifting strop around him, clip this to the lifting carabiner on the gantry, then with the block and tackle to help reduce the weight (Hugh was not skinny!) two of us pulled on the rope, it was a struggle, Tim emerged from the wheelhouse he said, *"want a hand?"*, *"get on the rope"* Pete said as he leaned over the railings on the flying bridge.

The three of us got Hugh over the railings and lowered him onto the side deck... he was still playing unconscious.

I said to Tim *"get the scoop stretcher we will get him onto the after deck"*... I guess this was what Hugh wanted to hear, even if not he did not relish being heaved into a scoop stretcher, anyway he made an instant recovery and said *"let's have a chat on the after deck"*.

We all stood around Hugh for the briefing, hoping he was not unhappy, Alan was there, Pete came down from the flying bridge, we all listened as Hugh explained *"that went well, we will try it again, this time with a crew member in the dry suit, when approaching a casualty in the water, if he or she is face down the first thing to do is to turn them over and give them a quick puff of air, OK"?*

We all said *"yes"* at the same time, Pete looked at me, he didn't say anything, I curled my bottom lip and said OK, he had asked me with the look to get a dry suit on. I didn't mind the action, but the dry suit with tight rubber neck seal was like walking around with someone trying to strangle you, also it gets bloody hot sealed in a rubber over suit.

Pete took the boat up to about half speed, Hugh stepped outside the lifeboats rail, looked at everyone, gave me the *'big eye'* then fell off the stern like a log, splash and as we were moving at around ten knots was disappearing quickly, *"man overboard"* we all shouted, as the boat turned to starboard two of us walked around the starboard side towards the

Inside the wheelhouse on the Holyhead Arun class all-weather lifeboat *Kenneth Thelwall* 52-37. The orange coloured scoop stretcher can be seen in its storage position. Photo: Royal Bank of Scotland/Rick Tomlinson

bow, never for a second taking our eyes off the casualty, losing sight of the casualty can result in a disaster.

In rougher weather to give younger crew a chance to manoeuvre the lifeboat we will do a man overboard exercise using one of the lifeboat's big fenders, this would disappear from view in every trough and re-appear as it goes over the wave. It is very easy to lose sight of the fender, in choppy seas we could soon be looking everywhere for it, a useful reminder of how important as many of the crew as possible keeps an eye on the casualty!

It was very easy to see Hugh bobbing around, to keep an eye on him the two of us felt our way around the boat as it turned, each with one arm out stretched and pointing.

We both moved around the bow as Pete lined up to bring the boat into a position where we could move slowly towards Hugh and ready to recover on portside.

Hugh was abeam the lifeboat about 10 metres off, I stepped over the railings and launched myself into the water and as I swam towards Hugh. Just before I arrived he turned himself over '*face down*'. I thought right, you said a quick puff of air … I came up to get him, got hold of his head, spun him over leaned forward and blew into his gob! If only you could have taken a picture, I blew bloody hard, difficult to get a '*lip seal*' due to the bushy beard, Hugh's eyes bulged, looked at me as if I was insane… "*you didn't actually need to give me CPR*" he said! I didn't reply, just grinned, trying hard not to burst into laughter… I dragged him back to the side of the lifeboat, I looked up and caught Alan and Pete's eye, they both nodded with big smiles, full approval.

I have recalled the exercise many times, saying Hugh is the only man I have ever kissed on the lips!

As we all gathered on the after deck for a de-briefing, Hugh said *"we don't need to try that again"* everyone burst out laughing, Hugh looked at me and grinned.

"Fire in the engine room" he screamed, he stood back so as not to get crushed in the scramble to put the drill into practice. Tim went below to turn off the electrics, leaving the alarms ringing. As he came back into the wheelhouse he closed the flap to seal off the tiller flat and starve the engine room of oxygen. In the meantime two of the crew were now out on deck shutting off and blocking all air vents.

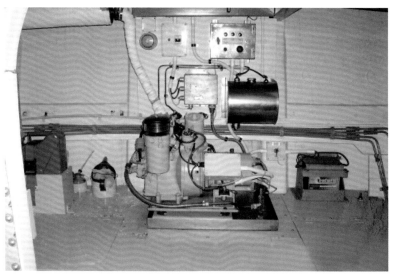

Tiller flat with access through a hatch to the after deck.
Photo: Gulf Group Marine Brokers Ltd

Tim went forward to get the breathing apparatus ready, Hugh and Alan stood by the aft wheelhouse door looking in from the after deck to make sure everyone was busy... the exercise went like clockwork, no one needed to shout out orders. Tim, as Mechanic, was in charge, fire on board was his responsibility, he said to Pete *"made contact with the Coastguard on Zulu"* Pete nodded. "Zulu" is the hand-held radio, this made sure that if we had to take to the liferaft or *Y-boat* we would have contact with the shore and could upgrade our problem from '*advisory*' to '*Mayday*'... of course as this was an exercise, the check with the Coastguard was only for a radio check.

As expected Hugh had all the kit out and tested, very thoroughly, everything went like clockwork. I got my dry suit off, and could breathe normally again, there was a lot of puffing from the crew, there was no time for relaxing.

Eventually 2000 hours, I noticed Hugh was having a word with Alan, I could tell Hugh was happy, not an easy face to read, but when he is not pleased you can just tell.

Alan came into the wheelhouse;

"Right lads, let's get everything put away and tidy the boat up, we will run in, Tim give Clifford a call, we want to re-fuel".

Pete took the boat back in towards the docks at around 14 knots, then when abeam of the Northern Wharf knocked the engines into neutral, as the boat slowed, the wash we were dragging behind us caught up, lifted the stern slightly, then both engines ahead to just over tick over and motor into the harbour doing around 8 knots, no wash, so no complaints from the Pink Gin brigade as they enjoyed the evening sun, having conversations about yah, gosh and cocktail sticks.

As we rounded County Wharf, we could see Clifford on the pontoon, fuel line ready, Pete knocked both engines into neutral, a touch astern on both engines, then back to slow ahead. This is a habit that has been custom through many Coxswains, just to make sure as we approach the pontoon the brakes can be put on and we don't ram it!

With the lifeboat re-fuelled, engines switched off, shut down with the Coastguard we were ashore and into the boat house.

Tim came into the changing room, beaming grin *"the station has passed inspection"* he said *"we are going over to the mission for a pint, everyone is invited"*. The Mission for Seafarers is two hundred yards from the boat house, small bar, plenty of retired sea farers enjoying a pint.

We all strolled over with Hugh, and as usual he got the first round in. A perfect way to end a DI's exercise, boat and boathouse passing inspection with no issues is a testament to Tim and John (our Second Mechanic) and their hard work and dedication to the job. It's easy to take it for granted that everything will work when the boat is launched in heavy weather, failure of a key piece of boats equipment could have terrible consequences for the boat, crew or casualty.

Falmouth is very lucky to have top RNLI inspector making sure our top mechanics keep both the boats at Falmouth in top condition!

Falmouth's Arun class all-weather lifeboat *Elizabeth Ann* on exercise. Photo: Falmouth RNLI Collection

Hugh's RNLI C/V is impressive: 1984/5 Assistant Inspector (Training) operating a mobile unit (MTV3, Radio and Navigation), 1985/90 Deputy Divisional Inspector West (Barrow to Tenby),1990/93 Deputy Divisional Inspector South West (Burry Port to Weymouth), 1993 Deputy Training Officer (Poole), 1994/96 Divisional Inspector South West (Ilfracombe to Selsey), 1996/2001 Staff Officer Training, 2001/04 Staff Officer (ILB), 2004/08 Staff Officer (Fleet), 2008/11 Head of Operations (Operational Support), 20012/14 Head of Operations (Operational Development). Photo: Nathan Williams

Falmouth's Arun class all-weather lifeboat *Elizabeth Ann* on exercise with with the station's Atlantic 21 inshore lifeboat *Elizabeth Bestwick*.

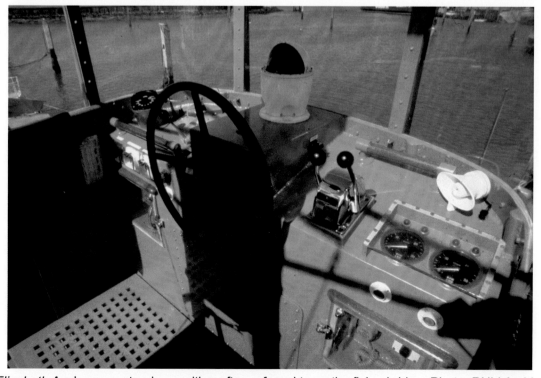

Elizabeth Ann's upper steering position often referred to as the flying bridge. Photo: RNLI Archive

DIVERS OVERDUE

A typical Sunday afternoon, late summer, warm, stiff breeze, a hard work out on the morning lifeboat exercise for a new intake of trainees to give them a flavour of what it takes to crew a large powerful lifeboat.

With a new intake of potential crew we look for strong tides where there are some decent waves, turn the boat side on and stop the engines. When the boat gets a good roll on from side to side we take the trainees below to try some rope work.

In the forepeak it is very uncomfortable I normally wait until it is obvious some are feeling ill, then back up onto the after deck for some fresh air... I feel their pain... and of course I am keen to not embarrass myself by puking! It was a good exercise, it gave the trainees a chance to see how the motion of the boat could affect their ability to contribute to a team, a pleasant run home from the exercise, cups of tea all round, boat put to bed and back to the *'Black Hole'* for lunch.

After an early lunch I wandered down to the quay to see what was going on, plenty of boat movements in the harbour.

Tim was busy in the boathouse checking the new lifejackets, making sure they were packed and folded properly ready for use.

The old lifejacket was brilliant, on long jobs in rough weather, your head could be supported by the ring that went around the back of the neck and, the front protected your chest, a bit like body armour. If you were plunged forward in the wheelhouse when ploughing into a steep wave you just move your arms out of the way and let the front of the lifejacket take the impact.

However, the RNLI had recently introduced a new all-inflatable lifejacket in place of the old Beaufort lifejacket, which had inherent buoyancy as well as the ability to add additional inflated buoyancy. The new lifejacket was instantly named *'the bog seat'*, a U shaped contraption with no inherent buoyancy, relying on CO_2 gas cylinders, a bit like oversized sparklet bulbs, firing off if the jacket was immersed in water, and blowing up the air bags contained within the jacket, great, as long as it inflates!

Tim was inspecting the crew's bog seats, the crew had a lot of faith in the jacket, not because of the design, but because they knew Tim was meticulous with his inspections, and during DI's visits every jacket is inflated and signed off by the DI as all in good working order.

To be fair we only get the best kit issued by the RNLI, never cheap but always the best, and thoroughly tried and tested by boffins and crew alike before being brought into general use.

Tim spun round as I entered the crew room. *"all right Mr P?"* he said ..."*yeah*" I replied, *"did you see the big guy this morning, the one with the tattoos around his neck, and a pig tail hair cut?"* Tim replied *"yes, he looked pretty pissed off when he came up from the forepeak, what did you say to him?"* I smiled. *"Bugger all, we were doing rope work, it didn't take long before he looked like he was going to shoot the cat. Looking at the size of his belly we would all have been hosed down with whatever he had for breakfast, so I suggested we go up on deck to look at the towing gear, I nearly got trodden to death in* *the struggle to get out of the forepeak!"*Tim said *"bet we don't see him again"*… I nodded.

I gave Tim a hand putting everyone's bog seat on their hooks. They are a personal issue item, and are adjusted properly for the various sizes lifeboats crews come in.

"Got their capsules in?" I asked as we hung them up, *"of course"* Tim replied grinning, it was only a couple of months ago that I had a pop at the D I. for requesting the capsules were removed when crew took the *Y-boat* for a run when we were on exercise, I said *"that is dangerous and I want the crew to keep them in"*… the crew on the after deck where the discussion was taking place all stopped talking and looked shocked… it looked like I was about to have a row with the D I.

Luckily District Inspectors are not selected from a line down the job centre, they are carefully selected for their knowledge of the sea and ability to understand the complexities of lifeboats and lifeboat stations. They get to visit a lot of stations and have to work with a complete range of human beings that crew lifeboats, short, tall, thin, fat, loud, quiet, young, older, all dedicated to the job.

"Give me one good reason why they should not be removed Chris" my reply *"for the safety of the wearer"*, the D I frowned, I went on to say *"the Y-boat comes alongside boats, it's never flat calm, a good bang on the head and a crewman could end up in the water unconscious, no buoyancy in the lifejacket, no capsule, and its curtains"*.

The D I raised his open hand, *"case made, happy with that, capsules remain in"* I grinned, held out my hand, the D I grinned, he had a good hand shake. Fast forward from that exercise ….. Tim grinned, *"you are funny about the capsules aren't you"*… *"yeah, fancy a pint"* I said… *"OK I'll lock up"*.

We strolled across to the Chain Locker, a good pub, bit of a stroll but worth it, Tim had a Guinness, I had a pint of orange squash, having stopped drinking alcohol once I joined the crew.

We sat in the bar, talking about diesel engines, how responsive Elizabeth Ann would have been with V8's, and wouldn't it be great if we could get a 20 horse outboard for the *Y-boat*.

Then when you least expect it off go the bleepers. It was 1410 hours, I left what was left of my orange squash, Tim went to gulp the last half of his Guinness, missed with most of it and shot it all down his neck and over his jumper, I nearly peed myself laughing.

We half ran and walked fast past Trago Mills, through Port Pendennis housing complex and into the boat house. By the time we got there, cars were screaming through the town, horns blaring, despite being warned by the Hon Sec to slow down on the roads… not much point in killing someone in a dash to try and save someone else. He had a point.

Alan came out of the engineer's room, he had phoned the Coastguard. *"It's a hurry up job, 2 divers missing in the Manacles, the dive boat cannot locate them, the sea is too choppy, Tim flash up the engines"*.

Tim grabbed his gear, didn't bother to put it on, rushed down the pontoon to the lifeboat to get things started.

I was right behind him with two others from the A team while Alan sorted out the rest of

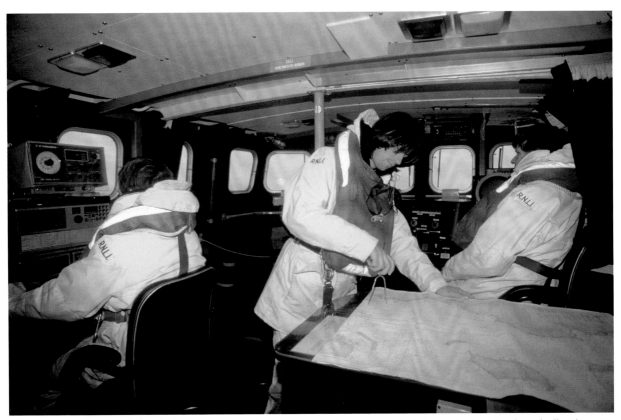

The chart table on Howth's Arun class lifeboat *City of Dublin* 52-35. *Elizabeth Ann* had a similar layout.
Photo: RNLI/ Rick Tomlinson

the crew, the Second Coxswain didn't turn up, and so as the next most senior crewman it was now my job acting as Second Coxswain to look after the general workings of the lifeboat whilst the Coxswain deals with the major decisions.

Being a Sunday afternoon, crew were thin on the ground, Mark and I were untying the springs and stowing ropes, four more crew and Alan came galloping down the pontoon and onto the boat, the engines were running, radar on, "*let go aft*" Alan said as he went up to the flying bridge, the steering position cover was off, we were ready to slip our moorings and a few seconds later we were away.

I went up to the flying bridge, Alan said "*take the boat out of the harbour I'm going below to look at the chart*"… I took the wheel and Alan went below.

By now Tim had passed the crew list and had an update on the job. The dive boat *Explorer* had advised they had two divers missing, a husband and wife. They should have surfaced 25 minutes ago; *Explorer* had done a search but could not see them, so they called the Coastguard who tasked the Lifeboat.

The Arun sits high in the water; the flying bridge is a perfect viewing platform.

If the divers had surfaced 25 minutes ago they will have drifted quite a way in the strong tides that run through the Manacles. Alan is an absolute master on the chart table; he taught all the crew navigation and made sure everyone knew how to navigate. Nearly all the exercises day or night have a navigation element, occasionally we would get the old paper charts out and with a stop watch start '*dead reckoning*' to get to positions marked on the chart, then plot search patterns again with the stop watch, and the steering disabled so emergency steering gear has to be rigged.

Luckily the lifeboat was running as sweet as a nut. Alan had plotted the position he reckoned the divers would be at having taken into account the tides, this would be the datum to begin the search.

I had taken the boat out past Pendennis Point and made a course for the Manacles, Alan came up to the flying bridge, squeezed past me and adjusted the small repeater screen of the plotter on the bridge. The datum was clearly marked, that was the mark we were heading for. My job was below on deck getting things ready for the search, I asked John if he could grab someone and get the *Y-boat* cover off and stowed, just in case we needed it,

Alan Barnes Coxswain 1991-2005. He was awarded an MBE in the Queen's Birthday Honours List in 2005 in recognition of his service with the RNLI. Photo: Simon Culliford

then into the wheelhouse to see that everything was running smoothly.

For a dive boat to not be able to find their divers as they surface is not a good sign. Divers usually carry a long orange balloon they can inflate that sticks out of the sea a couple of feet; you can usually see it quite a way off.

The sea state was choppy, probably marginal for a dive rib due to them being so low in the water.

The Manacles are notorious for claiming the lives of divers, the currents on the sea bed are strong, visibility low when the tide is running, and many divers have come to grief by getting tangled in monofilament nets, all but invisible to divers.

Divers can become disoriented or run out of air, many reasons for getting into serious trouble.

We were now a good 10 minutes into the job, so the two divers are now missing for 35 minutes, this is not good. In the distance we could see the dive boat manoeuvring in the Manacles, but no radio call advising they had found the two missing divers so things were not looking good at all.

We were approaching Porthoustock, Alan called down on the intercom "*everyone in the wheelhouse on deck*", the crew took up position on the deck, bow, and up top to keep a good look out.

The lifeboat slowed, we were entering the search area and making our way to the datum… there was a scream from the flying bridge "*there*", everyone on deck looked up, the outstretched arm could be seen. All eyes followed the direction the arm was pointing in "*there they are*" Mark called out; Alan had taken us straight to the position, a superb navigator! We approached the two balaclava clad heads, I could see them clearly, I knew instinctively there was something wrong.

They looked like a couple of round pot marker buoys, just bobbing in the tide.

Alan carefully manoeuvred the starboard side up to the two divers, three of us went down the three steps from the aft deck to the low cutaway on the starboard side, the low gangway is about a foot above the sea which allows lifeboat crew to get hold of people in the water, I went down onto my knees, one hand on the bottom safety rail and the other outstretched towards the divers.

I looked into the husbands face, he was holding his wife's head above water, he stared straight at me, big eyes, white face, he was in deep shock, he didn't say a thing, our eyes locked together.

I beckoned him towards me with my free hand and said to him "*come to me*", he didn't respond, Alan nudged the lifeboat towards the two of them, then, when the wife was close enough I grabbed her dive bottle carrier and pulled her close to the lifeboats side, we were still staring at each other, I said "*I've got her*"...still no change in his face, blank stare, I cannot imagine what he had been through during the last half an hour or more.

I looked to my left, the inshore lifeboat was manoeuvring by the stern of the lifeboat, Alan called down "*the ILB will take the husband*" one of the lads on the side deck called back "*OK*".

I was hanging on to his wife as hard as I could with one hand, and said to the two with me Mark and Glen, "*we need to get her in now*". I could see her face – Whilst I thought instantly she was dead, I'm certainly no expert, our job was to get her breathing again!

I looked back at the husband "*you can let go now*". There was no change in his face, he kept hold of her, I said a bit more forcefully "*let go now, the ILB will pick you up, we need to get your wife aboard now*".

He let go staring straight at me, he slowly drifted towards the stern of the lifeboat, we kept eye contact for at least ten seconds. I nodded to him, trying to say '*don't worry we have got her*',

She was too heavy to get on board with her dive gear and bottles, I said "*we need a line with a carabiner to clip onto the dive gear, then I can unclip her and we will get her on board*".

No sooner had I said it and one appeared, Mark clipped it to the dive gear and between us we unhitched her. She was not breathing, never the less I was desperate to keep her face above water, there is always the chance we can bring her back.

I had hold of the wetsuit and really struggling to hang on to her, then with all three of us getting hold of a bit each, we hauled her on board, the relief for me that she was safely on board was considerable, if I had let go I'm pretty sure she would have gone down and disappeared, which would have been a disaster.

By now Dave, Helmsman on the ILB had picked up the husband and taken him around to the other side of the lifeboat.

All of the crew are well trained by our Doctors on resuscitation, like all training it kicks in when needed. Mark was at the head end giving mouth to mouth and Glen was busy giving compressions.

I sat back and watched, nothing else to do until the helicopter arrived to transport her to Treliske Hospital.

The boys worked tirelessly, all three of us desperate for a sign that gave hope, but unfortunately nothing.

Alan leaned over the side of the flying bridge *"helo is coming in; get her to the after deck"*.

I said to Mark *"keep going, as soon as they start to lower the diver and scoop we will move her"*.

Mark looked up and nodded, he like Glen was totally focused on the job at hand.

The lifeboat was heading on a fixed course at around 10 knots I could hear the chopper running in, as we felt the downdraft I said *"let's move her now"*, without further talking between the three of us we carefully move her along the side of the lifeboat, up the steps and had her ready to transfer to the scoop stretcher that was on its way down with the diver.

Mark Pollard. Mark worked hard to revive the female diver, he went on to become the lifeboat's coxswain 2005-2015. Photo: Simon Culliford

Mark and Glen continued with CPR until everything was ready for the transfer.

The diver now on board looked at the casualty and said *"let's get her into the stretcher"*. If I had a stop watch I expect it took no more than ten seconds and she was in, and in another ten seconds the diver had her strapped in and called for the helo to lower the wire ready to hitch up…. A few seconds later the diver and scoop stretcher were off the deck and away.

Alan turned the boat back towards Falmouth. The helicopter was now also making in the same direction heading for Treliske Hospital where a team would be waiting to try and resuscitate her.

Far in the distance was the ILB making full speed to Falmouth with the husband, he needed care not just for shock but they needed to get him in the boathouse to warm up.

Most of the crew were chatting on the after deck, I went up to the flying bridge to have a chat with Alan *"didn't look good from here"* he said, I replied *"no, not good, the boys worked so hard to get her going, but no signs of life"*.

The rest of the run back to the harbour was in silence, everyone caught up with their thoughts.

As we rounded Pendennis Point the lads put the covers on the *Y-boat* and Tim got ready for refuelling. We hadn't used much but we always have the lifeboat ready with fuel tanks full to the brim, the next shout could be a 24 hour search!

We slowly rounded the docks, the ILB was tied up alongside the pontoon, I expect the HMA (Honorary Medical Advisor), one of our lifeboat Doctors had been called down from the Health Centre to check the husband over to make sure he was OK before he was collected by friends or family to care for him.

The lifeboat was refuelled and tied up alongside the pontoon. Those who didn't push off to get back to whatever they were doing went into the crew room for a brew and to chat the job over.

Alan and I were keen to make sure everyone on board during the job were OK …. Dealing with death is not what attracts volunteers to join a lifeboat crew, but on occasions as I've said before it comes with the territory.

Everyone handles their thoughts differently, for some it can mean nightmares, others just another day at the office.

Over the years quite often I get flash backs of moments that really affect me, the wife's distress during her visit to the lifeboat house to thank the Coxswain and crew for bringing her husband's body back to shore, and now the eyes of the husband who held his wife waiting for rescue and not wanting to let go. This was a shout that did not last long, just a couple of hours, but the whole crew will remember it forever.

Dave Nicoll and Mr Price on the stern of *Elizabeth Ann* a few years earlier when Mr Price had hair!

The Severn class all-weather lifeboat *The Will* approaching her berth at Falmouth lifeboat station on 16 July 1997, the day of her Naming Ceremony and Service of Dedication. Coxswain Alan Barnes in command with Mr Price and Tim Julian on the stern. Photo: Simon Culliford

The Will on exercise on 27 April 2008 while serving at the station on relief.
Photo: Simon Culliford

THE WILL

1996, there was a big buzz around the coast about the new Severn class lifeboat; it makes the Arun look small by comparison. All larger stations like Falmouth who have been operating Aruns for the last 20 years wanted one!

'*The Will*' was the first production Severn, order number 1201, it was built for Stornoway in 1995; due to a few teething problems Stornoway decided to hang on to their Arun for a while and '*The Will*' went into the relief fleet.

We found out our Severn wasn't due to be built and delivered to Falmouth until 2001.

Stations around the coast got a chance to look at *The Will* the new faster boat that was due to replace many of the Aruns. The Arun is capable of working up to thirty miles off shore with a speed of 18 knots (21 mph). The RNLI were working towards being able to work up to fifty miles off shore, and being capable of getting there in two hours in fair weather! The Severn class lifeboat was the answer, at 55 '9' long and a top speed of 25 knots (29mph)!

Alan got to have a ride in *The Will* as she went around the coast, giving everyone a chance to see what their boats were going to be replaced with… he was so impressed that he made the case for '*The Will*' to be taken out of the relief fleet and stationed at Falmouth until the boat we were scheduled to receive in 2001 was delivered.

The case was strong; Falmouth is a major station in one of the busiest and most dangerous patches around the UK and Ireland. Eventually RNLI HQ agreed and the deal was done; the Falmouth crew were to go to Poole HQ Training Centre to be introduced to the Severn… *The Will* ON 1201, operational number 17-02, 17 metres long, 02 designating the second Severn built. (01 being the prototype).

Alan selected the crew to go to the training centre; himself (Coxswain), Tim (Mechanic), Roger (Second Coxswain), myself, Dave and Peter, The six of us were to present ourselves at 0900 hours Monday 20th January 1997, a week's training and if all was well we take the boat back to the station, leaving Poole Saturday afternoon.

I was busy at work at the end of 1996, I had a lot of business going on in the Middle East, and more importantly I had a clutch of Parliamentarians who had adopted me as an expert advisor on firearms matters, the MP's were consumed with debating changes in the Firearms Laws following the terrible shooting of sixteen children and their teacher at Dunblane Primary school earlier that year.

The fax machine was the latest in communications, it was the way of sending letters and information, which only a few years earlier were sent by telex or post, it was much cheaper and easier to use than the old telex machine we had in the office… if you didn't have a fax machine you were a dinosaur when it came to communicating.

Alan rang me at work "*I want you on the crew to go to RNLI HQ, we are going to be introduced to our new Severn, one week training then we bring it home… OK with you?*" "*Of course*" I replied … "*when?*" "*In two weeks*" Alan replied… I paused… "*I need a fax machine, where are we staying?*" Alan replied "*give the Training Centre a ring, I'm sure they will sort something out*"… "*brill, count me in*".

The Naming Ceremony and Service of Dedication for *The Will* at Falmouth Lifeboat Station on 16 July 1997. Les Vipond can be seen taking the service. He drove all the way down during in atrocious weather during the St Simeon service just to greet us on our return and shake the crews' hands. An exceptional District Inspector, an absolute credit to the RNLI and hugely respected by all lifeboat crew who ever had the privilege to meet him. Photo: Simon Culliford

The Will moored up in front of the pontoon with the entire crew for the Naming Ceremony.
Photo: Simon Culliford

After lunch that Monday I gave the Training Centre at Poole a ring, a women answered the phone, "*Training Centre, can I help you?*"... "*My name is Mr Price, I am due to attend 1 weeks training with the Falmouth crew beginning on the 20th of this month. As I am up for a week, I need a hotel with bedroom where I can plug a fax machine in*" there was a long pause, I could hear the woman whispering to someone in the office, then she came back "*a fax machine?*" she said, I wanted to reply '*yes a bloody fax machine, don't you know what a fax machine is?*' ... luckily the several years under my belt as a diplomatic lifeboat wireless operator I contained myself... I replied "*I need a fax machine while I am away from my office as I have a lot going on at work at the moment*"... this time I heard the women in the office whisper to someone in the office "*he wants a fax machine because he is busy at work*". I had my ear pressed hard against the phone and heard "*ask him what he does at work*" I just about heard ... the woman came back "*what is it you do at work?*" ... Bloody woman I thought, I barked back "*I'm an arms dealer*"... "*He's an arms dealer*" she whispered loudly in the office .... Her boss told her "*give him what he wants*". By now I was jumping, being buggered about by some secretary ... "*I will see what I can arrange*" she said...I snapped back "*if you cannot arrange a fax facility I will not be able to attend, can I have your name please*"... "*Elaine*" she replied, with that I slammed the phone down... most unlike me, I think I actually wound myself up; I felt a bit of an idiot.

I gave it a week and decided to ring the Training Centre to see if there was any progress with my fax machine phone socket request, it was Elaine ... "*Mr Price here, any luck with finding me a room where I can plug in a fax machine?*" ...her reply "*I have spoken with my boss he says you can plug your machine into a socket in our office, will that be acceptable?*" I replied "*that will be perfect, thank you very much*". The conversation was short and sweet. No pleasantries, but a fax in the Training Centre was perfect, I could keep in touch regularly with my office, and more importantly I could keep my clutch of MPs informed and answer all their questions, most of which demonstrated they knew nothing about firearms.

Sunday early evening at the boathouse, five of us mustered outside, it was cold and dark, Alan turned up with a hire car; with a squeeze we all got in and we were off up to Poole for the week.

We were all booked in at Corkers, a small bar with rooms above, they obviously specialised in taking in visiting lifeboat crews, two or three single beds to a room, '*squeeze them in*' Alan grabbed a key with two singles "*Pricey you are with me*" he said. Up we went, beds were about two foot wide, probably ex-army, basic, squeezed into a single room with about 12 inches down the middle, typical RNLI for the end of the last century , '*best value, basic*', described the room well.

Monday morning, a short walk to the RNLI HQ, the training centre was down by the quay, the guard at the main gate said "*Falmouth lot?*" Alan said "*yes*" the barrier raised, looked like they were expecting us.

Several lifeboats tied up alongside, with a monster in the middle, '*The Will*'.

Although the Severn was only just under 4 feet longer than the Arun, it was massive, very modern, monster great whip aerials, plenty of deck space, big flying bridge, everything you could ask for, and that was just at a glance.

Tim's eyes nearly popped out of his head, he looked like he couldn't wait to get his

Falmouth lifeboat crew and station officials with the Severn class all-weather lifeboat *The Will* in 1997.
Photo: Simon Culliford

spanners out!

We made our way to the large building by the quay, the training and lecture rooms were upstairs, below was the ILB outboard testing facility, workshops and stores.

Hugh our 'old' Divisional Inspector was at the top of the fire escape, by the door into the training room, he came down slowly "*good morning Falmouth*", we all grinned, shook hands, then Hugh gave us a mini briefing, "*I am now Staff Officer Operations (Training), let's have a quick look around before we go up to the lecture room to meet with all your instructors for the week, I expect you have spotted The Will*"...we all looked over the Severn... "*we will go aboard a little later*" Hugh said.

We followed Hugh up the stairs to the main office, as we marched in I recognised Graham Wagstaff (Waggers) in the corner, next to him was Dan Nicholson, a tall Naval type and sitting at her desk was this goddess, I had to look twice, this couldn't be Elaine the starchy secretary that gave me a hard time over my fax machine.

Hugh was busy moving us all over to meet Dan and Waggers, I broke away and made a bee line for who was probably the most beautiful girl in the whole world.

"*My name is Mr Price*", I held out my hand, Elaine stood, put out her tiny hand, her hand shake was very powerful, she must have taken lessons from Hugh, "*I'm Elaine*"... then she pointed to a big envelope selotaped to the front of her desk "*this is your fax pouch, all your faxes will go in there, you can collect any time"...* I was speechless, very aware I was staring, which of course was rude... eventually I let go of her hand, she smiled... I nearly fainted.

"*Right Mr Price*" Hugh beckoned me over to the gang in the corner, I shook hands with Dan and Waggers and we all went into the training room.

Straight away I spotted amongst the RNLI bods our current DI. Les Vipond. There was another five up at the front, Dan asked us all to take a seat and introduced everyone: "*Right, we have met, I am Dan Nicholson, Training Officer Operations, you all know Hugh, most of you know Graham Wagstaff Deputy Training Officer Technical. This is Richard Price, Assistant Training Officer Operations, Keith Thatcher Naval Architect, Stuart Welford Research Development Manager ... and Ian Benham Comms Support Manager... and of course you all know Les Vipond*".

The RNLI team of top brass all mingled with us and there was a lot of hand shaking.

The boys had spotted me as I introduced myself to Elaine, Alan mentioned when it went quiet "*Mr Price has met the secretary in your office Dan*", a few giggles from the crew, all knowing I'm single, I knew I was blushing, my ears were on fire.

Dan gave us a briefing on what we were in for in the week, and he said "*to kick off this morning Bob and Keith are going to brief you in the design of the Severn, its capabilities and why it is particularly suitable for the kind of weather you encounter in the south west*".

We were all keen to know how good *The Will* was, especially as the crew in Stornoway (right up in the North of Scotland) didn't want it!

Bob began to talk, "*you have heard The Will fell off a large wave and suffered some damage, let me explain what happened. The extent of the damage and what we did to put things right*".

We all listened intensely to what happened, the lessons learnt, what was done to strengthen certain area's in the boat, then Keith explained what the hull was made from, a new concept called FRC (Fibre Reinforced Composite), with the massive reinforcing stiffeners and carbon fibre the hull was almost unbreakable, the talks and slides projected onto the wall went on for around one and half hours. I was so pleased we had the top experts to explain it to us all in great detail, I looked across to Tim, he was beaming, any doubts about *The Will*'s quality and ability to take the seas we have off south west Cornwall were gone, this boat can take anything, and travelling at nearly 30 miles per hour she is going to have to.

Dan came into the room "*right lads, tea and coffee in the office*".

We all shuffled into the office, I looked around... where is she... in the corner was Elaine, she looked across and smiled, my knees went to jelly, I smiled back, I felt a nudge in my side, Alan leaned over "*I think she likes you Pricey*" he said, I looked at him and whispered, "*don't be silly*" at the same time hoping he was right.

After more technical briefings we had a buffet lunch, Dan and Elaine joined us, I mozied over to her and due to lack of experience in chatting up spoke a load of rubbish, but managed to get her to talk about her work at the RNLI; she loved the job, met dozens of

William Hague, who was Leader of the Conservative Party at the time, with members of Falmouth Lifeboat crew. Left to right: Phil Rogers, Carl Beardmore, Tim Julian, William Hague, Jon Blakeston and Mr Price. Photo: David Barnicoat Collection

crews, worked with the RNLI filming unit run by Edward Malinson and quite often got to go up in the local search and rescue helicopter, she even features in some of the video training aids… so not just a pretty face I thought, she had some experience on inshore and offshore lifeboats!

Monday afternoon and we were aboard *The Will*…Tim was in the engine room with Waggers… there's not much Graham Wagstaff doesn't know about machinery and engines, he is ex Naval, submarines!!!… A specialist in firefighting and solving major problems at sea, the sort of guy you want on-board if things go seriously wrong with mechanical stuff.

The rest of us were being introduced to all the safety equipment and communication gear, intercoms, radio's, and so on.

In the afternoon back to the lecture room for a debrief and what was going to happen on Tuesday; with the debrief over I walked over to my envelope on the front of Elaine's desk and grasped my faxes, then as we filed out I looked back, Elaine was watching us leave, I caught her eye and waved … yes… she waved back.

That night I had a job to sleep, not just a huge fabulous lifeboat to play with for a week, but the loveliest secretary in the world to look after my faxes.

Tuesday morning, extra careful shave, combed what was left of my hair, not easy to look handsome when you don't have much to work with… but I did my best.

We were waved through the security gate at the RNLI HQ, everyone in the yard and security gate knew Falmouth was up to collect *The Will*... over to the Training Centre, Elaine's little Ford was parked outside, we filed upstairs, previous crews group pictures were on the wall up the stairs, ours was at the top with the word '*shedless*' written under '*Falmouth Crew*', the nickname going back to the time we were moving from our old boat house to our new one and operating out of a shed for a while.

We walked through the office into the lecture room, I peeled off like a spitfire pilot making an attack, I dived for Elaine's desk (not an actual dive!), I managed to slow down before crashing into the desk, looked into my envelope to see if there were any faxes... I wasn't really interested in the faxes, I just wanted Elaine to see how handsome I was close up (I wish), no really I just wanted to give her a big smile

The '*shedless*' crew on board *The Will*. Left to right: Alan Barnes, Tim Julian, Mr Price, Dave Proud, Peter Wood and Roger McClarity.

...she was warming to me, I could tell.

The morning's brief, Richard stood by the flip chart, "*this morning we are going to talk about the machinery, we have firefighting equipment, pumps, two capstan winches, we will also be looking at our nav aids, after lunch we will be going afloat to put what we have talked about into practice, back for the 1830 bridge*".

We had all been to the RNLI HQ Poole before, delivering and collecting passage boats, collecting from stations around the coast and bringing them up through Poole harbour; at the top of the harbour the Middle Ship Channel' leads to Town Quay alongside the main road of the town, at the end a road going across the short stretch of water leading up to the RNLI quay.

The Poole bridge opens up at set times during the day to let vessels moored in Back Water Channel pass, rules of the sea governed in a similar way to the rules of the road, traffic lights, hooters, lifeboats passing under the bridge always giving a hoot of thanks and a wave to the 'Bridge Master'.

Anyway we plan to get back to the bridge by 1830 hours to be able to moor up and get away for dinner by 1900 hours.

During the morning tea/ coffee break we were all milling around in the lecture room, chatting, that is all except me, I was milling around by Elaine's desk.

The phone rang, Elaine picked it up "*RNLI Training Department, Elaine speaking*"... she looked at me… "*it's for you*", she said with a surprised look on her face, "*you have a call from the House of Lords*", I took the phone having no idea who it was "*yes*" I replied, "*I have a question for you, what is the rate of the fire of a Sten Gun?*" I replied "*500 to 600 rounds a minute*" … "*Thank you Mr Price*" and that was it the phone call was over, what a strange question I thought, perhaps they are debating gun matters in the House of Lords, how on earth did he know where to get hold of me, probably someone from my office had passed on the RNLI number.

I handed the phone back to Elaine, we exchanged big smiles. I looked around, everyone was back in the lecture room, the crew all looked at me as I entered, grinning like idiots.

That afternoon we went afloat, out under the bridge, through Poole harbour which is huge, and out to sea… The Severn is a very powerful boat, twin V12 turbo charge Caterpillar engines, 25 knots. The lifeboat was flying!

We spent the afternoon trying all the kit out, we all had a go at driving, the plan was to repeat this on Wednesday, then a long sea exercise on Thursday with some night navigation and a 2130 hours bridge.

Thursday night after we put the boat to bed, we all went around to Hugh's house for some food. We were greeted by Hugh's lovely wife Judy who had obviously been very busy putting on a big spread; it was a great evening talking about lifeboats of course!

Friday morning in the lecture room first thing we had a nav aid de- brief, everything was going well, the training staff were pleased with us, after tea/ coffee break we were due to have a helicopter exercise brief and then a tour of the RNLI HQ.

We filed into the office I looked around, no Elaine… Dan caught my eye and made a big head movement suggesting I look out of the window, I strolled over to the window, well I tried to make it look like a stroll, I almost ran, looked down, Elaine was washing her car… I strolled down at high speed and walked up to her, "*need a hand?*"…"*No its OK, but thank you for asking, helo exercise this afternoon?*" "*Yes*" I said. We smiled at each other, my heart was thumping.

"*Pricey*" one of the lads called out of the upstairs window, I was running late, up the stairs two at a time and into the lecture room for the helo brief.

At the end of the briefing Hugh stood up and said we are all meeting up for a drink at Cranberry's tonight. You will be very busy tomorrow, and then you will be taking your boat back to Falmouth.

The tour of the RNLI HQ was great, we had a look around the workshops, the machine shop was huge, big lathes and other modern engineering machinery, we were introduced to the workshop foreman and the engineers, then off to the store to be introduced to the ladies who make sure we get all our spares, stores and equipment, everyone seemed to know we were the lot from Falmouth, up to collect our Severn.

Then across the road to the head office and ops room, whenever we are up in Poole on passage (collecting and delivering lifeboats) we always call into the ops room, one wall covered in the names of every lifeboat station with markers to show which stations are launched on service at any time of the day or night.

Les Vipond enjoying banter with a lifeboat crew. Les was one of the very best lifeboat inspectors of his time

The feeling of '*family*' is overwhelming, the pride the whole RNLI staff take in their jobs, supporting the boats and crews is pretty obvious, everyone greeting us as if we were long lost best friends!

That afternoon the helicopter exercise went well, back to Corkers to wash up and get ready for the evening drink.

Elaine had left the office by the time we returned from the exercise, I hoped she was going to be at Cranberry's for a drink this evening… and there at the bar was Elaine… stunning, what can I say.

The evening flew by, Elaine and I talked and talked, about everything, and before I knew it we were all shaking hands and saying good bye. Elaine smiled at me, she said "*thank you for a lovely evening Chris*"… I was smitten.

Saturday was going to be a busy day, 'consolidation exercises at sea', during the day, back to the training centre for a course de- brief, refuel then off home, via Alderney, a night stop over then across to Falmouth.

The Saturday exercise was a good workout, every piece of kit was used, the *Y-boat*, fire hose, emergency steering, everything, it was exhausting, there was a fair wind blowing, a freezing cold January day.

Back to the training centre for the final de-brief, it was a great day, all the RNLI training staff were there, Dan addressed us all. "*Well, Falmouth it has been a pleasure having you*

Mr Price taking *The Will* into Coverack on Lifeboat Day.

up for the week, I am pleased to advise you that the RNLI is passing 17-02 The Will into your care, in the knowledge you will look after her, we are all delighted to see her go to Falmouth".

There was big round of applause, then lots of handshakes, we were all keen to slip the moorings and get going to Alderney. It was going to be a fast rough passage across the English Channel! As we left the office I gave a wave to Elaine, we smiled at each other, then having lingered smiling, I ran and caught up with the others who were making their way to the pontoon.

We all got aboard *The Will* , Les Vipond gathered us all in the wheelhouse, *"right, I want a course in the plotter for Alderney, we should arrive in time for an evening meal"*, we had almost 70 miles to run, so at least three hours by the time we get out of Poole harbour and into Alderney.

It was just still daylight, 1630 hours, we were off, it was a lumpy crossing, strong winds, lots of sleet and heavy rain, not the best night for a passage! Not much moving in the shipping lanes, so the run was fairly uneventful. I'm pleased to say Les did not set fire to his stinking pipe in the wheelhouse. My tummy was holding up… just… the movement of the Severn in reasonably large seas was completely different to the ride of the Arun.

It had taken me eighteen years to get used to the Arun, I knew instinctively exactly how the Arun was going to land when it came off a big wave, how to stand, how to bend knees. The Severn is a different beast, much more violent ride, in big seas you have to strap into the big sprung hydraulically dampened seats, whilst they protect you from the violent slamming, you bounce up and down constantly.

The three hour run soon passed, we were entering Alderney harbour, a couple of the lads from the Alderney lifeboat crew had turned out to let us know where it would be OK for us to moor up for the night, it was blowing half a gale and plenty of sleet too!

With the boat moored up alongside the quay we shut down the engines, switched off the electrics, and went ashore, making our way up to the local hotel.

In through the front door the seven of us piled in, dripping wet, windswept and freezing cold, a woman came up to the reception desk, I noticed she had what could pass for a beard!... "*What do ya want?*" She said looking at Les, I instantly grinned; it must be obvious we were booked in for the night, seven lifeboat men in the middle of January for God's sake… Les didn't bat an eyelid… "*we are booked in for the night, seven from the RNLI*"… she looked down at her book, the finger ran down the only entry on the page "*ah yes*" she muttered to herself… she leaned back grabbed two keys off a hook, as she put the two keys on the desk, she said "*I have two singles*", before she muttered another word I leaned forward and grabbed one, "*this will do me*" I muttered, my arm moved so quickly it must have resembled the tongue of one of those animals that shoots out and catches a fly in mid-flight, Les slammed his hand down on the second key before anyone else could move…

She leaned back again and grabbed another three keys, put them on the desk and said "*three twins*"… Les and myself made our way to the stairs whilst the rest debated who was going to sleep with who.

I'm not fussy about sharing a room, but as a light sleeper if I draw a short straw and end up with a heavy snorer I don't sleep a wink and start the next day knackered.

At the top of the stairs Les leaned over the banister rail, "*in the bar for a meal by eight*", everyone nodded.

I found my room, it was small, basic, but in my worn out state just fine, a quick wash, dry clothes and I made my way down to the bar.

The hotel was empty apart from us, not many holiday makers in Alderney in January; the bar was a different story, four or five tables were occupied by locals, they were all chatting away, the chatter noticeably diminished as the crew made their way down for 'pre dinner drinks'. As they got used to our presence the chatter got back to normal.

We found an empty table; I went up to the bar with Les to get the beers, no one behind the bar, then out of nowhere appeared the bearded receptionist…"*what do ya want?*" she said, looking me right in the eye, I completely forgot what to say, I wanted to say '*a bloody drink beardy*' but forced myself just to smile, she must have thought I was as barmy as she was, after a ten seconds or so staring match Les said "*can we have some drinks please*"…she spun around, looked at Les and said "*what do ya want?*" I looked over at our table, there were a few giggles, it was as if the receptionist/ barmaid was an alien being that knew only the words '*what do ya want*'!

I had a side view of the barmaid as she started pulling pints, she was about twenty four inches from my face, I couldn't help but stare at her head, I was convinced she had a cone shaped head, it was difficult to tell, her hair was a similar profile to a police man's helmet, and was styled on a thatched roof at the very end of its life…Looking around the bar at the locals I came to the conclusion there was no resident barber on Alderney.

Left: Elaine kitted up ready for a helicopter lift. As well as working in the RNLI Training Department, Elaine was very popular in the Filming Department!

Below: The helicopter diver clips on the strop ready for the lift.

Left: The helicopter moves away from the stern of the lifeboat and begins the hoist. Note the earthing cable dangling below.

Elaine being lowered from the helicopter.

Elaine driving the Severn class lifeboat *The Will* with Alan.

There was a fair old blow outside with the sleet tapping at the large sash windows in the bar. I noticed some meals coming out from behind a door at the end of the bar that I thought was the door to the toilets, guess who was serving… yes, it was the beard.

10 or 15 minutes passed the beard glided over to our table and dropped some well-worn menu's, fish and chips, steak and chips, scampi and chips, prawn salad and chips… so lots to choose from, within 5 minutes we had all decided; we sat and waited, eventually into the bar came the beard, up to our table, not looking at anyone she stared at her notebook with pen poised… *"what do ya want?"*… Everyone grinned, one or two giggled… I gave it a few seconds, then I couldn't help myself, I blurted out in a similar accent *"what do ya want"*, even Les smiled before saying *"4 fish and chips, 3 steak and chips please"*.

Out came the meals, served as if we were inmates in an eastern block prison, the experience was worth the slog to Alderney, one of the most bizarre meals I have ever had, the whole stay was Fawlty Towers but with John Cleese swapped with the amazing bearded lady.

The next morning we all came down to the bar for breakfast, one or two of the crew tucked into the selection of boiled eggs, curly bread, Weetabix and Corn Flakes on offer, I passed, not because the food looked like it had been trotted out every morning and was at least six months old, more because it was blowing a hooley out there and eating anything would be a waste, and I was desperate not to pebble dash the after deck!

The run out of Alderney proved to be an interesting navigational experience, good sized seas as we made our way into the shipping lanes, a long slog back to Falmouth, five or six hours, nothing to see except the odd ship.

We were all looking forward to getting back to Falmouth, refuelling and getting home for a good meal and warming up, it was 1530 hours, we were coming in towards just east of St Anthony light house, Les looked towards Alan *"reduce speed, I want the Y-boat launched a short run and recover before we enter Falmouth"*… If it wasn't for the noise from the engine room you would have been able to hear a pin drop, everyone looked at each other in disbelief, we had been beating our brains out all the way to Alderney from Poole, then today from Alderney to Falmouth, freezing cold and worn out, *"right lads, launch the Y-boat"* Alan said, trying to sound enthusiastic.

Without any moans or complaints we all clipped on our lifejackets, out onto the after deck and launched the *Y-boat*, Tim and myself jumped in Tim took a couple of spins around *The Will* and we were beckoned back to the boat for recovery.

Having just spent the week working the boat's gear, recovery was slick. We had all been working together for around fifteen years, so no orders required barking out, within a few minutes the *Y-boat* was recovered and lashed down; we piled back into the wheelhouse to see what Les had in store for us next. *"Right, let's get the boat refuelled and put on her moorings"*, there were grins of relief all round as the engines were put in gear and we headed in at full speed.

Dave gave the boathouse a call on the VHF, Clifford came straight back *"the fuel lines are ready for you"*, before Dave had even asked for them!

The boathouse was packed, the crew left behind to look after the Arun for the week, ILB crew, reserves, everyone was keen to look over our station's first Severn.

Clifford Atherton n 1997 at the helm of boarding boat with *The Will* and *Falmouth Round Table* behind. Cliiford was a stalwart member of the shore crew for many years. Photo: Simon Culliford

I was keen to get back to the '*Black Hole*', have a hot bath, a Fray Bentos pie, and begin to compose a letter to Elaine.

Later that evening, after a big meal, I sat in front of the electric fire with all three bars on, I sat down and began to write my letter, it took a couple of hours to get the words right and then five or six attempts to write the letter in my very best handwriting, finally done and sealed in an envelope, addressed to Elaine at The RNLI Training Department, Poole, I crawled downstairs, carefully piled my clothes as they came off into a heap so I could step straight into them if the bleeper went off during the night, into bed and within a few seconds I was asleep.

A week had passed, every morning sifting through the post, nothing from RNLI HQ, then at last a letter, I just knew it was from Elaine, neat handwriting, I nearly turned it into confetti trying to open the envelope… yes!…. if I'm passing through Mere in Wiltshire we could go for a drink.

Where the hell is Mere I thought… yes of course I will be passing through Mere very soon… I spent the rest of the day trying to think what I was going to write.

I had a meeting in two week's time in London, so I wrote and suggested I took her out the night before, and picked her up at 6 o'clock in the evening.

The big plan was to run into London and go to see Carmen at the Royal Albert Hall, I'm not a great fan of watching fat people screaming at each other, especially if it's in another language, but Elaine is sophisticated so a pint in a spit and sawdust pub was out of the question.

It was agreed, I would collect her from Mere at 6pm on the dot. I cleaned the old Range Rover, polished it, got a haircut, ironed my trousers, went to M&S and got a new shirt, everything would have to be perfect. As always I prefer to be an hour early rather than a minute late, so I sat outside Mere for around 40 minutes, then cruised in and arrived at the front door at exactly 6pm… knocked on the front door and there she was… perfect, "*you look lovely*" I said, Elaine smiled, looked at the old Range Rover and pointed at it, I nodded, and opened the door for her, like an idiot I slammed it shut (it had a sticky lock) she looked at me with a look of surprise… I got into the driver's seat, slammed my door and said "*the doors are a bit sticky*" trying to excuse my desire to get a move on.

We needed to be at the Royal Albert Hall by 1930 hours at the latest!

We began chatting as we hurtled up the A303 towards London, usual stuff, busy at work? We had a good run to Alderney, the boat runs well, then as we got onto the M3 motorway it was obvious we weren't heading for a local pub.

"*Where are we going*?" Elaine said, "*It's a surprise, you will enjoy it, I'm taking you to a concert*". I wanted to re-assure her I was not kidnapping her, a hundred mile fast drive to the destination for our first date was probably not normal.

We joined the M25 in fast moving traffic, onto the M4, past Heathrow doing between 80 and 90 mph, I cannot imagine what Elaine must have thought, a first date with a complete lunatic.

"*London*" she said, "*yes*" I replied "*we are heading for the Royal Albert Hall*", she nodded, I could tell with a look of relief, it wasn't just a road race, or me trying to impress by driving like James Hunt.

I drove into Earls Court, to a carpark where I knew I would find a space, I rushed her up into the main street, a lot of traffic, there in the distance a cab with his light on, I took out my clean carefully ironed hankie, waved it like a crazy man, he spotted me, flashed his lights and pulled over.

We piled in, I said "*Royal Albert Hall please, we are tight for time*" "*alright mate, let's see what we can do*" the cockney geezer replied, we crawled along in the heavy traffic, the clock was ticking… "*the traffic this time of night is very heavy, I know a shortcut we can try, it's up to you*" the driver said.. "*go for it*" I said… well he whizzed around some narrow streets and within 5 minutes there it was The Royal Albert Hall!

The clock showed £14.50, I gave him a £20 note, "*keep the change*" not because I spend money like water, but because we were about 4 minutes before the opera started.

We pushed through the door and up to the ticket office, the place was deserted, "*you have two tickets reserved for Mr Price?*" I said. She looked at her computer, "*yes here they are*"… by the time they were printed I had paid.

Around the corridor to door six, opened it, the place was crowded, thousands of people all seated… *"you've just made it"* the usher said, she waved the instruction to follow her, she pointed at the only two empty seats in the hall, I nodded and smiled and muttered *"thanks"*. Everyone in the row stood as we squeezed past, then just as we sat the lights dimmed and the opera began… how lucky was that!

I was sat close to Elaine, totally oblivious to the screaming that was going on on the stage in the centre of the hall that was surrounded by the audience… it could have been the worst opera in the world, it wouldn't have mattered, I was in heaven… Luckily it was actually pretty good, Elaine was loving it, how sophisticated she must have thought I was… I wish.

An hour and a half passed, it seemed to go so quickly, the lights went on, it was half time, or probably called something a little posher at an opera, anyway I suggested we had a drink, as it seemed customary for everyone to stampede to the various bars situated just off the corridors within the building.

We found a bar, *"what would you like"* I said, *"gin and tonic please"*… I left her at a large pillar and began to wriggle my way through the crowd to the bar, eventually emerging with a gin and tonic and a ginger beer (drink). I took the notes I got in the change from my £20 note and took out my wallet, it was a wreck of a wallet and still wet from the previous Sunday lifeboat exercise.

Elaine looked at the wallet and soggy notes, *"it's wet"* she said, *"it's a long story"* I replied.

We finished the drinks, dumped the glasses on the nearest shelf and made our way back to our seats and settled down for the second half of the opera, it was great.

At about 2220 hours it was over and

This month we are featuring Christopher Price, who is deputy 2nd coxswain of the main boat. Chris has been with the RNLI for 24 years, one of the crew's longest serving members. He started out at the Coverack Station but transferred to Falmouth after Coverack closed and has been at Falmouth for 20 years. At the age of 53 he knows he has only two years left before compulsory retirement, something he is not looking forward to, the body may be getting slower but the spirit is still very strong!

Chris spent 14 years as radio operator and emergency mechanic before promotion to deputy 2nd Cox, this means that he will Cox the boat if he is lead hand on a shout. As Chris runs his own business in Helston, he is mostly available for evenings and weekend shouts, unless on-call as duty Cox, when he works from home near the station. Chris met his wife while on a visit to the Poole Lifeboat Station, where she was a valued member of staff, and has never been forgiven by the Poole crew for stealing her away to Cornwall.

Chris has a full and very interesting business lifestyle in that the company he runs produces firearms and ordnance for the Army. Chris himself is an expert on firearms and is often called upon by the Police and Customs to be an expert witness in incidents involving firearms.

The new boat the "Richard Cox Scott" has been thoroughly cleaned and T-cutted in preparation for the Queen's visit on the 1st May.

The whole crew are looking forward to meeting the Queen when she comes to officially name the new boat, this will be followed by a service of dedication for the boat in the afternoon. All these events will have occurred by the time you receive your News & Trader, but we will bring a full report and pictures in June's edition.

RNLI Donation

Lifeboats
Royal National Lifeboat Institution

I / We wish to donate the following to the work of the RNLI in Falmouth

☐ 50p ☐ £1 ☐ £5 ☐ £10 ☐ Other (Please specify)------

Name:..

Address:...

.....................................Post Code..................

Please return to: RNLI Falmouth, The Boathouse, Falmouth, TR11

Falmouth and Penryn News & Trader

we were outside the opera house looking for a taxi, we walked about half a mile and eventually flagged one down, "*is there a good restaurant open at this time of night?*" I said as we climbed in, "*yes mate, I know a good steak house, will that be OK?*" I looked at Elaine, she nodded, poor soul. She was probably going to bed about this time of night, what with a long drive from Mere to Poole in the morning to be at work on time, and we were going to eat before a one hour speed trial drive from London to Mere.

We arrived at the cabbie's recommended steak house, almost deserted, not a good sign, but we were both starving.

We sat down and ordered a meal, listened to a couple having a blazing row on the other side of the restaurant for a while, then Elaine said "*why is your wallet wet?*"

I had forgotten all about it... "*Well, we took the Severn up to the Dodman on our Sunday exercise to show it off to Fowey, it was a rough day with some very short steep seas off the Dodman, we thrashed both big lifeboats around, and Fowey's D class came out for a spin too, the seas were marginal for a D class lifeboat but there were two big boats there to look after it.*

I was asked if I would like to have a go in the D class, we whizzed around having a great time, I concentrated on climbing a big wave, then from nowhere a wave came at us from the side and we flipped over, the guys with me were washed out, I ended up under the boat breathing in the small air gap. I could hear both lifeboats moving close by so I decided to try and pass under the sponson and come up outside the upturned hull. No such luck my lifejacket got snagged, I was on the outside of the boat but about a foot under the surface with no way of getting myself free, I lay there for a few seconds trying to decide what to do, try and remove my lifejacket or keep struggling, I was running out of air, desperate to breathe, I swallowed a gulp of sea water and thought I'm not going to make it, for some reason I brought my knees up which pulled me back under the boat, I wriggled and got back to the small air trap, gulped in the air, and decided to stay where I could breath. Then a hand came under the boat and grabbed my yellow welly, I leaned forward grabbed his hand and between us he got me out by the stern. I looked up at the crew who were almost hovering over me, all had white faces, they dragged me aboard, soaked and completely knackered, stripped me off and put me in a 'woolly bear', it took a while to understand how close I came to passing out; so there you have it, my wallet got soaked!"

We finished our meal, got a cab back to Earls Court and back into the Land Rover, a much slower cruise back to Mere in Wiltshire, empty roads, Elaine was nodding off, it was around 0230 hours by the time I got her back to her front door, we had a little kiss and agreed to meet again, it was a perfect evening.

I turned around and got back into London at around 0400 hours, so 4 hours kip and off to my meeting.

Master of the Worshipful Company of Gunmakers 2005. Chris and Elaine at Ladies Night.
Photo: Lawson, Gibbs and Co. Ltd.

Falmouth's Arun class lifeboat *Elizabeth Ann* in Falmouth Bay in April 1987. Photo: Simon Culliford

P&O Nedlloyd Encounter ex *Elizabeth Ann* after she arrived in Australia. Note the former RNLI operational number 5211 on the bow. Photo:Royal Volunteer Coastal Patrol

PASSAGE TO LONDON

A lot happened in the months following *The Will* arriving at Falmouth and adopting the call sign *'Falmouth Lifeboat'*, one of them being one of the most important things to happen to me, my clumsy attempts at courtship worked. I persuaded Elaine to come to Cornwall and we were married.

It took a while for Elaine to get used to the lifeboat routine, not folding my clothes neatly when I get into bed, choosing what to eat depending on the weather, and so on.

The *'Black Hole'* was not a place to live in, so we moved to a new house, very close to the lifeboat house. It was perfect, we got a puppy, a border terrier called 'Luke', he was brilliant but had one bad habit, he made it his business to try and stop me getting dressed in the middle of the night if the bleeper went off, I'm sure the next door neighbours could hear me shouting *"control this bloody dog"* a minute or two before hearing our front door slam, and two maroons going off to signal the lifeboat was about to launch on service.

Elaine was brilliant, understanding that when there was a lifeboat shout, I was gone, and having no idea when I could be back, a lot to ask for, I was very lucky. There wasn't much Elaine didn't know about lifeboats, she has been used as the casualty in many RNLI training videos, being saved by ILB's, ALB's, and the helicopters!

I was now formally elevated to the position of a Deputy Second Coxswain and capable of being 'Duty Coxswain'; this was due to the quality of training by all the Coxswains I served under, Viv, John and Alan.

Alan was a superb Coxswain who spent all his spare time training the crew to the highest level, having a Second Coxswain and Deputy Coxswains gave him the ability to turn off his bleeper and not be tied to Falmouth. Our Second Coxswain Roger works on the Pilot boats and is often not available for shouts so the Deputies were often 'holding the fort' and were required to take the boat to sea if there was a shout.

Another opportunity for Deputy Coxswains to command the lifeboat was on exercises, and occasionally DI's exercises, which gave the DI's the chance to observe how the crew and Deputies work together.

Not long after being appointed to the position of Joint Deputy Second Coxswain I got the chance to complete the Coxswains course at Poole HQ...A gruelling course with other lifeboat men from around the coast, a real eye opener!

During the next year or so the station was busy, the usual, tow jobs, medivacs, flares sighted, even the odd EPIRB (Emergency Position Indication Radio Beacon), occasionally set off by accident. We even had one that was eventually located by the Search and Rescue helicopter in the boot of a car in a Truro car park!

One Saturday morning Alan rang me at work *"I've got a job for you; take our Arun from Poole to London, she's been sold out of service by the RNLI to the Australian Lifeboat Service, up for it?"*

I replied instantly *"you bet, who's my crew?"*... *"Choose your own crew, you'll need a Mechanic, I can spare Tim, you will need a navigator and two crew, drive up next Sunday to Poole, stay the night, set off Monday morning, stopping the night at Eastbourne, then*

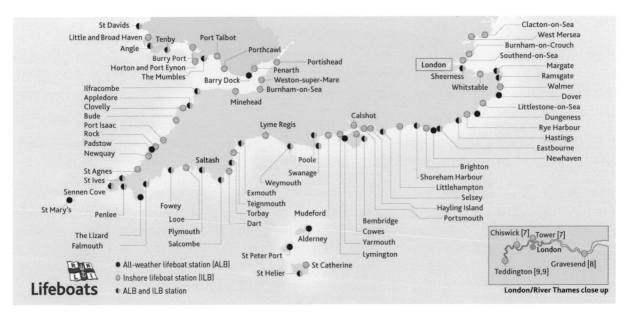

Lifeboat stations along the south coast.

to Ramsgate, stop the night, then deliver to Tilbury Wednesday afternoon, Poole have sorted the accommodation".

So, I needed a navigator and two good crew. Having taken the lifeboat to sea as Coxswain, if it was my turn on the rota, it was always reassuring to know the crew were going to take care of me.

Being responsible for an all-weather lifeboat at sea is not something to take on lightly, not because of the value ranging from many hundreds of thousands of pounds up into the millions for the Severn's, the responsibility is for the safety of the crew, and taking decisions that will not endanger the crew or the lifeboat.

As an employer I am responsible for the welfare of staff, but that is on dry land in a factory, not at sea in all sorts of weather conditions.

I needed a mechanic who would make sure the boat kept working, Tim was the perfect choice, he knew Elizabeth Ann inside out. Next I needed a navigator who would make sure we were in safe waters, I gave Dave a ring, he was looking after the inshore lifeboat so wasn't available, the next on my list was Alastair, known by the crew as 'Lily', (I have no idea why), Lily was a good all-rounder, occasionally a little excitable but a good navigator. I rang him at work "*got a passage*

Mechanic Tim Julian on *Elizabeth Ann*.
Photo: Falmouth RNLI Collection

Crew members left to right: Alastair 'Lily' Heane, Mark Pollard and Mark Waters. Photos: Simon Culliford

job, taking Lizzie Ann from Poole to Tilbury Docks, it's a 3 day trip I need a navigator are you available?" … *"sure, when?"* Lily replied, *"leave Falmouth next Sunday afternoon, a couple of stop overs and arrive at Tilbury Wednesday afternoon".*

That was mechanic and navigator sorted, now two solid crew and I am sorted. I was lucky, two of the best on the crew list, the two Mark's. Mark Pollard, great sense of humour, a lifeboat man that was to move on to become Coxswain when Alan retired in July 2005 and Mark Waters another great guy who could be relied upon 100%.

This was a huge relief to me, to be responsible for an offshore lifeboat and its crew is a big responsibility. Luckily I have learnt over the preceding twenty odd years the Coxswain and crew are a team, each member of the team with their own responsibilities but always able to share their concerns and responsibilities with each other, for the good of the job, boat and crew.

Alan had everything sorted for me, the charts, hire car the lot, this left me to concentrate on the needs of the crew, enough grub and drinks on board, so a trip to the supermarket.

Lily was to look after navigation, he obtained the charts for the trip, not a problem for him as he worked at a ships chandlers that supplied charts for ships and yachts sailing all over the world. I needed to know times for the departures to enable us to arrive from Poole to Eastbourne for the first leg, Eastbourne to Ramsgate, and finally from Ramsgate to Tilbury Docks. We needed to arrive at the time slot we had been allocated for lifting the Arun out of the water and into its cradle, ready to be put on a cargo ship as deck cargo, and delivery to Australia.

This included tides and moorings for us at Eastbourne and Ramsgate, the whole crew had a hand in organising everything. A big load off my mind! The week flew by, before we knew it the time had come, we all met at the lifeboat house, into the hire car and off to Poole.

We stopped off on the way up for a bite to eat arriving at Poole at 2200 hours… We left the hire car in the main car park. As always when we arrive at Poole we make our way up to the Ops room to say hello and see what's going on around the coast.

The Ops room is the hub of the RNLI, shift working ensures there is always someone there day or night, they are the first to be alerted when a lifeboat launches, a small marker is put up on the board showing the lifeboat station and time of launch.

Mark P was first into the Ops room the rest of us right behind him, "*Dick, how's it going? Much happening around the coast?*" Mark said, Dick replied "*not much on today, Humber lifeboat has been out most of the day on a search, just making her way back to station, a couple of inshore jobs, but apart from that a bit quiet*"... Mark knew Dick well; Mark often gets chosen for passage jobs and knew just about everyone at Poole HQ. Dick is a huge man, big hands, very firm handshake, if I had to describe him in four words it would be 'salt of the earth'! "*So you are taking your old Arun up to Tilbury Mr Price?*" Dick said, I replied "*yeah*".

We chewed the fat for around 15 minutes, then a crushing handshake before we left... Knowing I was in for a big hand squeezing contest, when I came to shake hands with Dick I squeezed like mad, looking him straight in the eye, teeth gritting, veins popping out of my neck. Dick gave an extra squeeze but stopped just before I would have screamed for mercy, we both gave each other a big grin... salt of the earth!

We wandered from the RNLI HQ towards our digs, all four of my crew were keen to get a couple of pints in before we bedded down for the night; they even asked for my permission which I thought was sweet.

At least 3 pints each later (except me) and we were saying good night, into our rooms, "*0800 sharp for breakfast!*" I said. My young crew agreed and that was it, a good kip, fine weather so for me a good English breakfast, I was looking forward to the passage.

After a hearty breakfast we all gathered up our bags, Lily with his big tube of charts, a couple of supermarket bags of grub. We started a slow walk from the digs to the RNLI main gate, "*Falmouth?*" the guard said, "*yes*" I replied back. We exchanged smiles and shuffled the gap between the gate and the security window.

As we made our way over to the quay, the *Elizabeth Ann* was tied up amongst a range of different off shore lifeboats. Having got used to the huge Severn lifeboat the Arun looked small, three RNLI staff were gathered on the boat, "*all fuelled up Tim*" one of the workshop staff in a boiler suit said. As we gathered round him he explained what was aboard "*the wheelhouse is a bit crowded, there are boxes of spares, some collecting boxes, spare ropes and fenders, enough kit to get the guys in Australia started, new oil and filters, she's had a thorough service, and a bottom scrub and anti-foul too!*" This was good, the boat was in top condition, typical for the RNLI, no 'sold as seen' as you might get with a second hand car. The lifeboat was going to be delivered in perfect working order, also reassuring for us to know we won't be limping into Tilbury in a worn out banger.

Tim leapt aboard, through the wheelhouse door and into the engine room like a ferret down a rabbit hole; I could hear the aluminium chequer plates that covered the sea cocks clatter as they were flung open. I asked Mark W to check the throttles were set in 'detent' (neutral), Mark P and myself went up to the flying bridge, Lily went to the chart table and took out his charts, setting them in order to take us all the way up the south coast to Tilbury.

Before we knew it Tim had both the engines started. We all mustered on the after deck for the farewell with the shore staff who had got everything ready for us. It was almost emotional, (well for me anyway), the clanging of the exhaust flaps, growl of the straight six Caterpillar engines, the smell of the diesel exhaust, a good friend I came to know well over 18 years.

"*20 minutes for the bridge*" boiler suit man said as he looked at his watch, big handshakes all round. I went upstairs, ready to take the boat off the pontoon, shore staff let go of the ropes, both Marks got the ropes put away, tidied up the deck, and we were off.

I managed to get the lifeboat out into the river without ramming anything. We pootled down towards the bridge on tick over, all five of us crammed into the flying bridge. For me it was like being with my best school mates, all who appreciated my dry sense of humour. As we stood off the bridge waiting for it to open and let us into Poole harbour and out to sea, I couldn't help myself looking at the bridge I felt a poem coming on:

"*The boy stood on the burning bridge,*

A pocket full of crackers,

One slipped down his leg,

And blew away his knackers"

Everyone went into a fit of uncontrollable giggles, including myself; we were like a bunch of 10 year old school boys.

Hooters blared, lights started flashing and the bridge slowly raised. We got a green light and we went through, waving to all the power boats and yachts patiently waiting for their turn to get through.

Lily went below to set the plotter up for our passage out of Poole harbour. The repeater screen on the flying bridge was a super bit of kit, a big map with the picture of a small boat (us) showing where we were.

The safe deep water channels are well marked with cans and cones so you would have to be an idiot to run on to a mud bank, but it was comforting to know I had an excellent navigator on board to make sure I didn't lose concentration and stray from safe waters.

As we passed the ferry out of the harbour I put the throttles forward and we were away. Clean bottom (boat) anti fouled, we were on the plane making a full 18 knots, low swell, blue skies, a perfect day for a passage.

We were due to arrive at Eastbourne at around 1700 hours, so a full day at sea, telling jokes, ham rolls, plenty of tea, everyone had a go on the wheel. Tim called up the Coastguard every hour, our call sign "Lifeboat 52-11", advising each Coastguard station on the first communication that we were on passage to Eastbourne, and that the boat was fully manned and available for a job if required. It made sense to declare ourselves available for the first two legs of our passage as it wouldn't interfere with our arrival at Tilbury on Wednesday afternoon.

We arrived outside Sovereign Harbour, Eastbourne at 1715 hours, the harbour was huge with lots of pontoons. One of the harbour staff waved at us wildly from a long pontoon and pointed to a space just big enough for us. We slowly made our way over to the pontoon, the crew got the fenders out and the ropes ready. As I brought the Arun up to the gap the breeze just slowly blew us into position, a perfect arrival, no damage, no hard landing, such luck. Everyone watching must have thought I was a brilliant driver, if only all arrivals were this perfect.

With the boat tied up, engines turned off, sea cocks closed; we began to muster on the after deck. Mark P lit a fag, but before he had a chance to suck in a lung full, over the tannoy came a booming voice *"no smoking in the harbour!"* We all looked around; no one to be seen, but obviously Mark was in full view of the smoking police.

He pretended to put the fag out, stamping on the imaginary cigarette on the after deck like a John Cleese pogo stick dance…then climbed down to the pontoon, hid alongside the side of the lifeboat and began to suck on his fag… *"I can still see you!"*…the smoking police screamed. Everyone looked at each other and smiled. I said to Mark *"put the fag out Mark, we don't want a black mark with Disneyland"* (RNLI HQ)… Mark put his fag out, tucked what was left behind his ear, held both hands high as if he was facing a bunch of armed police, I'm sure the Harbour Master saw him.

As we locked up the wheelhouse after everything was shut down, we decided to visit the Eastbourne RNLI boathouse to see if they were game for an exercise first thing in the morning. We were not due to arrive at Ramsgate until the afternoon the next day and had a few hours to kill.

Luckily some of the Eastbourne crew were in the boathouse, we had a cup of tea with them and agreed to have an exercise outside the harbour, meeting at 0900 hours.

The crew we met were great, no huge men amongst them; the Coxswain had a good London cockney accent. I reckon they had been working together for many years, very comfortable in their own company.

I shook hands with the Coxswain and said *"see you outside the harbour at 0900 then"*… *"we will be there"* he said with a big grin.

We left the lifeboat house and made our way to the hotel, passing the Zimmer frame brigade who were everywhere. The town was certainly old age pensioner friendly, the hotel foyer was crowded with groups of OAP's some were checking in, other groups checking out, coaches lined up outside, it was a busy hotel.

Anyway we all booked in and agreed to meet downstairs at 1930 hours to walk the town and find some grub.

The young cubs dragged poor old Mr Price from bar to bar, after a few pubs my back teeth were floating. I had consumed so much orange squash…I was starving!

We shuffled out of the Crown and Anchor, hopefully heading for a 'chippie' when I spotted a cyclist walking towards us in full racing lycra, speed crash helmet, poncey racing gloves, the lot!

I screamed out *"Courgette"*, a normal reaction when I see cyclists. As the cyclist walked by with his racing bike he looked and probably wondered if I was all there.

Mark P said *"what was that Mr Price?"* I replied, *"it goes back a long way, we had a customer known by everyone as Mike The Bike, he often came in to see us in full push bike racing kit, including the clip in clogs that made him walk as if he was walking slowly over hot coals, or filled his nappy. One day he came in with new thin body hugging lycra, I couldn't help noticing he dressed to the left, and the clue that gave that away was what looked like a courgette tucked in his lycra pants, from that day on he was known as Courgette, as were all cyclists"*.

Mike moved up country a year or two later, he is now one the best rifle makers in the UK!

The crew laughed, and obviously made allowances for my idiocrasies. Tim decided he wanted a kebab and broke away from the group, the rest of us decided on fish and chips, we found a chip shop and munched them as we strolled back to the hotel.

We gathered at 0800 hours for breakfast, the hotel restaurant was laid out with large round tables and a few small tables filling the gaps. I pointed to a table near the window overlooking the marina, only four chairs but enough room for five.

Tim was late, we sat around the table waiting for him, eventually he appeared and made his way through the maze of tables. Each large table had a large label, reservations for the various Darby and Joan gangs who were beginning to come down for breakfast.

We were next to a table with a large label 'Tulip'. Tim reached our table, no chair for him, Mark pointed at the chairs around the Tulip table, Tim grabbed one and sat down. As we waited for the waiter the Tulip table began to fill until all seats were full round the table. A large women began to circle the table looking for a chair, there was a gap with a chair missing opposite where Tim was sitting, our table was set for four and I guess it was obvious Tim had the missing chair.

The big hand tapped Tim on the shoulder, *"you've got a Tulip chair"* she bellowed with a blokes voice. We all looked at Tim awaiting his reply, he looked at all of us for help, then he focused on me as the boss… I shrugged my shoulders and grinned which didn't help, Big bird had spotted my indifference, this wound her up, she got hold of the top of the back of the chair and began to drag Tim away from the table, he hung on to the base of the seat determined not to let go.

It was obvious who was going to be the winner; Tim did not have the build of a sumo wrestler. The big bird was obviously a female cage fighter from the last century, not the sort to mess with. She gave an almighty tug, a bit like you would see when a drunk tries to remove a table cloth but leave the cups and saucers on the table, Tim was left in mid-air chair less. There was a round of applause from the Tulip table as big bird walked with a swagger clutching her chair as if it was first prize in a wrestling match final.

Tim looked as if he has been abandoned on a desert island, we were all laughing. I noticed a waiter making his way to our table, I raised my hand, caught his eye, he came up to me, *"may we have a chair for him please"* pointing to Tim, *"yes sir I will fetch one"*… back came the waiter with a chair. Tim sat down, looking as if he had been beaten up by a night club bouncer. Big bird looked over to our table with a look of superiority, she looked at me straight in the eye, I folded the fingers on my left hand so that only my middle finger stuck out, then stroked my chin. It was a mild way of giving her the 'finger', I guess it went over her head as the smug grin remained as she looked away.

Eastbourne's Mersey class lifeboat *Royal Thames* 12-36. Photo: RNLI Archive

We had breakfast, got our gear and strolled down to the pontoon in the harbour, pulling Tim's leg mercilessly about chairs and tulips, and the good thrashing he received from big bird.

We found out where to refuel from the Harbour Masters Office, got aboard the lifeboat and got her flashed up. It was a pleasant morning, not too cold, but as usual when both Caterpillar engines coughed and splattered into life there was plenty of noise and lots of black smoke.

Our stern was level with the bow of a reasonable looking super yacht; the moorings were full so no room to space out.

Out of the smoked glass surrounded cabin of the super yacht came Captain Birds Eye, obviously not impressed with our smoke. He stood on his bow arms folded, shorts, fat legs, a red face that had no doubt guzzled his fair share of best whiskey and Pimms… "*how long are you going to be here*?" he grunted. I was on the afterdeck looking up at him "*not long sir, apologies for the smoke it will clear shortly*" thinking at the same time and desperately forcing myself not to say '*you tosser*'.

Up to the flying bridge, I waved to the crew to let go all ropes as they looked up at me. No doubt they were thinking how's he going to get the boat out without ramming Capt Birds Eye… I looked across to Birds Eye, he was obviously thinking the same.

After a lot of to-ing and fro-ing plenty of revs and smoke, somehow I managed to exit the gap without ramming anything, or worse still the paint of Birds Eye's floating gin palace.

We pootled out of Eastbourne harbour at 0850 hours, in the distance was Eastbourne lifeboat, a Mersey Class, 12-36 named *Royal Thames*. More modern than our Arun, but a bit smaller.

The sea state was slight, we were far enough out to sea to make our way over and tie up alongside them.

We rigged our fenders port side and came alongside Eastbourne lifeboat's starboard side; the deck crew took our ropes.

I shouted from the flying bridge to the Coxswain *"let's look over each other's boat, OK with you?"*... *"yeah"* he replied.

Tim was first to jump aboard the Eastbourne boat, like a rat up a drain pipe, he was straight into her engine room.

I left the flying bridge and made my way down to the afterdeck, by now all the Ramsgate crew were aboard the Arun. We all shook hands, I'm pleased to say not a limp handshake from any of the crew! We chatted away about recent jobs and wandered into the wheelhouse, *"loads of room in here"* one of the Eastbourne crew said, I thought wait till he gets a chance to look over the Severn lifeboat!

We decided that once we could extract our mechanic Tim from the Mersey class engine room we would have a thrash around, launch our *Y-boat*, then rig for tow, the Mersey towing the Arun.

For the next 20 minutes we were moving around outside Eastbourne harbour at top speed, the Mersey was slower than us, we were churning up the sea. From the shore it must have looked like the two lunatic dogs running around in a garden.

We launched our *Y-boat* and Mark P took a couple of the Eastbourne lads out to show them how manoeuvrable the small inflatable boat was. Whilst this was going on we showed the Eastbourne crew how we tie a casualty up alongside the lifeboat to take it onto its mooring. Leaving the lifeboat back end sticking out to give the unit complete manoeuvrability.

With the Mersey stern sticking out behind the Arun by around six feet and both boats tied together with tight springs to stop the boats sliding against each other when the Mersey moves ahead and astern. The Eastbourne Coxswain began to move the boats around, we had plenty of sea room, the Eastbourne boat was tied portside to our starboard side.

We were making our way towards ten or more small sailing dingies, heading in our direction. I was stood on the Arun's foredeck with one of the Eastbourne crew, the Second Coxswain, a thin medium height confident man, half a roll up fag smouldering away in his gob.

"Starboard" the guy in the leading sailing dingy screamed, *"starboard"* he screamed again. I looked to the Eastbourne Coxswain who just grinned... I knew the next 2 minutes were going to be exciting.

The idiot in the dinghy was now almost upon us, we were obviously not going to give way. The idiot looked up at the Second Coxswain of the Eastbourne boat and me, he waved his arm as if to push us out of the way, screamed at the top of his voice *"starboard!"* His eyes were bulging, mouth opened so wide it was about all you could see, his tonsils were clinging on for dear life as the scream passed them... I looked at the Second Coxswain who still had his arms folded, fag clinging on to the corner of his gob... As the dinghy bounced off the lifeboat's bow and started to bounce down the side of the Arun we both looked down at the top of the head of the screaming dinghy man... the Second Coxswain said *"we are towing you must give way"*. The dinghy idiot was busy fending off the Arun as he scraped past us, obviously livid *"I'm going to report you!"* he screamed... I looked at the Second Cox, he just grinned, obviously he had come across these types before, the 'ya brigade' yacht club lounge lizards who own the sea.

It was a brilliant exercise, lasted about two hours in all, great to meet a new crew from a station we would not normally meet on a passage. Good to see how well they worked together, we had a lot in common with each other, comforting to know if we needed help off Eastbourne the best were there. The same going for all stations around the coast, one thing in life you can rely on 100% is the crews of the RNLI.

Tim and the Eastbourne mechanic were like a pair of lovers, no doubt discussing spanners and oil filters. I said to the lads as we mustered on the after deck, *"let's get the Y-boat stowed it's time to make our way up to Ramsgate"*. I looked at the Coxswain on the Eastbourne boat on his after deck, we moved towards each other leaned over our respective railings and shook hands *"I enjoyed that exercise, great crew you have"*, he grinned, nodded and said *"you too"*.

As we parted, the Eastbourne boat making its way to the harbour, us moving off to the east, we all waved to each other. We were all brothers with the same aims and aspirations.

Another lovely day, throttles set to full speed, I introduced a driving rota of 1 hour so everyone had a go on the helm. A five hour run we were looking to arrive at Ramsgate harbour around 1630 hours.

Well we arrived right on time, into the visitors pontoon area. I arrived at the pontoon a little faster than I should have and had to give both engines full astern to avoid destroying the pontoon. Luckily I got away with it, a few smiles from the crew as we tied up.

With the boat locked up, we jumped down onto the pontoon, the boys walked on ahead. They went through the gate and onto the path that led to the main road. A cyclist passed them pushing his bike, he was about 10 yards from me, I looked at him at the exact time the 4 crew turned round behind the cyclist and screamed in unison *"Courgette"*... the cyclist turned around and looked at the crew who were all giggling then looked back at me, we were almost passing... as he passed me I muttered *"they're a bunch of idiots"*, we passed, I kept my eyes forward and waved a clenched fist at the crew who burst out laughing.

I caught up with them as we got onto the main street, Lily said *"there's our hotel"* so we didn't have far to walk.

I was first through the revolving door, as the boss I made my way directly to the booking desk, there was a young lady sitting in front of the computer screen. We were all now at the long desk, I noticed a name tag on her blouse, so I thought I would show off and exude confidence *"good afternoon Ramada"* I said. She looked up at me, looked down to

Arriving in Ramsgate, looking for our mooring. *Elizabeth Ann* with number 52-11 removed and painted in Australian markings. On the flying bridge, Mr Price and Tim, on the foredeck the two Marks.
Photo: Ray Noble

the badge on her chest, smiled, pointed at it and said *"this is the name of the hotel"*… Well I was shrinking into the size of a mouse at the same time the crew burst out laughing. It was just not my day… the receptionist looked at me and smiled, obviously thinking 'what an idiot'!

We agreed to meet up to try a few pubs and find one that served food… I was interested in the food, the rest were focused on the beer!

Tim amazed me, he was not a big guy, where did the beer go once he drank it?. How was he able to be in good working condition the next morning?, I could say the same for the rest of them, it was like being the judge in a drinking contest of the world finals!

The next morning, down for breakfast 0730 hours, we found a table with five chairs. The hotel was modern, not too many 'tulip people' and no chance of Tim being dragged backwards clinging for his life on his chair.

After breakfast we all stood, up to our rooms, back to the foyer, handed in our keys and we were off.

No need to refuel, we had plenty of diesel to make the short trip from Ramsgate to Tilbury.

Lilley passed up a course on the intercom; I acknowledged with a couple of presses on the mike button, we were on our way to Tilbury.

As we made our approach to the estuary I couldn't help noticing the water colour, mud, no chance of encountering snorkelers here!

A light breeze, cool, clear skies, we motored towards the channel, there were so many cones and cans, red and green, I could see all the old forts in the distance, they are 'Maunsell Forts' they were armed and used to defend London during WW2.

Maunsell Forts in the Thames Estuary Photo: Hywel Williams

The structures are just amazing, stuck in the middle of the sea, 80 years old and still in good nick!

Tim and Lily nipped up to the flying bridge to join Mark and myself for a look around. We were motoring at around 12 knots, we had plenty of time and wanted to enjoy the trip. Lilley went back down to the wheelhouse to check the chart and echo sounder. As we entered the narrower channel we were all concentrating on the channel markers, it became a little confusing. Not far ahead was a small coaster making its way up the Thames. I suggested we close its stern and followed it in, if it went aground we would still have enough water, it meant reducing our speed but it was worth it!

By now we have passed the forts and structures, buoys marking sunken WW2 ammunition ships and entered the Thames. Time to overtake the small coaster and begin the trip up the river, back to 14 knots, dragging a lot of wake behind the lifeboat.

The reed beds were swaying as our wash went through them, I was aware there was a speed limit due to the big 12 knot speed limit signs.

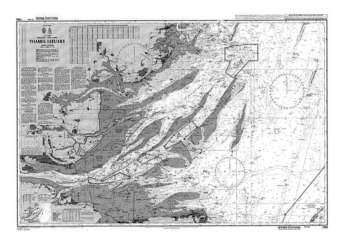

As usual we keep a listening watch on VHF channel 16 and 0, and 2182 on the MF wireless.

On channel 16 came a call "*lifeboat reduce your speed*", I looked astern and there they were, the water cops, a big black craft something like the pilot boats used back in Falmouth… I instantly throttled back, I thought bloody hell, I'm in big trouble if we get done for speeding.

I shouted down to the crew on the after deck, "*If they come along side speak in Australian accents and apologise*".

The cops motored past us, obviously speeding! The driver wagged his finger at me, I gave him a bow like you would if you meet a member of the Royal family, it did the trick, and he nodded and accepted what was my visual grovelling apology.

Police launch on the Thames. Photo: Adrian Pingstone

We crept up the Thames at around 8 knots, our wash was much better.

In the distance we could see Tilbury Docks, huge cranes in a long line; I guessed this was where we were heading so we slowly cruised up the long warf. About half way up there was a guy waving both arms, we pulled up opposite him "*you're early*" he shouted down to us… "*the crane drivers and the divers will arrive in about half an hour*".

I said to Mark P who was alongside me, "*we will tie up here for a while*". I noticed the huge crane had two big strops, they're going to lower those into the water and we were to manoeuvre the boat into position over the strops. There was a fair tide running, so this wasn't going to be easy.

We sat alongside, engines on tick over. I noticed Tim was unscrewing the RNLI order number from the board between the engines panel and MF set, "*this is for you Mr Price*" Tim said as he presented it to me. I have to say I was quite touched "*thanks mate*" I replied.

He had unscrewed the RNLI plaque Viv made for the boat. It had underneath the boats motto '*Festina Lente*' meaning '*Hasten Slowly*'…"*This is for the boat house*" Tim said.

Tilbury Docks. Photo: Ashley Dace

RADIO CALL SIGN

WHEN OPERATING ON STATION USE STATION NAME
FOLLOWED BY "LIFEBOAT"

WHEN ON PASSAGE OR TRIALS USE CLASS

OPERATIONAL NUMBER: 52-11

The 52-11 radio call sign plaque from between the engineer's panal and the radios.
Presented to me by Tim the mechanic.

Outside we heard someone call out "*anyone there*?" We all filed out of the wheelhouse, it was the dive boat with 4 big guys aboard, 2 in diving gear. "*We are ready to get the boat into the strops*" one of the divers said, I gave him the thumbs up, the crew let the bow rope go and we moved away from the quay.

I looked up at the crane, the crane driver stood up and gave us the 'thumbs up', I nodded and he lowered the big gantry then lowered the two heavy strops into the water. There wasn't much room for error if we were going to position the lifeboat in the strops.

I lined the boat up, a little on the skew to allow for the ebbing tide, made my move, buggered it up completely, came astern and had another go… after 3 or 4 goes I wondered how on earth am I going to hold the boat in position while the tide was washing us out of the strops.

Then suddenly I noticed the tide stopped, the river went smooth, a short burst ahead with both engines and we were in. I gave the crane driver thumbs up, he wound in the wire and suddenly we were in the strops, the boat lifted about two feet, then stopped.

I looked down to see the two divers lowering themselves into the water from the dive boat… I looked at the skipper and shouted, "*keep them there until I cut the engines*"… he said "*they will be OK*"… I said in with a very stern voice "*keep them there until I say it's OK to go under the boat*" he shrugged his shoulders and said "*OK*", he then told his divers to hang on.

I called down to Tim "*switch off both engines please*"… Just the thought that there were two divers under the boat with both engines running made me shiver. The props are huge, they hang low of 'A' brackets and if for some inexplicable reason they were to slip into gear they could chop a diver up in seconds!

The engines stopped, alarms rang, Tim silenced them, then we were ready.

I gave the dive boat skipper the thumbs up, he nodded to the divers and down they went. Their job to inspect the strops and make sure they were not twisted and were in the correct position.

After what must have been a couple of minutes they popped up like a couple of seals, black rubber balaclava covered heads, they signalled to the skipper all was well.

We felt the boat judder, the crane

Elizabeth Ann's plaque on the front of the upper steering position, made by Viv Pentecost, Coxswain 1980-1989. It was carefully removed and now has pride of place in the crew room at Falmouth Lifeboat Station. Photo: Simon Culliford

driver began to lift us out of the water, to a position about 20 feet above the quay. Then we swung across and were lowered into the purpose built cradle, that together with the Arun would eventually be loaded as deck cargo, cradle and lifeboat together… ready for transport to its new station in Australia.

One of the dock yard workers rolled up with a long ladder, we lowered our gear down, climbed down and that was it, the job was complete.

Tim rang the RNLI HQ to let them know The *Elizabeth Ann* was delivered, and on the quay in its transport cradle.

"Well lads, I really enjoyed the last couple of days, thanks for looking after me, sad to see the old girl go, hope they look after her properly". The crew nodded, Lilley said *"let's go to the main gate and collect the hire car"*, Lily was the driver, his first job was to drop me at the railway station. I was due in London for a meeting the next morning, also pleased not to be travelling back to Poole for a stopover before returning to Falmouth, not because its cramped in a small hire car with five plus gear, but because Lily is better situated on a race track than cruising in a hire car, he drives like a complete loon.

We left the docks with a 'bleach burn out', two strips of smoking rubber left on the tarmac as we passed the main gate. The guard looked out of the window, eyes on stalks, obviously not impressed… I hid my face so I couldn't be recognised in a line up if we were arrested!

At the railway station I piled out the front passenger seat, Mark P jumped out the back where he Mark and Tim were squeezed in, I said to Mark, *"See you at the boathouse on the next job"*… he replied *"Amen to that Yitzhak"*, I grinned, *"cheeky git"* I said, he was grinning too. We had the same sense of humour, the Amen bit was due to us being the inaugural two who started off the '*late Amen's*', at church services or when we took the lifeboat to '*Sea Sunday*' type events there was always, a vicar, padre or preacher who would say a prayer, the contest was who could say the loudest and latest '*Amen*'... often I would count slowly up to five, after everyone in the congregation had said amen after a prayer, then scream out '*AMEN*' in an American accent of course the crew would piss themselves, the vicar would spin around with a look on his face of shock, the rest of the congregation would look at each other as if there was a lunatic yank amongst the giggling crew, then often Mark would blast out '*Amen*' which brought the house down.

Yitzhak was his polite way of responding to my habit of stroking my beak when discussing financial matters!

Anyway, I thanked Tim for my present, the call sign plaque I had looked at for around 18 years (situated above the VHF wireless), something I will treasure for ever.

All the windows of the car wound down, the rev's mounted, Lily was obviously looking for a spectacular getaway, the crew all shouted at the same time "*Mr Price*", the tyres spun, for a split second the car didn't move, then it was gone leaving the smoke from at least 1lb of smouldering rubber on the road!

P&O Nedlloyd Encounter ex *Elizabeth Ann* at Ulladlla, Australia now repainted but retaining the former RNLI operational number 5211 on the bow. Photo:Royal Volunteer Coastal Patrol

Elizabeth Ann's bell, builders plate official number plate and the Festina Lenti motto removed from the lifeboat before depature for Australia and now in the crew room at Falmouth Lifeboat Station. Photo: Simon Culliford

Falmouth's Severn class all-weather lifeboat *The Will*. Photo: Royal Bank of Scotland/Rick Tomlinson

TWO SAILORS

A couple of years have passed since we collected *The Will*, Elaine and I were married and living in our own little house close to the lifeboat house, plenty of shouts, most in the middle of the night.

Elaine's parents had come down from Mere to join us for the weekend so we had a full house; it was Saturday around 1830 hours, midsummer, a bit of a southerly blow. We had just sat down for supper, the last thing I expected was for the bleeper to go off, Bleep, Bleep, Bleep, I pressed the buttons, up flashed 'ALB call', I had expected it would be an ILB job but that's life. I stood up, "*It's blowing hard*" Elaine's Dad said, I smiled "*it won't be too bad*", "*I'll have my tea when I get back*" I said to Elaine. I fought my way past the dog and got out of the kitchen door just as the first maroon went off.

I arrived at the boat house to the explosion of the second maroon. At the same time John the Second Mechanic had arrived. Just behind him, Alan drew up in his car. Within minutes four or five reserve crew arrived.

Tim had phoned the Coastguard, "*there's plenty of time, we need to meet up with a bulk carrier off the Ten Mile Buoy to receive two yachtsmen that they picked up in mid Atlantic from their dismasted and sinking yacht . Time 2000 hours*", "*OK*" Alan said, "*we will give it 5 minutes to see who turns up, then take a slow run out to the Ten Mile Buoy*".

By this time as well as four main crew there were at least six reserve crew, all circling Alan like wildebeest circling a wounded animal. Each was letting Alan know they were available with their desperate looks.

I expected Alan to pick two or three who hadn't been on many shouts to give them some experience. For this sort of job they weren't expected to do too much, perhaps break out kit when asked but otherwise, unless the job developed into something complicated, just keep out of the way and observe.

The four of us on the main crew or '*first team*' as it's often referred were all dressed up; jackets, trousers, yellow wellies and bog seats (life jackets). Alan looked at his watch, then looked up to the six reserves, by now all looking like Starling chicks in the nest, desperate for food from the parent. "*You, you and you*", Alan said pointing to three of the younger reserves, bitter disappointment for the other three. I remembered the feeling from years ago as a reserve, turning up to every call and not always being picked.

The three lucky ones got dressed within a few seconds and followed us down to the pontoon. Tim the Mechanic and John the Second Mechanic went into the wheelhouse, I took charge of the deck and Alan went up to the flying bridge to remove covers.

"*Get ready to let go fore and aft on Alan's instructions*" I said to the reserves, "*Mark, you come with me, we will take the cover off the Y-boat, I doubt we will need it but just in case*".

We got the covers stowed, Mark went down to the after deck and I stood in the flying bridge with Alan as he took the lifeboat slowly out of the docks. I looked back to the lifeboat house, the three reserves who were not lucky this time were stood outside watching us leave. There would be plenty of shouts for them as they rose up the pecking order and joined the main crew; in fact if they remained with the lifeboat for ten or twenty years there would be hundreds of shouts of all types in all weathers to come.

As we rounded the docks we could see the rollers lining up behind each other, some with white surf crests.

We made our way out towards Black Rock Buoy at the entrance to Falmouth, the lifeboat slowly climbing the waves and falling into the troughs, a bit of spray coming up over the boat.

Pendennis Point was crowded, lots of cars and spectators, a bonus for them to see Falmouth Lifeboat launched on service and making its way out of Falmouth into what probably looked like rough seas.

It certainly would have looked spectacular if we were motoring at full emergency speed of around 25 knots; that would require the crew to strap into the wheelhouse seats to avoid being injured.

Unbeknown to me, Elaine offered to drive her Mum and Dad up to Pendennis Point to see the lifeboat go out to sea. She had no idea where we were going, how long for or what the job was.

Elaine told me later that night her Dad said *"cor! It's bloody rough, look the lifeboat is disappearing behind each wave"* once we were out of sight she took them home to finish supper.

By now Tim had opened up with the bulk carrier, she was making good time. The two sailors they had picked up were husband and wife, uninjured and well. We had the ship on radar and could just see her on the horizon.

Alan called down on the intercom *"Tim, ask the Captain how he would like to transfer the two sailors"*. Tim called the bulk carrier, asked him the question, he replied *"we have a loading hatch four meters above sea level mid-ship on the starboard side, if we swing around and head to the west we should give you a good lee"*. Alan gave two clicks on the intercom button to acknowledge that he heard his transmission, Tim replied to the bulk carrier *"all copied"*.

We slowly closed about one mile south of the Ten Mile Buoy, so outside of the pilotage area where if a ship enters it has to pay for pilotage whether it uses it or not.

It slowly circled around to port until it was facing west and gave three short blasts on its horn to signal it was engaging astern propulsion, which when moving ahead means in layman's terms it was applying its brakes.

The bulk carrier slowed to about 5 knots, just enough to maintain its course. Alan looked at me *"get John and go forward to receive the casualties"*, I nodded and went below. John was in the wheelhouse, kitted up and all ready to go. We were the two biggest crew on the boat, excluding Alan who was driving. The boat was far from steady due to the sea conditions, assisting casualties onto the deck would not be easy. We had all worked together approaching fifteen years so knew each other's abilities well.

John is a huge man, no fat, stronger than two men put together, known as 'the *Winch*'. If when hauling the anchor or heaving on a heavy rope, someone says use the capstan, John would grab the rope and pull it in as if he was just pulling in the rope with nothing attached.

We slowly approached the bulk carrier. Around about amidships two large doors began to slide open, 'the *Winch*' and myself on the foredeck. Alan moved the lifeboat in slowly, getting a feel of how we would ride the swells and position the port bow of the lifeboat firmly against the ship, to make sure there was no gap where a casualty could slip between the lifeboat and the ship and get crushed.

I was nearest the bow of the lifeboat; 'the *Winch*' stood next me, then out came what looked like a baby whale being born, slowly making its way out of its mother. It was a leg, probably the biggest leg I have ever seen! I looked at John, my eyes were bulging, he looked at me, pursed his lips. I'm not sure what the expression meant, probably translated into "*cor blimey look at the size of that leg*". We both looked back to the hatch, then alongside the first leg out slid a twin, another leg, I thought, thank god I've got 'the *Winch*' with me, this casualty is going to weigh 30 stone minimum!

Alan held the port bow onto the ships side, we were just under the hatch, two massive legs protruding over the edge, a face appeared between the legs, it was a woman, she looked pretty worn out after her ordeal on board a sinking yacht and being rescued from the middle of the Atlantic.

"*Don't worry darling, we will get you onto the lifeboat and soon have you ashore*" I said.

This was just one of those jobs where you just need to get on with it, not overthink how many ways it can be achieved.

I looked at the 'the *Winch*' "*the left legs mine*", obviously meaning the right leg was his.

I went in like a rugby tackle, both arms wide open. I crashed into the inner thigh just about the knee, wrapped my arms around the left leg, hands just meeting around the other side, big mistake! I should have approached from the outer side, but it was too late, 'the *Winch*' had done the same but took the right leg from the outside.

As the woman felt we had her she began to slide out. I gripped like mad, determined not to let the leg slide from my grip, not just because it could be dangerous for the casualty, but because I could disappear into the ladies internals!

I now had a leg each side of my head, I was facing away from 'the *Winch*', I spun my ahead around, scraping my beak against what was the ladies' inner thigh. I knew my eyes were bulging under the immense strain because I had a panoramic view of the woman's buttocks (clothed I'm pleased to say)… I caught John's eye, he was red in the face, and I could see he wanted to burst out laughing.

The woman had both her hands on top of my head, her leg was beginning to slip through my arms, my head went deeper. I knew that another few inches and daylight would disappear and I wouldn't be able to breath.

I decided to let my knees buckle, rather than disappear. Having a large woman as a hat was not what I was expecting when the bleepers went off!

By now I was sat on my bum, 'the *Winch*' keeled over clutching the woman's right leg with a grip like a tourniquet, we all ended up in a heap on the lifeboat foredeck. I crawled out from under and we both stood up. 'The *Winch*' had tears in his eyes; he was desperate not to burst out laughing.

I said "are *you* OK *madam*?" she nodded, totally unaware I had nearly died due to failing to stay around the vicinity of her left knee!

At the front of the wheelhouse the three reserves and Tim were up against the windows watching the floor show on the foredeck, Tim was grinning!

I gave two fingers then pointed towards the reserves, and waved them to me, signalling I wanted two of them on deck now!

Out popped two reserves from the wheelhouse and up to the three of us on the foredeck, "*help this lady into the wheelhouse please*". They escorted her to the safety of the wheelhouse. I looked up at Alan who was working the lifeboat's controls from the port side position where the bow thruster lever was situated; he looked at me, nodded and smiled.

Alan looked up, then back to me, and flipped his head up, telling me without words to look up. Out slid two more huge legs, it was the husband, another 30 stoner if he was an ounce. I moved right up to the very front of the bow, this time the left leg was mine, but from the outside. I had seen enough inner thigh to last me a lifetime.

'The *Winch*' was controlling his giggling (just) we both moved in simultaneously grasping a leg each, both heads to the front, our noses almost touching. As the weight came on I couldn't control myself. We both burst out laughing, the husbands left hand on my head, his right on 'the *Winch's*' head.

As he slid out of the ship's side we took the weight and both slowly sunk to our knees, the husband's feet hit the deck and was safely on board.

I looked up to Alan, gave him a single nod which told him we were on board and happy. He took the lifeboat away from the open hatch, we all waved to the crew of the carrier who helped with the operation. The rescue was not normal, it wouldn't have made a good PR video clip for the RNLI, but it was a success, no one died and no one disappeared!

'The *Winch*' and myself escorted the husband back along the side of the lifeboat and onto the after deck. He stepped into the wheelhouse, gave his wife a big hug. She began to cry, that almost got me going, but I looked at John just in time, he grinned, (he was always grinning), I had to look away before I burst out laughing.

Tim was thanking the Captain of the bulk carrier on VHF channel 67 for his excellent seamanship and help in passing the two casualties to us, and advised him we would take good care of them.

I went up to the flying bridge to keep Alan company. He stood away from the wheel and pointed to it with both hands. I took the wheel and he went below to check on the husband and wife. I took the boat back to our pontoon, the three reserves that didn't make the shout were there with the fuel line. I knew looking at them as they helped tie up the boat that they would turn into a solid, reliable and competent crew.

We took the husband and wife ashore, they were from up north, accents difficult to understand, but body language that was very easy to read, They were so grateful to be ashore, probably having been resigned to dying alone in the middle of the Atlantic.

With the lifeboat put to bed and boat house tidied up and everything put away, the two survivors taken off by taxi to a hotel, I walked home. As I got in the front door… *"you stink"* Elaine said, I replied *"it's been a long hot sweaty evening, I'll go up and have a shower"*, as I passed her in the hall her nose creased up with my odour… If only she had seen what I had on my head on the foredeck of the lifeboat that evening and the effort it took to receive the husband and wife from the bulk carrier, she would understand why!

John Murray ('The *Winch*') being presented with a signed framed photograph of Falmouth Lifeboat *Richard Cox Scott* by Coxswain Alan Barnes to mark his retirement from the crew. Photo: Simon Culliford

Richard Cox Scott heading out into Falmouth Bay in February 2002. Photo: Simon Culliford

RICHARD COX SCOTT

The Will, a lifeboat the crew grew into, over the 5 years that we had her, carried out 91 services, saved 24 lives and rescued 111 people, it was time to transfer our tea pot to our brand new Severn class lifeboat *Richard Cox Scott.*

She arrived in Falmouth in December 2001 and was placed on service on the 18th. This was Tim our mechanics first brand new boat, you would think he was guarding the crown jewels! We had to keep the boat spotless for the naming ceremony and dedication due in May 2002.

The main crew were sworn to secrecy on who was going to perform the naming ceremony, but it became obvious to everyone on the crew as the date drew close, the town smelt of new paint, new street signs, Falmouth railway station refurbished, everything at the lifeboat station painted, it was going to be the Queen and Prince Phillip.

During the winter there were plenty of exercises, almost every Sunday morning and at least one night exercise a week, the Severn is a very complicated boat for Tim and John the second mechanic to maintain, on the odd occasion when computers flagged up a bug in the system a specialist would come down to Falmouth plug in the laptop and clear all the faults, and of course a run out into Falmouth bay to check that everything worked OK.

District Engineers, just like Divisional Inspectors (formally known as District Inspectors)… still DI's for short, were as dedicated as the crews, they would turn up when requested to fix a problem no matter what time, if the lifeboat was put on 'restricted service' or declared 'off service' it was imperative it was fixed or a relief boat was collected from anywhere around the coast to get the station operational as soon as possible.

A couple of years earlier we were bringing *The Will* back from Southern Ireland on a 3 day shakedown trial in bad weather, we passed Lands' End, approaching the Lizard in heavy weather, total darkness, travelling at full speed of around 25 knots, we fell off a particularly large wave, the lifeboat landed on its port side and stopped dead in the water, luckily everyone was strapped into their seats, "*everyone OK?*" Alan shouted, we all looked at each other, wondering what had happened, in turn everyone confirmed they were O.K.

The D.I. had stuck his elbow through some electrical trunking on the inside of the wheelhouse, I was strapped into the 'doctors chair', my left leg flew forward and I gave a fire extinguisher a good kick with my shin, (still bear the mark) and sprained my left hand, most of the crew were shaken, but luckily nothing broken and no blood.

Alan took the Will in towards Cadgwith, just to the east of The Lizard for some calmer water so we could assess the damage. Tim stood in the aft of the wheelhouse and pointed forward, "*look at the seats*" he shouted, everyone by now had unstrapped and were gathering bits and pieces off the floor, I looked forward, all three forward position seats were bent over considerably to the left!

A couple of the lads had put on their lifejackets and ventured out onto the deck, Tim had put the deck lights on, we could see damage to some forward stanchions (rails) and the lifeboats anchor leaning out over the rail, still well lashed in position, but the impact had done some damage there too!

With a full assessment of the damage and a quick cup of tea, we reported to the boathouse what had happened and limped back to Falmouth at half speed.

On arrival later that evening with the boat tied up alongside, Tim began to list everything that required repair or replacement and relayed this to RNLI HQ at Poole.

The RNLI engineers went into action, lorries were loaded with replacement seats and all the equipment required to replace them, in the meantime engineers were paged and making their way to Falmouth to help our DE and Tim, the team worked through the night, and by early morning the lifeboat was declared seaworthy, all seats replaced with new, anchor stanchions replaced, everything shipshape again…So for the 'staff engineers' a 'shout' with a successful outcome!

During the naming ceremony Alan Barnes introduced the crew to Her Majesty The Queen. Left to right: Snowy Angove, Peter Wood, Chris Price, John Murray, Tim Julian and Roger McClarity. Meeting the Queen was a great honour. When Prince Philip asked me what I did for a day job, I did notice his bodyguard look me in the eye!

As the naming ceremony day approached, the crew were issued with new kit, I got a pair of new size 12's, marking them in best handwriting 'Mr Price', the main crew even got new hats!

We practiced entering and leaving the National Maritime Museum pontoon, the weather forecast was perfect, we were going to take her Majesty and the Duke of Edinburgh for a short tour of the harbour from the pontoon to the Prince of Wales pier as soon as the naming ceremony was complete.

Her Majesty The Queen on board *Richard Cox Scott*.

As we passed HMS Cornwall who were moored in the harbour the sailors all lined alongside her starboard side gave a cheer, it was a perfect day.

We arrived at the Prince of Wales pier and duly tied the boat up, tightened the springs to make sure the boat didn't surge and was firmly alongside, engines switched off. I was on the bow, close to group of top brass from the town, all lined up to be presented to Her Majesty. I noticed standing close to the bow of the lifeboat in the line up was the Chief Constable of Devon and Cornwall Police, he glanced in my direction, obviously didn't know me

The crew lining up for the afternoon dedication service at the lifeboat station after the Queen's naming ceremony held that morning. Left to right: Dave Nicoll, Mark Pollard, John Murray, Tim Julian, Chris Price, Alan Barnes, Roger McClarity, Peter Wood and Snowy Angove.

Falmouth lifeboat crew 1 May 2002. Left to right. Back row: Alastair Heane, Nick Lewis, Jonathon Blakeston,Mark Pollard, Ken Avis, Neil McClarity. Middle row: Mark Waters, Alan Rowe, Andrew McInnes, Geoff Gill, Phil Rogers,Tom Bird, Carl Beardmore, Marc Thomas, David Proud, Tim Kemp, Mike Lowres, John Lower, David Burgess, Dr Phil Slater, Dr Richard James, Dave Nicoll, Lifeboat Operations Manager Graham Pearce. Seated: Peter Wood, Roger McCarity, Coxswain Alan Barnes, Chris Price, Mechanic Tim Julian, Andrew "Snowy" Angove and John Murray. Photo: Falmouth RNLI.

from Adam, I gave him a big smile and winked at him, the expression on his face was priceless, I think he must have thought I was making a pass at him, his head swivelled round to the front, he wiggled a bit as he stiffened up, standing to attention, Pete was stood next to me, we looked at each other and grinned, I did think to myself that the Chief Constable didn't get out a lot, or wasn't used to interfacing with the lower echelon!

I was now in my early 50's, heading towards the dreadful day when I reach my 55th birthday and would have to retire. I was the oldest in the crew, only Alan and myself left from the St Simeon days, how time flies. Elaine was counting the days when my life wouldn't revolve around the bleeper,

'Coxswains course'. A very tough week, a total of 8 2nd coxswains and deputy 2nd coxswains from Falmouth to Lerwick. Elaine looked after Dan Nicholson's diary when she worked in the Training Department (before I stole her away to Falmouth).

no more shouts in the middle of the night, no days away as a relief Coxswain for stations on the south coast, no more Sunday morning exercises.

It was agreed that on my birthday the crew would take me out in the lifeboat for a trip down to Coverack, then back for a pint in The Front, a little pub on Custom House Quay.

The dreaded day arrived, I arrived home early from work, had a wash, got changed, went downstairs, "*don't look so miserable*" Elaine said, I didn't reply for fear of having to gasp

Richard Cox Scott passing St Anthony Lighthouse. Photo: Simon Culliford

and having a meltdown, I composed myself and strolled over to the boat house.

Well it was packed, most of the crew were there, all milling around like you would do at a funeral, I'm pretty sure everyone present felt my pain, it was old Pricey's last trip on the boat.

Tim came up, gave me a smile, didn't bother to say anything as he could see I wasn't in a fit state to reply, anyway I managed to remain composed, got kitted up with the rest of the crew and we all wandered down to the pontoon and aboard the Severn.

I hung around on the after deck with the lads as the boat was flashed up, the moorings let go, a slow run out past the docks and out towards St Anthony lighthouse.

Everyone was painfully aware I was not enjoying the trip, but rallied around, not knowing what to say. I went up to the flying bridge to join Alan and couple of the lads, we all jostled around and crammed in, enjoying the summer evening trip down towards Coverack, a couple of laps around Coverack Bay then Alan stepped back from the wheel, pulled me across and said "*take the boat back to Falmouth and put her to bed*", we were travelling at full speed, a perfect evening, "*we've had some good times over the years Chris*" Alan said, I looked him in the eye and nodded, not trusting myself to speak, Snowy recalled a couple of occasions when I had had a spectacular pizza moment on the after deck in heavy weather, I remembered them well, we all started laughing, Ken the Tea Pot chipped in recalling one or two of the funnier moments we have all shared over the years and before you knew it we were all laughing.

I brought the boat alongside the pontoon, luckily without ramming into it, the boys tied her up, Tim refuelled, closed down with the coastguard, and that was it, my last trip as a

'Respect'. My final trip on the Severn. Photo: Tom Bird

lifeboat man on a RNLI lifeboat.

A gang of us poodled over to The Front on Custom House Quay, to mark the end of an era with a pint or two, it is inevitable that things evolve with time, I had a great innings, very lucky to be part of a great team at Falmouth, it seemed like only yesterday Viv invited me to join the crew, after being taken out on an exercise and having been vetted by the crew.

THE RETIREMENT PARTY

When long serving lifeboat crew retire it is customary to organise a secret surprise retirement party, to commemorate the occasion, and present the retiring crewman with his or her 'Certificate of Service'.

Eventually the date came around for 'my leaving do', I was to arrive at St Michaels hotel with Elaine for a 'meeting'.

Chris being presented with his Certificate of Service by Divisional Inspector Simon Pryce.
Photo: Simon Culliford

The evening arrived, into the hotel we walked, down the passage and into the big meeting room… there were the crew and wives,… *"surprise"* , I grinned at Elaine, it was just so nice of everyone to make such an effort, all for me. A few weeks had passed since my 'last trip', which by the way wasn't my last trip, (I was asked a year or two later if I would like to join a small crew on a passage to a collect a lifeboat, as an honorary crew man, I got permission from Elaine and had a trip to Poole in the evening, five crammed in a small car built for four, driven by Lilly, or as I nicknamed him 'Fangio', at around 100 miles per hour all the way! Then back to Falmouth, I can mention it now as most of the crew on that passage have retired, and won't get into trouble for having me along).

I have now got used to the new life without the bleeper, and was quite relaxed, as long as I didn't have to make a speech I was going to survive the evening.

All the old crew came up in turns to chat with Elaine and me, we recalled old shouts and some of the hundreds if not thousands of special moments we shared, young crew, 'cubs' as the older of us referred to them as, were enjoying the evening, I could see myself in them, some 27 years ago.

Then later in the evening it was time for the presentation and speeches, it was a surprise to see the Coxswain and wives from our two flank stations there, Keith Stuart and Phillip Burgess.

ROYAL NATIONAL LIFEBOAT INSTITUTION

CERTIFICATE OF SERVICE

THIS IS TO CERTIFY

THAT

Christopher David Price

served as a Deputy Second Coxswain,
Emergency Mechanic and Crew Member of the

Falmouth Lifeboat

and previously a Crew Member of the

Coverack Lifeboat

for a total of 27 years and 6 months, during which
period the Lifeboats rescued 73 lives from shipwreck.

The Council are glad to place
this testimony to his personal participation in
the Lifeboat Service.

Chairman

January 2004

Chief Executive

Our DI Simon Pryce called for order, he handed the microphone to Alan who said some nice words about my time on the lifeboat, then on behalf of the whole crew he presented Elaine with a big bunch of flowers and me with a massive painting of the Elizabeth Ann steaming away from Coverack lifeboat house and Coverack harbour. Well needless to say I was blown away with the framed painting (it sits on the wall in my office as reminder of some of the best times and best mates anyone could ever have).

Simon regained the mike, and presented me with my Certificate of Service, a big round of applause, then as you would expect a scream from the back of the room from Snowy… "*Speech*"…

Simon held the mike out to me, I stepped back and shook my head, he could see there was no chance of me uttering a word, I must have looked as if I was going to pass out.

There was probably 5 seconds of awkward silence, then everyone started clapping and the moment passed, I wasn't required to speak, Elaine sensed my inner distress and came up and stood beside me, and within seconds I was surrounded by crew, all hell bent on cracking a few ribs as they patted me on the back and all had a go at getting the better of my handshake… no chance!

On the way home that evening I was relieved, it was all over, now to a life without lifeboats, a new world.

Some years later I was asked to become chairman of the Falmouth Lifeboat Management Group, this is an RNLI appointment, and a great honour, which of course I accepted, so I remain to this day involved with the RNLI.

'Air Chief Marshall' Price and Elaine at the fancy dress retirement party held for John Lower to mark his retirement from the active crew in November 2012. Photo: Simon Culliford

EPILOGUE

This book is to give an insight into the types of shouts and jobs undertaken by an offshore lifeboat, through the eyes of just one of the crew.

The jobs selected are typical of the hundreds of shouts I have been on, certainly enough for another book!

Luck... very lucky when my Mum declared she was pregnant that my grandparents didn't call for the knitting needles, which was the standard reaction to the possible introduction of a bar steward into the family in the middle of the last century. Lucky...I wasn't bundled off to an orphanage. Lucky...I had a Mum who loved me so much she would never let me go. Lucky... to have joined the Falmouth boat and to have met Elaine at the RNLI HQ, and that she saw something in me... so very lucky.

Fear... never on a shout, the heavier the weather the more exciting, respect for the sea, of course, its power is overwhelming. The RNLI lifeboats are powerful, maintained to perfection; the confidence of a crew in its lifeboat is total.

The fears I have are letting my crew mates down, not arriving on scene in time to help someone in great danger at sea, leaving the scene while there is still a chance of finding a survivor or body, and of course, heights!

Regrets, on lifeboats... none. In life... just the one, never telling my Dad how much I loved him.

My Dad

Elizabeth Ann on exercise in Falmouth Bay in 1987. Photo: Simon Culliford